I0626875

Me, Bobbi Nell

*Buckner Orphans Home
Faith and Romance*

Written by

**Bobbi Nell Richardson
Parson Batchelder Austin**

*Edited and Compiled by
Dennis Austin*

BOBBI NELL PRESS
Woodside, California

Me, Bobbi Nell

ISBN: 979-8-9993431-0-9 (Hardcover)
ISBN: 979-8-9993431-6-1 (Paperback)

Some names and identifying details have been changed to protect privacy.

Every effort has been made to obtain proper permissions for the use of copyrighted materials appearing in this book. All photographs, articles, and quoted materials are used with the express consent of the original copyright holders or are believed to be in the public domain..

Published by

Bobbi Nell Press

Woodside, California

Printed in the United States of America

First Edition: July 2025

Cover and interior design by Dennis Austin

Introduction

People often tell me, "You should write a book." After sharing pieces of my life, both the heartaches and the moments of joy, I've heard that phrase more times than I can count. Maybe it's because my story is full of unexpected turns or reflects so many untold stories.

Years ago, I sat beside a kind stranger on a plane. We exchanged stories, as travelers sometimes do, and by the time we landed, she asked if she could help write my story into a book. I agreed. We met in person, shared long talks, and she began the process of writing. But life, hers, took a difficult turn. With a husband in poor health and a son who needed her care, the project was quietly set aside. I never heard from her again.

More than a dozen years have passed since then, and though time has softened many memories, the desire to share my story never faded. It has grown stronger with age.

You'll meet my parents, Virgil and Velma Richardson, whose presence and absence shaped my heart in ways I'm only beginning to understand. You'll walk with me through the cotton fields, the chapel pews, the orphanage halls, the tennis courts, and into the lives of those I've loved and lost. You'll hear the laughter, feel the tears, and see the beauty I've come to recognize.

This is me,

Bobbi Nell.

Dedication

For my mother, Velma Richardson

This is for you, Mama. You made me feel deeply and unforgettably loved. Though you were taken from me far too soon, your memory has never left me. Your strength lives in my bones. I was just a little girl when I lost you, and I longed for your arms on nights that felt too long, too quiet, and too hard.

This book tells the story you never got to see unfold. But in every chapter of my life, I carried the imprint of your resilience, your warmth, and your gentle way of mothering.

We are all bound for the Promised Land.

The seventh of nine children,

Bobbi Nell

Acknowledgements

To **Dennis James Austin**

My lover, my partner, my husband, my editor—with all my heart and deepest gratitude, I thank you. You are the reason this book came to life. When I wanted only to share the facts, you coaxed, cajoled, pleaded—and came just shy of bribing me—to let emotion find its way into these pages. Had the book remained as I first imagined it, it might not have held anyone's attention—not even mine.

Thank you for your patience, your gentle encouragement, and your unwavering belief in my voice. What a gift it is to share this season of life with you. Bless you for loving me so faithfully.

To **My Dear Family and Friends**

It hasn't taken much to get a Buckner Orphans Home story out of me! Over the years, many of you have patiently listened to tales from my childhood, and some of you appear within these very pages. If you recognize yourself, please know how much I honor and cherish the role you played in my life.

To **Gracie Hawkins Williams**

You are deeply loved and admired by every Buckner alum still with us—and many who have passed. Since the day you joined our lives, your dedication, your thoughtful communication, and your tireless research have kept us all connected. The newsletters, emails, and roster updates you compile so faithfully help us remain a family, no matter the distance or the years.

Thank you, Gracie. And thank you again. Each word of gratitude comes straight from the heart.

My Family

Me, Bobbi Nell

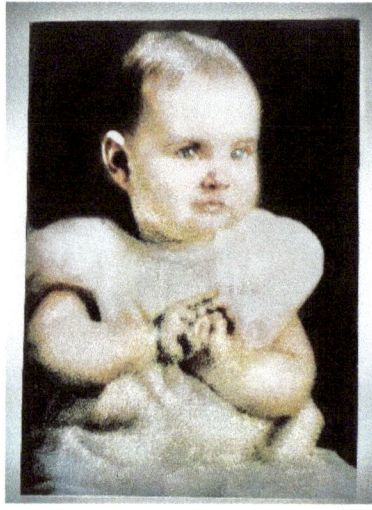

My name is Bobbi Nell Richardson, and I was born on August 24, 1933.

My daddy, Virgil Richardson, was 42 years old then, and my mama, Velma Teer Richardson, was just 25. They had already been married for seven years when I came along. I was their seventh child out of nine, in the middle of a big, beautiful, and often heartbreaking family.

1_Photo: Me, Bobbi Nell (1933)

My Daddy

My daddy, Virgil Richardson, was born on Groundhog Day, February 2, 1891, in Freestone, Texas. He was the fourth oldest among ten children: three sisters and seven brothers. His father, William Harvil Richardson, was a hardworking farmer who died when Daddy was just 15, only a month before Daddy's youngest brother was born. His mother, Susan Willard Richardson, was 29 when she gave birth to him.

2_Photo: My Daddy (1926)

I only know bits and pieces about my father's early life before he married Mama. He had been married once before, though I never learned many details. There was some whispering that he may have fathered a child either before or after that marriage. The facts were never made clear to me.

Daddy served in World War I. He enlisted in the U.S. Army on May 27, 1918, at the age of 27. Less than two months later, he was shipped to France and assigned to the 36th Infantry Division. They were thrust into one of the shortest but bloodiest episodes of trench warfare in American military history. The losses were staggering on both sides, German and American, but the outcome helped bring an end to the war.

Before returning home on May 21, 1919, Daddy's unit was reassigned to the 34th Division. He was honorably discharged on June 30, 1919.

Many years later, I saw a video reenactment in London showing what those 21 days of trench warfare might have been like. The cold, the mud, the constant threat of death, it stayed with me. Watching that film helped me understand the fear and trauma my daddy must have endured. It gave me a window into how those few weeks could forever shape a person's thinking.

War changes people. For my daddy, the mental toll was heavy. Though he wasn't physically wounded, the fear, the noise, and the horror left him what they called "shell-shocked." In today's language, we'd say he suffered from PTSD. He spent time in and out of the Veterans Hospital in Texas during the early years of my life.

I remember standing with my siblings outside the hospital window, each taking turns speaking to Daddy. He sat there with his face pressed to the glass, talking softly through the barrier. I don't remember the exact words we spoke, but I'll never forget how it felt to be in that moment.

Despite everything, Daddy was a gifted farmer. He worked hard and provided well for us. At harvest time, he hired extra hands, his brothers and other local men, because there was always plenty of work. He was a sharecropper, which meant we didn't own the land we worked. We lived on property owned by my mother's uncle, Dean Cockerel, who was also Daddy's relative.

Dean Cockerel was a descendant of Henry Cockerel, a man who had acquired vast land in and around Fairfield. His heirs managed the land and leased it to farmers like Daddy. Our family lived on a generous portion of that land, in a well-built farmhouse with good fields.

Daddy's reputation as a farmer was solid. He raised healthy crops, livestock, chickens, hogs, workhorses, and milk cows, many of which we named. The farmhouse was tidy and painted. The well gave us clean drinking water, and the creek nearby supplied water for washing. We had no electricity, but we always had enough wood to fuel our stoves and fireplaces.

Daddy wasn't deeply religious, but he respected those who were. He came to church with us. I remember one Sunday, fidgeting in the pew beside him. I wiggled too much, and Daddy gave me a light tap on the head to settle me down. I learned that day how to sit still in church.

My Mother, My Heart

My mother was born Mary Velma Teer on December 29, 1904, but everyone called her Velma. She was strong-willed and determined from a young

age. At 14, she ran away from her parents, Ellen and J.B. Teer. We children always called them "Big Mama and Big Daddy." I don't know much about her life before leaving home, but she never finished high school. Still, she possessed more practical wisdom and life skills than most educated folks I've known.

3_Photo: My Mother, Mary Velma Teer (1926)

What I remember most about Mama was her ability to make a home run smoothly, even under the hardest conditions. We had no electricity or indoor plumbing, just a deep well for water. But somehow, Mama managed to use that water for cooking, drinking, cleaning, and teaching each of us how to be self-sufficient. Her organization was remarkable. Every child knew their role in keeping our home running, and she trained us all with patience and care.

Her meals were simple but delicious. One dish stood out above the rest: her cornbread. We loved it so much that her recipe has been passed down through the generations. To this day, it still brings comfort and memories of home.

Mama was a deeply religious woman. We attended church regularly, and she was even my Sunday School teacher. At home, she tirelessly cared for our garden and orchard. She canned jams, vegetables, fruit and lined the jars neatly in the storm cellar alongside onions, potatoes, spices, and flower seeds. Her frugality was legendary, and nothing ever went to waste.

Velma was pregnant nearly her entire married life, from 18 to 37. Nine children in nineteen years. Every one of us was born at home. Without birth control, large families were common, especially on farms where every hand helped. I can't imagine how hard that must have been, but she handled it with quiet strength.

And oh, how she could call the hogs! She'd clasp her hands tightly, raise her thumbs to make a whistle hole, and let out a piercing sound that echoed through the countryside. Then came the call: "Here, piggy, piggy, pig!" followed by banging a pan with a stick. That sound meant dinner for the hogs, and they'd come running. Billy and I tried to imitate her whistle for years. Even now, Billy's pretty good at it. The trick is getting your fingers tight enough so no air

8

escapes. Then, in your best Southern voice, holler, "Here, piggy, piggy, piggy, pig!"

That was my Mama, strong, smart, resourceful, and full of love. Everything we knew about working hard, respecting others, and caring for one another started with her example.

Marriage of Virgil Richardson and Velma Teer

I don't know exactly how or under what circumstances my Daddy and Mother met. Perhaps it was through family connections; they were second cousins after all. What I do know is that they married in October of 1922. Daddy was 40 years old, and Mama was just 18.

When Kinfolk Fell in Love

Interestingly, my parents were second cousins. Their common ancestor was John C. Cockerel, my father's great-grandfather and my mother's great-great-grandfather.

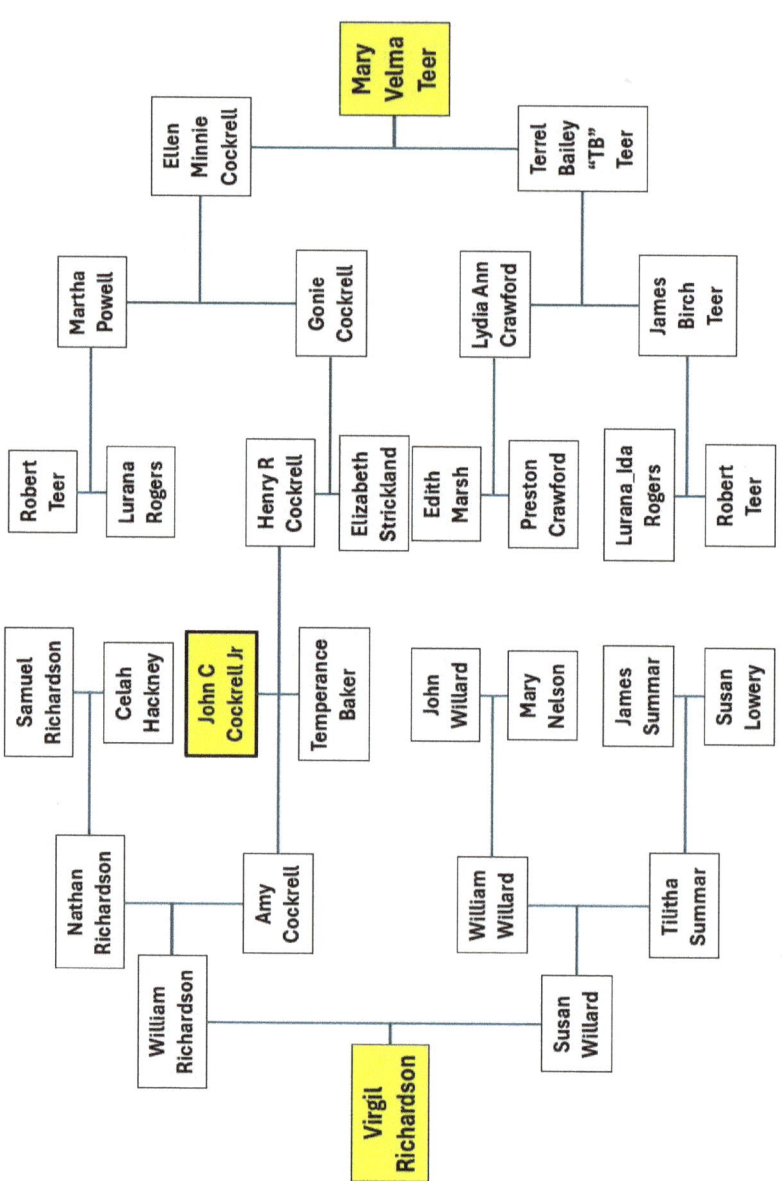

My Brothers and Sisters

When I arrived, Velma and Virgil had already brought six children into the world. Three of them died young, and three were still living when I was born. All of us were born at home, delivered with the help of a relative or an older child; there were no hospitals for country folks like us back then.

When I first opened my eyes to the world, my living siblings were Dottie Jean, Ray Edwin, and Billy Dean.

I grew up in Fairfield, Texas surrounded by my two brothers and two sisters. We shared a house, chores, and countless memories, each carving out a unique role in our family's rhythm.

Sister Dorothy (Dottie) Jean

Born in 1924, Dottie Jean was the eldest of us all. When I was born, she was

nine years old and quickly became a kind of second mother to me. I clung to her like a shadow. I can still remember the feel of her steady hand and the way she made me feel safe, even in uncertain times.

4_Photo: Mary-Velma and daughter Dottie (1924)

Dottie was the firstborn and took on a tremendous amount of responsibility. With Mama often pregnant and busy keeping house, Dottie became a second mother to Billy, Angie, and me. She was nine years older than I was, already in school by the time I was born. I looked up to her with both admiration and awe.

Dottie attended the local school across the country road from our house and was granted freedoms that the younger three of us didn't have. She seemed to be Mama's confidante. They shared a closeness resembling friendship rather than the usual mother-daughter bond. One evening, I watched them comb each other's hair. Mama's hair was long, past her waist, and I had never seen it down before. I asked if I could help. Dottie handed me the comb, and I stood with Mama at the mirror, brushing her hair. That's the first time I remember seeing myself in a mirror.

Brother Ray Edwins

Ray, born in 1926, was the second child, seven years older than I. I don't

remember having many close moments with Ray when we were growing up; he always seemed a little older, a little farther away. But I remember him being gentle and kind, and I always felt warmth in his presence. Even if we didn't talk much, I loved him dearly.

5_Photo: Velma, Dottie, Ray, Virgil (1926)

He helped Daddy with the farm and spent much time with Billy. I don't remember much about his relationship with the rest of us, and I'm not sure how he was affected by Daddy's hospitalizations. Dottie and Ray had a kind of privilege the rest of us didn't; they seemed set apart, older and freer.

Ray was a sleepwalker. He'd get up and leave the house without knowing it. Sometimes, he'd wake up at a relative's home, and someone would return him to us the next morning.

Brother Billy Dean

Billy Dean was born in 1931, just two years before me. We were closest in age,

and that made us special. We were constant companions, playmates, partners in mischief and discovery. Billy has always held a deep place in my heart, not just as my brother but as a true and lifelong friend.

6_Photo: LR: Ray, Billy Dean (1939)

We played constantly, building imaginary towns under the house, pretending rocks were people, and making cinnamon-sugar "snuff" to put in our bottom lips like the grown-ups. Of course, we'd spit it out, but not all of it; we wanted to taste the sweetness too.

12

Billy and I played "horse" often. He'd tie a rope around my waist and use a switch to get me to trot or gallop. I'd paw the ground and toss my head, mimicking the horses we saw on the farm.

Billy and Ray had their adventures, too. Once, they dragged Mama's #2 wash tub to a deep stock tank and tried to use it as a boat.

Billy tells it best:

"Ray was four years older than me, so he was always talking me into things. One day, he had this brilliant idea to get Mama's #2 wash tub that she washed clothes in and go boating. We were little, and that tub must have weighed a ton since it was half of a wooden barrel. Ray conned me into putting it on my nice, new, red wagon, which I got for Christmas. Then,

We pulled and tugged for what seemed like hours across plowed fields to the six-foot-deep stock tank in the middle of the field. It just so happened that Daddy was plowing that field down at the far end.

Ray and I wrestled that tub off the wagon into the water. He asked me if I wanted to go first since it was my wagon that we used. I said, "No, go ahead." I held it still while he got in without any paddle. When he sat down, his arms weren't long enough to reach the water to steer him.

I pushed it out away from shore. It made about three or four complete turns in the water. He hadn't panicked yet, but it didn't take long. Knowing he couldn't get back to shore and I couldn't help him. The wind wasn't blowing, so he sat out there in the middle with the hot July sun beating down on him. He hated it, but his pirate sailing career had come to an end. The next thing was to get him back to shore. The only choice we had was to go get Daddy at the other end of the field. Daddy came to our rescue, but not to his liking.":

Ray remembered that story years later and gave Billy another little red wagon in honor of the memory.

Sister Angie

After I was born, two more siblings followed me. Angie was born on January 3, 1936. I was two years and seven months old at the time. Even as a toddler, I felt a sense of protectiveness toward her. We were young girls, and I remember watching her grow with a sister's pride.

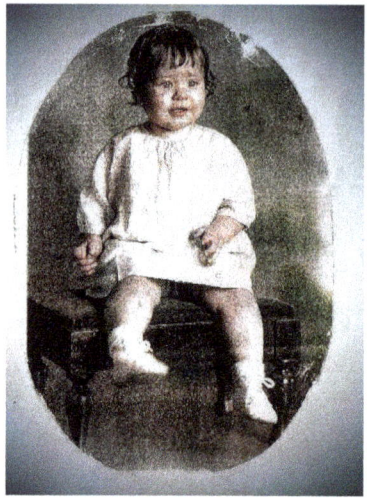

7_Photo: Angie (circa 1937)

Angie was two years and four months younger than I was. She was the baby of the family and cried a lot. Dottie was mostly in charge of her, but I desperately wanted to play with her. I saw her like a living doll with beautiful hair. Angie didn't appreciate my efforts.

My siblings and I cared for one another. Angie, though, was a bit different. She was adorable, always crying, always pretty, always a little resistant to our efforts to baby her. I think I tried the hardest, perhaps because I didn't have a doll of my own and wanted Angie to fill that role. But she would have none of it.

When I tried to get close, she'd throw rocks at me. Once I grabbed her hands and made her drop them. She screamed like I'd hurt her badly. Dottie came running and made me sit on the porch steps. My explanation didn't matter.

We started sleeping together when Angie got older and moved out of her crib. She wasn't potty trained and would often roll over me to find a dry spot in the bed. I'd wake up in the wet spot, cold and uncomfortable. The age gap between us then felt like a canyon, but we became best friends later in life.

Sisters Bonnie Joy & Freda Joyce

Before my arrival, Mom had twins, Bonnie Joy and Freda Joyce, but sadly, they passed away within a day of their birth.

8_Photo: Grave stone: Bonnie and Freda

Brother Other Neal

My baby brother was born on January 15, 1938. We called him "Other Neal," pronounced with a long "O", like *Omen*. His time with us was heartbreakingly short. He passed away just three weeks after he was born, on February 5, 1938. His little life, though brief, left a quiet ache in our family that never quite faded.

9_Photo: Grave stone of Other Neal

My mother and daddy had nine children. Four of them died young, and five of us lived to grow up.

Despite the stress and struggles, there was deep love in our family.

My Home

A House Without Water

I lived on land that Daddy worked as a sharecropper: the property and buildings were owned by Dean Cockerel, my grand-uncle, and a relative on both sides. As a sharecropper my Daddy gave Dean a portion of the harvest. My brother took his middle name from Dean Cockerel.

House
Our house was large and well-built, always in good condition, thanks to Daddy's handiwork and Mama's diligence.

Outhouse
Our toilets were outside with crescent moons carved on the doors. At night, we used chamber pots, "slop jars", which we emptied the next morning.

Lights
We had no electricity, so we used coal-oil lamps. They had to be cleaned after each use, usually at the dining table.

Heating
We kept warm with a fireplace. On especially cold nights, Mama would warm blankets by the fire and place them over us in bed. Sometimes, she'd heat bricks, wrap them in cloth, and put them at our feet.

Farm Animals
We had pigs, chickens, milk cows, and workhorses. The hogs were semi-wild; they'd roam during the day and return to be penned up at night. Every year, one hog was chosen, fattened, and slaughtered around Groundhog Day, also Daddy's

birthday. We used every part of that hog. Nothing went to waste: chitlins, sausage, ham, pig feet, brains, hog's head, skin, tongue, you name it.

Buildings

The property had stalls for livestock, pig pens, hen houses, and a smokehouse for curing meat. On slaughter day, Daddy would kill the hog, and Mama would handle the rest, preserving and storing what fed us all winter.

Storm Cellar

When a storm rolled in, Mama would usher us into the storm cellar, which was lined with shelves full of her canned goods. There was no electricity, so we lit a lamp to see. Sometimes, we stayed for just a little while; other times, we spent the whole night.

I'll never forget one visit to the cellar, when we emerged, we saw a little chicken, a bantam hen, with its throat cut. Lightning had struck nearby, they said. The poor hen tried to eat corn, but it kept falling through the hole in her neck. We felt so sorry for her. Daddy took care of her.

Well

We drew water from a well and kept a bucket with a dipper in the house. I don't remember using drinking glasses, just jars. We used that water for cooking, drinking, and, on cold Saturdays, heating bathwater for the entire family. In warmer months, our baths were taken in the creek.

Water had to be drawn from the well using a bucket tied to a rope and pulley. It took strength and skill to swing the bucket just right, lower it, fill it, and haul it back up. The older kids were trained to draw water, and the three youngest were not allowed near the well.

There were stories about cats being thrown into wells, but I don't believe anything like that happened on our farm. Still, we recited the old rhyme:

The Cat in the Well

Ding Dong Bell,
The cat is in the well.
Who put him in?
Little Johnny Green.
Who pulled him out?
Little Johnny Stout.
What a naughty boy was that
To try to drown the little pussy cat.

Creek

A freshwater creek ran along the lower edge of our property. We carried its water up to the kitchen, where it was boiled for household use. More buckets were hauled to a large black pot outside, where Mother would build a fire beneath it to wash clothes.

After scrubbing and rinsing, she hung the laundry on a line to dry. When everything was sun-dried and crisp, she'd unpin the clothes and place them in a basket. Sometimes, if something wasn't too heavy, she'd hand it to me to carry to the basket. Then, with the full load balanced in her arms, Mother would carry the basket back into the house.

We loved playing by the creek, but it wasn't always allowed. Only Dottie and Ray, the two oldest, could go there alone. The rest of us needed supervision, unless we'd been taught the safety rules.

Corn Bin

The corn bin was another special place, though only Dottie and Ray were trusted to play in it unsupervised. We had two types of corn: one for the animals and another, sweet corn on the cob, for the family table.

I remember days in the field when we couldn't wait to get home to eat the sweet corn. We'd build a little fire at the end of a row, fetch water from the creek, boil the corn, or roast it on a stick. It was some of the best corn I've ever tasted, and we ate our fill, whether in the kitchen or out under the open sky.

Transportation

Our main transportation was a wagon pulled by horses. I don't remember riding in a car until after I'd left home. But Billy recalls riding in one now and then. More often, the horses would take us home automatically, standing by the barn until someone came to unharness them. We'd be carried into the house, already asleep.

Schoolhouse

Across the highway from our home was the one-room schoolhouse. Billy, Dottie, and Ray went there while Angie and I were still too young. I sometimes tagged along. I remember climbing into the empty schoolhouse one day and stealing chalk. I hid it in my shoes, but walking was awkward with it stuffed in the sides. The guilt followed me home.

Church

Our church was a Pentecostal one, just down the road. We rode there in a wagon pulled by our horses, Rocky and Kate. We didn't just go on Sundays; services were held several times a week. I loved church. I especially loved sitting with friends, or even by myself, soaking in the singing and sermons.

One night, I fell asleep in the pew after writing on the back of the bench with stolen chalk. Someone gently lifted me and laid me on a pallet at the back of the church. I woke up surrounded by other sleeping children. I never got in trouble for writing on the pew. Maybe whoever carried me decided not to tell Mama. But I knew what I had done, and I felt guilty.

Sometimes, kids were carried home still asleep. Once, a neighbor accidentally took the wrong child wrapped in a blanket. That was the kind of community we had, close-knit, loving, and sometimes a little mixed up in the best way.

Playing on the Farm

Billy and I were already inseparable by the time I was old enough to remember anything clearly. We played constantly, under the house, in the shade, in the sand. Our "cars" were just rocks, and we made winding roads beneath the house with sticks and imagination. We also played on and under the furniture inside when we were allowed.

The long path that stretched from the house to the road became our racetrack. We rolled old tires down it and took turns climbing inside to be rolled along. We had almost no store-bought toys, so we made do with what we had. That yard held all the entertainment we needed.

I remember trying to pick up one of the big iron wheels left in the yard. I wanted so badly to move it, just like Billy could. But it was too heavy, and it landed on my foot when I dropped it. To this day, the toenail on my right big toe is deformed, a lasting reminder of that moment and that wheel.

Billy and I shared the same toys, and he's written about them in a way I can't improve upon. His memories match mine:

Billy:

'*My toys consisted of a lid from a syrup bucket, which was the steering wheel of my make-believe eighteen-wheeler (cattle truck). I could back it into some of the tightest places and climb some of the steepest hills by shifting the fifteen-speed transmission and straining the motor to its limit. I would play for hours by myself. Make believe.*

My other toy was a used snuff jar. Our house was partially off the ground, maybe four feet. The sand was deep in that part of the country, which made it pretty nice to play in the shade under the house. I would turn the snuff jar around with the open end to the rear and push it through the sand as a car.

I had other really nice toys, like old car tires that we found in the ditch. I chased that tire many a mile. The other toy I had was the outer steel rim off of a wagon, which was approximately twelve inches in diameter, and a stiff wire made with a "U" shape on one end and a twisted handle at the other. I would put the "U" shape against the wheel and push it.'

We'd sometimes hide in a shed just to get away from Dottie, who was supposed to supervise us. We weren't supposed to wander out of sight of the house, but we tested that rule often.

Billy:
"I played with my little sister, Bobbi, sometimes. We played doctor or made mud pies with her little play dishes.

One day, we heard a tractor struggling down in the field, so I grabbed Bobbi's hand and said, 'Let's go see what's going on.' Dottie was supposed to be watching us, but we slipped away. When she found us, she gave our fannies a good paddling.

Daddy usually treated his livestock well. But one day, one of the mules just wouldn't behave, and he smacked it with a plow line to get its attention.

A day or so later, Daddy and a neighbor went into the woods behind the barn to cut wood. I wanted to see what Daddy was doing, so I grabbed Bobbi by the hand, and off we went. We found him, and he asked if Dottie knew we were there. I said, 'Yes, sir.'

Right on cue, we heard Dottie shouting from the house: 'Billy! Bobbi! Where are you?!' Her voice could out-yell an Arkansas pig caller. Daddy realized I'd lied, and he walked us back home.

As we crossed the cotton field, Daddy cut a stalk, stripped the leaves, and made a switch. I was in short pants, and he tapped me on my bare legs, telling me to walk ahead. Bobbi ran, trying to escape the swats, but I stayed put, crying hard.

When we reached the barnyard gate, Daddy stopped to open it. I turned to him, tears streaming down my cheeks, and said, 'Daddy, if I was as big as you and you were as little as me, I couldn't whip you like you were a mule.'

Daddy's eyes filled with tears. He picked me up and carried both of us home. That's the only time I remember him whipping me. Not that I probably didn't deserve it."

Love in a House of Hurt

I loved being where my mother was, especially when she was working. On wash days, I would sit nearby and watch her tend the fire beneath the black iron pot, stirring the laundry with a stick. Other times, I'd wander over to the one-room schoolhouse across the road. It had one teacher for eight grades, and when Billy started school, they let me sit in on his class. The teacher would gather small groups while the rest of the students worked quietly. It felt like a little world of its own.

When Billy, Dottie, and Ray were away at school, I stayed close to Mama. She was always doing something, canning, scrubbing, tending the garden, hanging laundry, or cooking. I remember one sunny day when I lay my head on a mattress she had set out in the sun. I must've dozed off, and when I woke, I saw a little patch of saliva on the fabric. I felt ashamed, like I had ruined something. But Mama said nothing. She just looked at me with kind eyes, and I felt safe.

Sometimes, when she worked outside and I played in the house, she'd check on me through the window. One glance from her could say everything, stern if I was getting into something I shouldn't, gentle if all was well.

Mama was a master of order and tidiness. She taught us early to return things to their proper place, not just to avoid clutter but so that when something was needed, it was ready. We didn't have much, but what we had was respected.

One Halloween stands out. Mama made me a cat costume out of a flour sack, tracing the outline and stitching it to fit. I was so proud wearing it to the schoolhouse, but I wanted it off as soon as I got home. Later, when Mama had guests, I asked her to help me put it back on. Then off again. Then on again. I'm unsure how often I repeated that little game, but Mama always helped me. She had endless patience.

I never recall her scolding me, even when I did something wrong. Somehow, I always knew when she disapproved; her expression alone was enough. I admired her deeply, even before I turned five.

She taught me songs and Bible verses that I can still recite. She was my Sunday School teacher, my example, and my comfort. I remember brushing her long hair into a bun as she talked and laughed with Dottie. "Let me comb it," I said. She smiled and let me. That moment stayed with me.

Our "Daily Bread"

Our family went on Relief at some point, though I don't recall exactly when or why. We didn't feel ashamed. Sometimes it brought unexpected joys, like an overabundance of cabbage. I misheard a song in church: "Only Believe, Only Believe, All Things Are Possible, Only Believe." I thought it said, "On Relief, On Relief, All Things Are Possible on Relief."

We had cabbage every way you could imagine: boiled with ham, wrapped around sausage, raw with carrots, or with onions. Mama never canned it, though. She said it would blow up, and I believe her.

No matter how little we had, Mama always managed to put food on the table. We didn't always eat together, but we always had enough. Cornbread was our staple, served with beans, greens, soups, stew, syrup, and molasses. The cornbread was made with just cornmeal, baking powder, and buttermilk. My favorite was crumbled cornbread in a cup with buttermilk and onions. There was even a pan of cornbread made just for the chickens and pigs.

We raised chickens and hogs for our meat, and hunting dogs helped us get deer during the season. For church dinners on the grounds, Mama would always prepare a meat dish to contribute.

Hard Times at Home

There was often tension in our home. Daddy's repeated stays in the veterans' hospital left Mama to raise the children and manage the farm independently. Even as a small child, just four or five years old, I could sense the lack of harmony. But despite the difficulties, I never once saw Daddy mistreat us children. He showed us love and respect.

I remember one day when Daddy was home working, and Mama was in the field. Dottie was in charge of looking after Billy, Angie, and me. Angie, being the youngest, was a handful, and Billy and I had wandered off to the barn to play. Dottie couldn't find us, which soon got Daddy involved in the search. When they found us, Daddy marched us home. I was so scared that I ran ahead, crying, not from pain, but from fear. Billy stayed back with Daddy, who had a switch in hand, then Billy, brave as ever, said, "If you were as little as I and I was as big as you, I wouldn't whip you like a mule." Daddy dropped the switch, picked Billy up, and carried us back to the house.

I remember another moment when I played inside the house and everyone else was outside. Daddy called me over, picked me up, and patted me on the bottom. Thinking I'd done something wrong, I started to cry. He held me close and said, "I'm sorry. I was giving you birthday presents. Today is your birthday." I hadn't been hurt, just startled. Then we all laughed and celebrated.

When Daddy was home, Mama would often get pregnant. I remember one time when she was far along in a pregnancy, and Daddy was still in the hospital. She needed help with the farm and asked if the doctor would allow him to come home. The doctor agreed, and Daddy was released.

But soon after he came home, the fighting began again. I saw them argue, and then one day, I saw something that has stayed with me the rest of my life. Daddy took the bridle reins and began hitting Mama. She ran toward the house, and not long after, she had Angie and me with her and out the door. We caught a ride going in the direction of a relative's home. When we were dropped off, Mama carried Angie and began walking. Eventually, she stopped and placed Angie down. I saw how exhausted she was, her big belly heavy with the baby.

She asked me to walk ahead and check if the nearby house belonged to a relative. If not, I was to try the next one. The first one was familiar; I recognized it as family. When I turned back, Mama had already made it nearly to the doorstep.

We were welcomed inside. Angie was put to bed, and I was placed in a high chair and given cornbread and buttermilk. I lay my head on the tray to rest and heard someone say, "See, she's asleep. Let's put her to bed." I slept soundly.

Soon after, the baby was born. I was four years old. It was a boy, and they named him Other Neal, pronounced "O-thur Neal."

Daddy went back to the veterans' hospital, leaving Mama to care for all of us: Dottie, Ray, Billy, me, Angie, and now the newborn. That was her ninth birth. As before, she requested that Daddy come home to help.

Daddy returned, but something wasn't right. He didn't seem to believe that Other Neal was his child. I don't know if that was the source of their tension, but the fighting returned. One night, while the baby was sleeping between them, Mama suddenly screamed and jumped out of bed. Dottie ran in. Neal was dead. Mama said she had rolled over onto him. He was only 21 days old.

After Neal's death, everything changed. Mama was often gone, but Dottie took care of us. I don't remember feeling happy, though I couldn't have said why then. Sometimes, I was hungry, but never for long. Dottie would feed us. I imagine Mama had prepared the food ahead of time. It felt like Mama was hiding, maybe from Daddy, who was often in a bad mood. Yet they were still sharing a bed.

A Life Shattered

When I was five, something happened that changed everything. In March 1939, less than a month after Neal's death, tragedy struck.

Dottie heard Mama calling for help. She told me later that she ran toward her, just as Daddy reached for his gun. As Mama and Dottie turned to leave the room, Daddy shot Mama.

The noise brought Ray and Billy running. I woke up and saw them struggling with Daddy to take the gun away. Billy was bouncing around in his long underwear with the flap hanging down, his little behind showing. I remember that detail clearly.

When the gun was finally taken away, Daddy went outside, shouting, "What have I done? Oh God, what have I done?"

I could see Mama lying on the floor from my bed in the next room. Dottie was by her side.

Ray and Billy ran to the neighbors for help. We didn't have a phone. Dottie stayed with Mama. Soon, Aunt Arma arrived and sat with her. Mama asked for water. My aunt stood to get it, but Mama said, "I want Bobbi to get it."

It was dark, but I knew where the glasses were. I climbed onto a chair and reached into the cabinet. I found a glass and filled it from the pail with the dipper. Mama never drank it.

When the ambulance came, they carried her out on a stretcher, right past my bed. I reached over and put my hand over Angie's eyes. She stirred but didn't wake.

Daddy was still shouting. I whispered, "Please make Daddy quiet so I can sleep." Then the police took him away.

And I slept.

A few days later, I remember sitting with Dottie. She told me what had happened that night. She'd heard a sound and ran into the room. Daddy had the gun. Mama and Dottie tried to leave the room, and Daddy fired. Mama collapsed. Dottie struggled to take the gun away. Ray and Billy arrived and helped her.

Dottie later showed me the holes in the wall where fragments from the shot had embedded.

My mother died in the hospital just an hour or so after she arrived. It was Saturday, March 25, 1939. I was five years old.

Newspaper's Report

10_Photo: Fairfield Recorder

The County Newspaper – Established 1876
Fairfield, Freestone County, Texas
March 30, 1939 – Number 28
"Virgil Richardson Charged with Murder of Wife

A sad Tragedy Occurred near Fairfield When Mother of Five Children Fatally Shot Mrs. Virgil Richarson, 34, died at a Teague hospital Saturday morning about 8 o'clock from a shotgun wound received eight hours earlier at her home three miles north east of Fairfield. Her husband Virgil (Gould) Richardson was placed in jail here, and his examining trial was held before Justice Willis Young, Monday, and Richardson was remanded to jail without bail.

Some four months ago Richardson was sent to the Veterans' hospital at Waco for mental treatment, and he was allowed to return home about seven weeks ago. Friday, accompanied by his wife, he went to Corsicana for medical examination.

A daughter of the couple sleeping in an adjoining room states that she was awakened by her mother calling for help. She ran into the room, and her father had a gun; she took it away from him, but he again secured the gun and loaded it. Her mother and father were standing near the bed, and the gun fired while she was not looking. The entire load of shot passed through Mrs. Richardson's body.

Richardson, we are informed, stated he could not rest, and when he placed his hand on his wife she told him to let her sleep. He got up and got the gun, a single barrel shotgun, but had no intention of shooting his wife and did not explain how it happened.

Burial was in the Lake Chapel cemetery Sunday afternoon under direction of Burleson Funeral Home after services by the Rev.Robt. Hankins. Near surviving relatives are: five children; her parents, Mr. and Mrs. Terrell Teer of Dawson, and four sisters and one brother. "

In the Wake of Tragedy

I don't remember much from the funeral except for being lifted to see inside the casket. Whoever was holding me told me to "kiss her goodbye." But the woman in the casket didn't look like my Mama. I squirmed in their arms,

unwilling. I remember shaking my head and making it clear I didn't want to. There was pressure, but I refused. Eventually, they put me down. I was only five, but I knew my Mama could no longer see or hear me.

11_Photo: Angie, Bobbi Nell (1939)

I thought testifying in court would be more important, maybe even comforting. But it wasn't what I expected. Dottie and Ray each went in to speak with the judge, one at a time. I sat in the hallway alone, waiting for my turn.

When I was finally brought in, no one was allowed to accompany me.

A kind voice asked me questions, and I answered yes and no as best I could. But I never had the chance to tell my story, not the way I felt it inside. I was dismissed; I was too young to matter. That disappointment stayed with me.

12_Photo: Billy Dean, Ray (1939)

By 1937, the Great Depression had gripped rural Texas, and most families were already struggling. For our relatives, keeping all five of us children together was impossible. The Richardsons were hardworking farming people but didn't have the resources to care for more mouths.

The court decided we would become wards of the state. That meant being separated was almost certain. If any family could keep one or two of us, it would only be for a short time. Staying together was no longer an option.

13_Photo: Young to Old: Angie, Bobbi Nell, Billy Dean, Ray, Dottie (1939)

For about a month after Mama's death, the five of us, Dottie (15), Ray (13), Billy (7), I (5), and Angie (3), did not live together. We stayed with different relatives from the Richardson side of the family. I don't know exactly where my siblings stayed during that time, but I clearly remember the two homes I was placed in.

The first home I lived in was with my Uncle Harvel and Aunt Arma, my daddy's brother and sister-in-law. I was the only one of the five to stay there. They had two daughters younger than me: Shirley Sue (4) and Delia Vannette

(1). We often attended church services, sometimes right there in their home, and it brought me a sense of comfort.

One particular evening stands out. After returning from church, Uncle Harvel asked us to stay in the car while he went inside the house. I remember whispering the Bible verse my mother had taught me: *"When I am afraid, I will trust in Thee."* When he returned, he told us that he had frightened off an intruder who had come through the window. Nothing was taken, but I never forgot that moment of fear and faith.

My Aunt Annie Mae and Uncle Roy Pittman were the second family I stayed with. Aunt Annie Mae was Daddy's sister, and Uncle Roy was her husband. Living with them was Ruby Mae Cagal, the daughter of Annie Mae's sister, Ethel Richardson-Cagal, who had died in childbirth in 1922. They had adopted Ruby Mae and wanted to adopt me, too.

My time with them was peaceful and even joyful. They had a Victrola, and after showing me how to operate it, they let me use it on my own. I listened to songs like:

- "Can the Circle Be Unbroken?"
- "With a Banjo on My Knee"
- "That Silver-Haired Daddy of Mine"
- "I Want to Be a Cowboy's Sweetheart"
- "I Don't Want Your Greenback Dollar"

I'd play them again and again until I had memorized the lyrics. I can still hear the tunes in my head.

I've often wondered what swayed the court to grant custody of the five Richardson children to my mother's parents, Mr. and Mrs. Terrell Teer of Dawson, Texas. We called them Big Daddy and Big Mama.

14_and 15_Photos: Big Daddy, Big Mama Teer: (1939)

Maybe it was because they petitioned to keep us all together. Maybe it was because Big Daddy was a deputy sheriff. I don't know.

16_Photo: Big Daddy wearing his gun

I can only imagine that no Richardson relative could afford to take all five of us in. At least, that's what I presumed when I was old enough to reflect on why we spent the next nine months with Big Mama and Big Daddy in Dawson, Texas.

They lived in a "shotgun house," a narrow, rectangular home no more than 12 feet wide, with rooms arranged in a row and doors at each end. It was a tight squeeze for five kids and two adults. Big Mama worked at a sewing room.

Big Daddy was a deputy sheriff, but I don't remember him doing much with us during the weekdays. Dottie took care of Angie and me. She bathed us, dressed us, and fixed our hair. I don't know who watched Angie during the day while the older kids were at school and Big Mama was working. I spent a lot of time alone in the yard.

Big Daddy had about four peach trees in his garden which he was quite proud of. My brother, Billy Dean found Big Daddy's hammer and nails in his shed. He drove quite a few nails in his prize peach trees. Big Daddy gave him a hard whipping. I did the same thing Billy did: I drove nails into the trees but never got in trouble.

On Saturday nights, we went to the movies. Angie usually fell asleep, and Big Daddy carried us home. I'd replay the movie scenes in my mind for days and even made up my own endings while playing alone in the dirt with rocks and twigs.

Dottie would bathe Angie and me on Sundays, and we'd dress up for church. I walked to Sunday School on my own and loved it. I memorized Bible verses and songs, which I still remember today.

I even made a friend, a girl named Creassy, who lived up the street. She was often home alone. Years later, when I visited the State Orphanage in Austin, she was the same girl. She had become an accomplished pianist, and we sang together around the piano. It was a sweet reunion.

Life at Big Mama and Big Daddy's wasn't stressful. I had a lot of freedom. Maybe someone was watching me, but I never felt watched.

Big Mama and Big Daddy consulted the minister at my Baptist church. As a trustee of Buckner Orphans Home in Dallas, he explained that we could be placed there as wards of the court. Wanting to understand what that would mean, Big Mama and Big Daddy visited Buckner to observe how the children were treated. After their visit, they began incorporating some of the Home's practices into our lives.

They adopted a demerit system for discipline to manage the misbehavior we had developed. At the same time, some rules were relaxed. We were now allowed to hum or sing at the table, a change from previous silence. We were also encouraged to have light conversation during meals. Silence was no longer a requirement.

We stayed there for nine months, from April through August 1939. When I turned six in August, I was enrolled in school that September. It was like kindergarten, just toys and play. The teacher knew I wouldn't be there long, so she didn't teach me anything academic. I felt like I was on a waiting list. I didn't feel safe or settled; I was just in a state of waiting. "What's going to happen to me?" I kept wondering.

From Nowhere and No One—To an Orphans Home

As court-appointed wards, Billy, Angie, and I were sent to Buckner Orphans Home in Dallas, Texas, which only accepted children twelve and under. Sadly, Dottie and Ray were too old to be admitted.

Ray, just over the limit at thirteen, missed the chance for this structured refuge, and his life grew difficult. Too old for school and too young for work, he was caught in a painful limbo. Dottie, fifteen, was also ineligible and went to live with our Aunt Mattie. She never returned to school. She married young, divorced soon after, and eventually forged a life through sewing and hairdressing. Later, Dottie married Butch Townzen and became like a second mother to us younger three.

Although my heart ached at being separated from Dottie and Ray, it was a small comfort that Billy, Angie, and I were at least allowed to stay together in Buckner's Receiving Home—if only for a while.

What Billy Remembers About Growing Up in Fairfield, Texa

My brother, Billy Dean, wrote his vivid account of life growing up in Fairfield, Texas. His memories enhance my story and bring another voice to our shared childhood. I have included his full recollections, just as he wrote them.

"It started according to my birth certificate on September 7, 1931. It stated: Baby Boy born to Velma & Virgil Richardson on that date. Some families didn't name their children until later. I guess to see what you were like. So, I guess they found out I was hard-headed as a billy goat, so they named me Billy.

My memory relates back to when I was around five years old, maybe six, on a small farm in Fairfield, Texas, Freestone County. I had three sisters and one brother that lived. Dottie was 11, Ray 9, me, then 5, Bobbi 3 and Angie maybe 1. You can see there was some difference in our ages. My cousins were older, or about as old as Dottie and Ray. That left me to play with either Ray or Bobbi or by myself. My family was like other families in the depression years. We made it the best way we could with the help of neighbors, friends, relatives and hard work.

My toys consisted of a lid from a syrup bucket, which was the steering wheel of my make-believe eighteen wheeler (cattle truck). I could back it into some of the tightest places and climb some of the steepest hills by shifting the fifteen-speed transmission and straining the motor to its limit. I would play for hours by myself. Make believe. My other toy was a used snuff jar. Our house was partially off the ground, maybe four feet. The sand was deep in that part of the country, which made it pretty nice to play in the shade under the house. I would turn the snuff jar around with the open end to the rear and push it through the sand as a car.

I had other real nice toys, like old car tires that we found in the ditch. I chased that tire many a mile. The other toy I had was the outer steel rim off of a wagon which was approximately twelve inches in diameter, and a stiff wire made with a "U" shape on one end and a twisted handle at the other. I would put the "U" shape against the wheel and push it.

I decided to try my hand at rolling a steel cultivator wheel, which was much taller than I was and quite heavy. I was going pretty good until it started in a tight turn around and around right across my bare foot. I laid out in the road and cried so hard that I lost my breath and started to turn purple. Someone came and got me breathing again. I was always doing that. I don't know why. That is why I got my way some of the time and they had to keep an eye on me when they whipped me. Some of my kin folks said that it was to get my way, but I couldn't help it. I just could not catch my breath if I cried too hard.

My older brother and sister and cousins would want to go down in the woods to smoke grapevine and play. I wanted to go too, but they would run off and leave me. So, I would lay in the hot, sandy road and cry until they had to come back and get me. They said they would let me tag along if I wouldn't tell on them for smoking grapevine. Naturally that is the first thing I did to blackmail them. I played with my little sister, Bobbi, sometimes like a doctor or making mud pies with her little play dishes.

One day, we heard a tractor way down in the field trying to get unstuck; so, I got Bobbi by the hand to go see what was going on. Well, Dottie was supposed to babysit us, but somehow we got away. But, when she finally caught up with us, she paddled our fannies.

My daddy was pretty good about treating his livestock good. But, one day in the barnyard, this mule didn't want to do what he wanted him to do. So, in order to get his attention, he busted his butt with a plow line.

Later on, maybe a day or so, daddy and the neighbor went into the woods behind the barn to cut wood. I wanted to see daddy work, so I got Bobbi by the hand and went off to find daddy. We found him and he asked us: "did Dottie know we were up there". I said, "Yes, sir." About that time, Dottie called out "Billy - Bobbi, where are you?" She had a voice that was so loud, she made those Arkansas pig callers think they had laryngitis.

Daddy knew right away that I had told a lie, so he proceeded to march us back to the house. As we went through the cotton field, daddy cut off a cotton stalk, stripped the leaves off and made him a nice switch. I had short pants on and he began tapping me on my bare legs and telling me to strike out ahead. Bobbi ran ahead of me where she wouldn't get so many licks. But, I was hard-headed. I was crying so hard that I didn't run. When we got to the barnyard gate, daddy stopped to open the gate. Well, it struck me what daddy had done to that old mule the day before. So, I turned to daddy with tears streaming down my cheeks. I said, "Daddy, if I was as big as you and you was as little as me, I couldn't whip you like you was a mule." Daddy, with tears in his eyes, picked me up and carried both of us to the house. That is the only time I remember daddy whipping me. Not that I probably didn't deserve it.

I was really close to daddy. I tried to be grown up like daddy. He would let me sit between his legs and drive the team of horses. The horses were pretty tame. One was a male, which was named Rock and the female was named Kate. I could ride Kate, but Rock was a little spirited. When daddy was plowing in the field close to the house and it came quitting time, I would meet him. He would put me on Kate's back and I would ride to the barn. That was a lot of fun.

Like I said, I had a pretty big imagination growing up. I would imitate the horses pulling the plow. Daddy would sometimes lay the harness back on the plow to let them rest while he ate dinner. I would ask daddy to put the harness on me where I could pull the plow. So, he would put the harness around my neck, holding up most of the weight, and I would go through the motions of pulling the plow.

Daddy would let me drive the team while he pulled corn. I would turn them around at the end of the row and back in the next row to be pulled. That was quite a feat, being only five or six.

Ray and Dottie I guess were in school. When I could get Ray to play with me, I would get a string and put it in my mouth like a horse has to do with a bit. I would get a hoe and by holding onto the handle and turning the blade on its corner with the string back behind me, Ray could drive me like I was plowing a field. We made rows all over the schoolhouse yard.

Mom would give us small kids cocoa and sugar mixed dry. We would put it in snuff cans like older folks did snuff. We would put it between our cheek and gums and make believe we were dipping snuff. We had cocoa and sugar running out the corner of our mouths like grandma.

When It came cotton picking time, the grown ups would go to the fields. Neighbors and friends would help each other. Sometimes us small kids would ride on the cotton sack while they picked cotton. They wouldn't leave us alone by ourselves very long because big, red ants would bite us. They were everywhere. When they did bite, the elderly that dipped snuff would put it on the bite. It would help from hurting as much.

I had a dog like all boys do. Actually, we had two or three. One was named Justice. I can hardly remember if it was a shepherd or a cur (editor's note: a "cur dog" is a term often used to describe a mixed breed dog with a strong herding instinct), but we were inseparable. Ray says it was so named because daddy got it from the Justice of the Peace.

I decided to go for a walk. Justice followed me. It got dark. I must have gotten tired and sleepy. I laid down, Justice by my side. I don't remember being scared, but daddy and the neighbors were out looking for me, calling my name and Justice. Justice let them know where we were, which was in a graveyard. They were too glad to get me back to whip me, but I got a talking to.

All us kids were taught early in life to recognize a mad dog at a far distance by the way it moved. It trotted at a slow gate and in a straight line. So, if you stayed pretty still, it would pass you by if not too close.

One day, daddy was talking to Ellis Chapel who lived up the road from us. Ellis said something was getting his ducks. He didn't know if it was coyotes or wolves. Well, it wasn't long before he found out. It was Justice, My dog. They say once they start catching chickens and ducks, the only way to stop them is to shoot them. Well, guess what? Daddy told me to go to the house and get the shotgun. Justice was with me. I asked daddy what was he going to do. He said, "Do as I ask." I did. He tied a rope around Justice's neck and let him into the woods. He told me to go back to the house. I heard the shot. I cried and thought my world had ended.

Daddy hated it also because he raised hogs and that was one of the finest hog dogs in the country. Daddy raised hogs which he killed for meat. We didn't raise beef cows much. Maybe one milk cow. Daddy would mark his hogs by cutting their ear with a knife. Then, he would let them run wild down on the river bottoms. One day the neighbor came by and asked daddy if he had seen his hog that got away. Daddy said, "No, but come Sunday, saddle up your horse and come over to the house and we will go looking down in the bottoms and see if it is running with mine." The hog wasn't marked, but by the description, Daddy knew he had killed that hog a couple of days before and made sausage and ham out of it. He asked the neighbor, later, how he liked the meat he gave him. He said, "Real good." Daddy told him that was his hog he had killed.

Ray was four years older than me, so he was always talking me into things. One day, he had this brilliant idea to get mama's #2 wash tub that she washed clothes in and go boating. We were little and that tub must have weighed a ton since it was half of a wooden barrel. Ray conned me into putting it on my nice, new, red wagon which I got for Christmas. Then, we pulled and tugged for seemed like hours across plowed fields to the six foot deep stock tank in the middle of the field. It just so happened daddy was plowing that field down at the far end.

Ray and I wrestled that tub off the wagon into the water. He asked me if I wanted to go first since it was my wagon that we used. I said, "No, go ahead." I held it still while he got in without any paddle. When he sat down, his arms weren't long enough to reach the water to steer him. I pushed it out away from shore. It made about three or four complete turns in the water. He hadn't panicked yet, but it didn't take long. Knowing he couldn't get back to shore and I couldn't help him. The wind wasn't blowing, so he sat out there in the middle with the hot, July sun beating down on him. He hated it, but his pirate sailing career had come to an end. The next thing was to get him back to shore. The only choice we had was to go get daddy at the other end of the field. Daddy came to our rescue, but not to his liking.

Ray had another brilliant idea one winter day. We lived across the road from the wooden, shotgun, one-room schoolhouse. He and I decided to build a fire in the pot-bellied stove which was up close to the teacher's desk at the front of the room. So, before school opened, we did just that. After we got it started, we walked back across the road to the house. The stove got so hot, it was cherry red from its legs to the top of the chimney. School was delayed for over an hour until it cooled off to where we could enter school. We left that up to someone else after that.

We went to church once in a while. We would go by wagon or, sometimes, the Ward boys would come by and pick up us and the neighbor kids on their flat-bed truck. The truck didn't have sideboards, so the older kids would sit on the outside and they put us younger kids in the middle of the bed. Once in a while the sand was so deep that the truck would get stuck and the older kids would have to push it out.

We were members of the "Holy Rollie" church. When we got sleepy, they would put us on pallets at the back of the church until church was over. When the church was over with no electric lights, it was slightly dark. With quite a few kids wrapped up in blankets and quilts, they would pick up others for a joke, or not think which kid was theirs, put you in their wagon and drive off. You never knew whom you might spend the night with until the next day. They would feed and take care of you until they saw the rightful owner.

Sometimes my uncle that lived down the road would come by to see the family. His name was Dean Cockrell, on my mother's side. He had a pickup that had big lights on the fender. My middle name is Dean, which I was named after him. When he came to see us and he got ready to leave, he would pretend to take my red wagon with him. That would make me cry, but he got a big kick out of it. Daddy would tell him to quit making me cry. He would finally get me to go home with him. I would get to ride and straddle those big lights on his pickup, which was a lot of fun.

My mom would dress me up in short pants to go spend the day with my Uncle Dean and aunt. My aunt liked me a lot. She would take up for me when Uncle Dean aggravated me and made me cry. One evening while I was visiting him and I was all dressed up in my clean, white, short pants, we had to go milk the cow. Well, it had come a little rain and this cow had made cow piles all over the cow lot. Uncle let the little calf get its dinner when the cow would let the milk come down to where he could get it. After the calf sucked a little while, he usually tied it to a post in the middle of the lot, but this time, he decided he would let me hold the rope to keep the calf from going back to its mother. Well, about the time he got his stool and bucket to milk the cow, the little calf decided to get some more dinner. Well, I tried to hold the little calf, but I stepped in the cow pile and that little calf drug me through about two more. The calf knocked Uncle Dean off his stool. I thought he was going to be mad, but he turned and looked at me, and what I looked like, and smelled even worse, and he folded up laughing. Aunty cleaned me up and finally got me to quit crying.

Dottie told me that when I was little and in the baby cradle, she would have to rock me to sleep in the rocking chair. She wanted to play with dolls, but I wouldn't go to sleep until she rocked me. Well, about the time she thought I was asleep, she would lay me down and I would start crying again. So, she got this idea to put me in my cradle, which rocked, and she would tie a string on her big toe and to the cradle. When she moved her foot back and forth, the cradle would rock. But, sometimes she got preoccupied with her playing and quit rocking. Well, I would call out "rock, sitter, rock", not speaking too plainly, to say sister. It was customary for the oldest kid to take care of the little ones.

My Uncle Harold and Aunt Amy married the same year I was born. A tornado came a few years later and blew their house away. My aunt got her arm broken. They moved across the woods from us, maybe two miles. For a short cut, the trail led across a deep ditch, over a few fences and through a graveyard and woods. Ray and Dottie would run ahead of me and hide behind trees and gravestones. When I would come by, scared to death, they would jump out at me and make me cry. The next time we went to see my aunt and uncle, I would try to get Ray and Dottie to take the long way around the road, but, no, they had too much fun making me cry.

Ray and I slept in the same room. Ray would walk in his sleep. One night, daddy and mama went to church in the wagon. That night, Ray walked in his sleep. The house was about a quarter or so of a mile from the six-foot high gate at the road. He climbed over it, climbed through a five-strand, barbed-wire fence, walked another quarter of a mile down the trail, through the woods to the neighbor's house, and knocked on the door. They let him in and put him to bed without waking him. When they heard the wagon coming down the road, they stopped daddy and daddy and mama took Ray back to the house. Daddy started *locking the door, but Ray would get up banging on the door. Daddy would get up and make him sit by the fireplace the rest of the night.*

My mom passed away and daddy had to go to the hospital for a while. My uncles and aunts wanted us to come and live with them, but with different ones. My grandmother and granddaddy got custody of us kids. We called them Big Mom and Big Dad. They were my mother's daddy and mother. They wanted to keep us together. We went to live with them for a while.

I don't know just how long we stayed with them; maybe a year and a half or two years. It was okay, but not like being on the farm. It was pretty close to town.

I must have been about six or almost seven. I remember Big Dad had about four peach trees in his garden which he was quite proud of. I found his hammer and nails in his shed. I drove quite a few nails in his prize peach trees. That is one of the hardest whippings I ever remember getting.

Ray was quite a corker. Once, he made a small truck out of some boards and skate wheels. He went to the show and told me not to play with it. Well, you guessed it! I played with it and left tracks all over the yard. So, he decided to teach me a lesson by beating me up. Well, I wasn't going for it. So, I fought back. I wound up getting knocked in the wash pot which was in the backyard.

Dottie and Ray fought sometimes. One time they were fighting and I was in the next room. The door was closed. Ray called for me to come and help. The bed was next to the door. I opened the door quite fast and it hit him. He fell across the bed and didn't breathe or move a muscle. I thought I had killed him and Dottie made me think so too. So, I tried to wake him, but he would not move. I was scared and started crying. He jumped up and started laughing. I really could have killed him, but I was glad to see he was okay.

Ray and I made a little money to go to the show by picking up onions and potatoes that had fallen on the ground from when they unloaded box cars near our house. In some small towns, the townspeople would throw turkeys off the top of the show roof, which was one story high. The turkeys would fly and run. I caught one once, but it nearly beat me to pieces. (editor's note: just put "turkey drop 1924 chandler" in search bar of "YOUTUBE" to see a video of a "turkey drop", filmed in Chandler OK in 1924. It illustrates vividly a turkey "beating up" a small boy:

Big Mama and Big Daddy couldn't keep us anymore. They consulted with their pastor and decided to place us in an orphan's home. They picked Buckner Orphans' Home. They wanted us to stay together, but the age limit was where Ray and Dottie were too old, so Ray stayed with Big Daddy and Dottie went to live with my mother's sister, (editor's note: Mattie), who is my aunt on my mother's side. Bobbi, 5; Angie, 3; and I was 7 years old, so they say since I didn't know my birthday or how old I was."

35

Facilities Where I Lived from 6 to 17
First Days in a Strange New World

Before joining the main campus at Buckner Orphans Home, children lived at the Receiving Home, a welcoming facility that helped them adjust and

ensured they had no communicable diseases.

17_Photo: Receiving Home

The house parents, Mr. and Mrs. Saddler, created a warm, structured space to help grieving children begin a new chapter.

The Receiving Home had two sections with separate bathrooms, a shared dining area, a play yard, and a living room. When we arrived, another family, the Wallers, was there. Though their stay was brief, we bonded quickly. Betty Fern Waller would later become my roommate, and her older sister, Barbara, became a dear friend who took me to movies, the Starlight Opera, and visits to her family's home.

Shortly after, the Ward family arrived, five children in all. Prince and David were older and musically gifted. Alice Ann was my age, and Elsie matched Angie's age. Baby Joseph cried endlessly and was eventually taken in by relatives.

Major Thomas, a new orphan, couldn't stay at the Receiving Home because

it was full. Dr. Hal Buckner, the Home's director, took Major into his house for ten days. There, Major found a piano, taught himself a few songs, and impressed Dr. Buckner so much that a teacher was called to give him formal lessons.

18_Photo: Major Thomas

Major became a skilled pianist, studied music at Baylor, and later joined the Navy. Lacking a middle name, he adopted his late father's name, Owen, for military records, because they would not let him be called "Major". But to us, he was always "Major." We always knew when Major returned to campus, his spirited piano playing echoed across Buckner. His music turned Mana Hall into a place of joy, and we whispered to each other with excitement: "Major Thomas is here!"

Ironically, just as our ten-day intake ended, a measles outbreak struck the main campus. We stayed at the Receiving Home another ten days. So, instead of keeping disease out, we were kept from entering.

When the main campus reopened, we moved to separate dorms. This was heartbreaking. For the first time, I was not with Billy or Angie. My dormmates were my age, but I longed for my siblings. I often wondered if they were as lonely as I was.

Facilities and Buildings at Buckner

The Buckner main campus had a main entrance called the Main Gate. It opened at 8 a.m. and closed at 5 p.m. A gatekeeper and his wife lived in the brick gatehouse nearby. Entering the grounds meant entering a new world: structured, secure, and expansive.

18_Photo: Main Gate at Buckner Orphans Home

Buckner Orphans Home provided everything we needed to live, learn, and grow.

19_Photo: Main Campus

The main campus covered 60 acres, and most buildings were solid, red-brick structures, some one-story, others two or three stories high. Beyond the central campus were over 2,000 acres of farmland, a dairy, and recreation areas in wooded sections, one for boys and another for girls.

Visitors arrived through the Maris Welcome Center. This was the front-facing hub for guests and official business.

20_Photo: Maris Welcome Center

Behind it stood the statue of Father Buckner, a flagpole, and finally, the Chapel and auditorium.

The Chapel was central to our spiritual lives. Boys sat on one side, girls on the other, and there was space for a full choir. Behind the choir seats was a baptismal font. Summer revivals were especially memorable, culminating in baptisms.

21_Photo: The Chapel

I was baptized there at eight years old on July 4, 1941. After the ceremony, Brother Hal asked if anyone had something to say. I stood up and quoted the 23rd Psalm.

Next to the Chapel was the two-story building that housed both the educational rooms (upstairs) and Mana Hall (downstairs).

22_Photo: Educational Building

The classrooms were used for Sunday School, Training Union, and weekday Bible classes.

In those classrooms, we also played games, like "Knocking on Doors," a guessing game in which we hid in small rooms and tried not to be discovered. We could spend hours laughing and running between doors.

The dining room at Mana Hall served three meals daily to hundreds of children and staff. Each table had an assigned waitress on the girls' and boys' sides, and a matron was seated at every other table.

23_Photo: Mana Hall

Before every meal, we sang a hymn while someone played the piano. I once managed the entrance door for the girls' side of the dining hall. For three months, I opened the door at the start of every meal. Once the dishes were washed, the tables were reset for the next group.

For children under the age of six, there was the Sunbeam Home, boys and girls shared this space until they were old enough to move into separate dormitories.

24_Photo: Sunbeam Home: boys/girls: 0-6 yrs

The main campus was laid out in a large circular design. At the left of the circle was the Main Gate. On the top side were four boys' dorms. (see 19_Photo: Main Campus).

Boys' Dormitories:

25_Photo: Pires (Grades 1–3)

26_McElroy (Grades 4–6)

27_Photo: Freeland (Gr 7–9)

28_Photo: Cullum (Grades 10–12)

On the bottom side of the circle were five girls' dorms. These dormitories were more than just buildings. They were homes filled with routines, friendships, rules, chores, and quiet nighttime prayers. They were where we learned how to live with others and take care of our belongings.

Girls' Dormitories:

29_Photo: Hardin Home (Gr 1–3)

30_Photo: Crouch Home (Gr4–6)

31_Photo: Hunt Hall (Grades 7–9)

32_Photo: Buhrman (Gr 10–12)

33_Photo: Pender (Academy Srs)

School Buildings

34_Photo: Teacherage (Single teachers/staff)

The Grammar School housed grades 1 through 8. Each grade had its own classroom, and there was

also a study hall. A large play area surrounded the building, although no playground equipment existed.

35_Photo: Grammar School

The High School building stood

on the opposite side of the Chapel. It included academic classrooms, the library, science labs, and rooms for specialized programs.

36_Photo: High School

Girls learned cooking and sewing in the Home Economics wing, with stoves and sewing machines in connected rooms. The school newspaper was printed in a small press room, and a chemistry lab helped bring science to life.

At the end of the high school hallway were five piano practice rooms and one larger piano teacher's room. These were often filled with the sound of scales, hymns, or classical music being rehearsed.

37_Photo: Occupational facilities

Older students could pursue vocational skills in dedicated buildings for cosmetology, carpentry, and automobile repair. These programs gave children real-world skills, helping them transition into jobs after graduation. The cosmetology department trained many girls who went on to become beauticians.

Milk, Bread, Heat, and Healing

Located a mile or two from the main campus, the Buckner Dairy was operated by older boys. Cows were milked twice daily, and the milk was delivered to Mana Hall Milk from the Dairy early each morning. . At every meal, pitchers of milk and water were on each table. Cups and glasses were used depending on the drink. We drank a lot of milk unless it was cocoa morning. I remember the dairy crew working hard in the early mornings, no matter the weather. Their work helped keep the whole campus nourished.

Near Mana Hall stood the Bakery. Every day, the fresh scent of bread, cookies, or pies drifted from its wide receiving doors.

38_Photo: Bakery
The Bakery produced fresh loaves for every meal, toasted bread as a treat, and a weekly dessert rotation: cake on Sundays, cookies on Tuesdays, and pie on Thursdays. Syrup, butter, and warm bread made a fine dessert when the official one didn't quite satisfy.

The powerhouse controlled our heat and hot water. Steam radiators clanged and knocked as they warmed each building. We learned to place our clothes on them at night so they'd be warm when we dressed in the morning.

39_Photo: Steam radiator
Boys were trained to help operate the Powerhouse and maintain underground connections to every dorm and facility.

The hospital was at the far end of the campus.

40_Photo: The Hospital
On one side was a ward for girls, and on the other for boys. In the center were the kitchen and the

day clinic. There was an operating room, and upstairs were dental offices and an apartment for the dentist. There were two private rooms for children with special conditions or contagious illnesses.

I still remember Bobby Bray, who fell from the silo and was left paralyzed. He lived in one of those rooms. While working at the hospital, I discovered prosthetic leg forms with shoes attached, stored on a shelf. I was so startled, I thought they were real legs; it's a memory I've never forgotten.

The hospital laundry was kept separate from the campus laundry, and a special incinerator handled medical waste. Some jobs lasted three months, but the dental assistant position was different; girls who trained in it often kept the role until graduation.

Living in an Orphanage

Separated, Scared, and Wondering

My first day on the Orphanage's main campus marked the greatest insecurity I had ever known. I would sit looking past the fence surrounding the 60 acres on which the campus was built, wondering, "Will I ever adjust to this place and its ways of living?" "What is happening outside the front gate in other people's lives?" "What is my older sister, Dottie, doing?" "What about my older brother, Ray?"

After ten days in the Receiving Home with siblings, we were separated by age and moved into different dorms. That separation was painful. I remember entering the main campus without Billy Dean or Angie Darlene; it was heartbreaking. Once I got through it, I made it a point to show kindness to newcomers going through the same.

Angie was just three years old when she became a resident of Sunbeam Home, which housed boys and girls under six. It was comforting to know she was somewhere on the same campus, even if we couldn't be together daily.

Billy Dean, eight years old, was placed in the Pires Home, the dormitory for boys ages six through nine. After lunch each day, we were allowed a brief visit, about 15 or 20 minutes. Those small windows of time with Billy were precious.

When I was six, I was assigned to Hardin Home, a dormitory for girls ages six through nine. It became my first long-term "home" at Buckner. Hardin Home had the best playground on campus. The most exciting piece of equipment was a

maypole with four chains hanging down, each ending in a set of iron bars.

41_Photo: Johnny Strides

Girls would hold the bars, run around the pole to build momentum, lift their feet, and swing through the air in wide circles. Sometimes, others would push us higher and higher.

We had a set of swings and did various tricks on them. The boldest one was to swing so high and then launch yourself over the bar, a thrilling, jolting ride that was both scary and exhilarating. You had to hold on tight!

42_Photo: Swings

The seesaws were a daily favorite. We would "bump" each other, lifting our feet to give the other a sudden jolt as the board hit the ground. There were unspoken

rules: you never got off the seesaw unless your partner agreed. If someone was waiting, they replaced whichever girl had been on the longest.

43_Photo: Seesaws

These playground games were more than fun; they were part of the daily rhythm that brought some sense of joy and normalcy into our new lives.

Guided by Gentle Hands

There was a matron for each unit. I fondly remember my first matron, Miss Jennie Orr. She was the perfect person to care for a six-year-old girl adjusting to life away from home. Every evening, Miss Orr would gently wash our socks and underpants and lay them on the floor by our beds to dry, until we learned how to do it ourselves.

I never heard a harsh word from her. No girl ever spoke ill of Miss Orr. She cared for fifteen girls housed in four rooms, each pair of rooms sharing a bathroom. Her calm presence helped me through those early, anxious days.

Making My Bed, Missing My Brother

Even though Billy was two years older than I, I missed him terribly. We had spent nearly all of our time together before coming to Buckner. Angie, being much younger, was not a playmate in the same way. I once received a small toy I thought Billy would like, so I hid it under my dress, hoping to give it to him during our short post-lunch visit. As we lined up to walk to the dining hall, Miss Orr gently took the toy from my hands and said, "I'll carry it for you. I know you want your brother to have it, but you may want it back later and might not be able to get it again. You can tell him about it when you visit him and have it back to play with this afternoon." Though she was kind, I was heartbroken. I didn't want the toy; I wanted Billy to know I missed him.

Each unit housed a specific age group of girls, and with each move to a new unit came new skills to learn. Before leaving one unit for the next, every girl had to demonstrate self-care, personal hygiene, and housekeeping responsibility. Those who were slower or newer received help from others, and there was no teasing or unkindness.

After breakfast, we would meet as a group for instruction from our matron on physical and spiritual care. We learned how to care for our bodies, treat each other with kindness, and resist doing wrong. One of our guiding verses was, "As a person thinks in the heart, so becomes their actions." (Proverbs 23:7)

We each had our bed, which we made every morning and again after our mandatory afternoon nap. Once a week, we changed the bottom sheet and moved the top sheet down. The Texas Baptist women had sewn so many quilts that each child had at least four under their mattress. These quilts were rotated regularly, one brought to the top while another took its place underneath.

Miss Zapp was the head matron of Hardin Home. She was firm but fair, highly organized, and deeply kind. Being in her unit meant more structure and privileges. Unlike in earlier units, where two girls shared, each girl had her own toy box.

Every morning began with a devotional. We walked in pairs and in silence to all our destinations. We lined up three times daily to go to Mana Hall for meals.

Friday evenings were special. We walked the campus, bought a piece of candy at the gatehouse using money relatives sent us, and then gathered for a preview of the Sunday School lesson. Miss Zapp, a dedicated Bible scholar, taught us verses, hymns, scripture stories, and how to find Bible passages on our own.

From Guilt to Grace

One day, during free play, I sat quietly on my toy box, overwhelmed by a surge of guilt. I remembered our Bible lessons and felt the Holy Spirit nudging me. I thought of Jesus dying for my sins. I couldn't play. I needed to talk to someone.

I went to Miss Zapp's outer room, sat in a chair, and wept. She came to me gently. We prayed together, and she explained salvation in loving detail, that being sorry, asking forgiveness, and accepting Jesus's death and resurrection was enough. "You need not feel guilty anymore," she told me. "Rejoice and be glad, for great is your reward in heaven."

Joy flooded my heart. I wanted to tell everyone.

When Brother Hal offered the next baptism, I signed up. On July 4, 1945, I was baptized. I stood before the congregation, fearlessly declaring, "I'm a child of God."

I recited Psalm 23 in full. From that day on, I felt free and whole. Though I did not have a father or mother in my own home, I belonged to God. That was more than enough.

Rooted in Routine, Growing in Grace

At ten years of age, I began living in Crouch Hall.

My first dorm was Hardin Home, but the names changed once we moved to
Crouch Hall. They were now referred to as "halls," not homes.

There were noticeable differences in Crouch Hall:

-*We could play on the playground without a matron supervising, but only around the building.*
-*We could walk to the swimming pool without lining up or a matron accompanying us.*
-*We could walk around the 60-acre campus with visiting relatives, but not at any other time.*
-*We could visit other girls' dorm rooms on our floor, except at bedtime.*
-*We could go on a day trip to the Girls' Woods in the cattle truck after dinner during the summer.*
-*We could play outside and even grow a garden. I planted and grew beans.*
-*We still had to nap and be quiet during quiet time.*

If our chores were done, we could listen to the matron's radio on Saturday mornings.

-We still went to meals as a group, which were breakfast, dinner (noon), and supper (evening).

-We earned rewards for good school grades and were punished for poor ones. I was often punished for bad grades.

44_Photo: Saturday Night Movies

-We could go to Saturday Night Movies in the auditorium with fewer than four demerits.

One time, relatives came to visit and wanted a photo of Angie and me with some of our friends: 1st Row (L–R): Angie, Betty Jo Harwood, Bobbi Nell 2nd Row (L–R): Wanda Faye Godsey, Eluese Brinley, Dorothy Simmons, Alberta Disch (1943)

45_Photo: Angie Me Friends

During sixth grade, I was fortunate to have the support of several teachers:

Mrs. Dickey, the math teacher, helped me build basic math skills and arranged for a tutor, Miss Barnett. I finally began understanding addition and subtraction, although long division and multiplication remained difficult.

My reading teacher, Miss McCorkle, gave me small assignments that slowly built my confidence. She also gave handwritten notes of encouragement and even rewarded me once with a small paper sack of pecans.

Miss Swafford, art teacher. When I arrived at Buckner, Miss Swafford was an art teacher in 1940. She had been commissioned to draw portraits of students for display at the Texas Baptist Convention. I was chosen to sit for a portrait. As I waited, nervous and shy, I put my fist to my mouth. When it was my turn, she saw that and told me to keep it there; it became part of the portrait. I never saw it again, but that moment stuck with me.

Later, Miss Swafford became one of the most influential people in my young life. She saw potential in me when I didn't see it in myself. I often acted out, talking when I shouldn't, showing disapproval, even turning my back on teachers. One evening after Training Union, she asked me to stay behind. She handed me a mirror and asked me to smile.

"Do you see a different person than the one you've been acting like?" she asked.

I did. My resolve melted. As I sat there in shame, she gently listed my good qualities: "You have a beautiful face, you're neat and well-dressed, you study your lessons, and you're well-liked." I began to feel seen in a new way.

She continued, "You have great potential. Use it, develop it, and create opportunities for yourself."

Another time, during a camping trip for her class, she noticed I wasn't including all the girls in conversation. Quietly, she pulled me aside and said, "You show many qualities of a fine Christian, but excluding others is not one of them. Christian love includes everyone."

In fifth grade, I was in Miss Power's class, but I was often sent across the hall to deliver notes to Miss Swafford. I grew suspicious: "Am I the dumbest in the class? Is that why I'm being sent out?"

One day, I threw the note onto her desk. She had me pick it up and gently place it where it belonged. From that moment on, I delivered every note with a smile and care.

A classmate, **Frances Zackery**, struggled even more than I did. I admired her; she never complained, and she tried her best. One day, she was gone. She had been sent to the State School for the Retarded.

46_Photo: Frances Zackery (Middle 1st Row)

Later, our class wrote to her, and she wrote back. Her letter showed surprising growth. She had blossomed in the new setting. We all felt she had found the right place, which made me proud to have known her.

That experience left a mark on me. I realized how important it is to make room for everyone, even those outside the group. Frances showed us all what a loving heart and the right support can do.

I was only eleven when I moved to the second floor of Crouch Hall; most girls didn't make that move until they were twelve. At the time, I had secretly planted a few bean seeds in the play area and was quietly tending to them. I watched them sprout and grow, and when they were ready, I ate them raw, my very first harvest. But my math tutoring during playtime cut short any chance of planting more. My gardening dreams were put on hold, but the joy of those beans stayed with me.

As we grew, the commissary issued larger clothes. Sometimes, the matron would hang them in our closets. Other times, we'd go to the commissary and choose dresses from three piles, organized by size. Once, I went to the smallest pile, and the matron gently corrected me: "Bobbi Nell, you're too large for that pile." I was embarrassed. I had still thought of myself as the smallest one, but clearly, I wasn't anymore.

While I was still in Hardin Hall, my sister Dottie married Butch Townzen and began visiting us, Billy Dean, Angie Darlene, and me. She brought us things we couldn't get at Buckner. One Easter, she gave Angie and me white boots. We felt so loved and cherished. Dottie and her husband had no children, and when they took us out for our annual three-day visit, they treated us like their own.

That year, it became clear I wasn't one of the popular girls. I wasn't good in school, and popularity often followed good grades. I didn't have a special friend, so I asked myself what I liked to do. I loved singing, and that's how I found Alice Ann Ward. She had perfect pitch and loved to sing hymns. We met often in each other's rooms and set out to memorize every hymn and the matching Bible verses. It became our mission. We weren't popular, but that didn't matter; we had each other and our music.

Each year, the matron reassigned roommates. That year, I ended up on the first floor of Crouch with new roommates: Joy McCloud, Billie Juanita Graves, and a third girl whose name I can't remember. Joy was younger and had a close friend in another room, so I often felt like the third wheel. But we got along well.

We discovered our room was far from the matron's, and the parlor floor squeaked when she walked. So at night, after lights out, we whispered and giggled until we heard the creak. Then silence. She never caught us, but I wonder if she knew we were "good little girls" only because her steps gave her away.

Joy didn't like Buckner. Her two older brothers had already graduated, and she wanted to run away to find them. She even planned to take her younger brother with her. But someone told her scary stories about the dangers of leaving the campus at night. That changed her mind. She snuck out to get her brother, but found him asleep and safe in bed. The plan ended there.

Years later, her brothers had homes of their own. One of them took in Joy and her brother. Joy finished high school and later went to college. Her brother grew up to be a handsome young man.

Swimming was our favorite activity when I roomed with Joy, Billie-Juanita. We went to the pool three times a week for an hour and a half. I became a strong swimmer, especially in the sidestroke, which became my specialty. I even won contests for it.

47_ Photo: Pool (1943)

I earned ribbons for the swan, regular, and stunt dives in diving, including the backflip and headstand. Summer was filled with pool time and fun.

Twice a month, we took trips to the "Girls' Woods," where we rode horses, hiked, and waded in shallow streams. Sometimes, I sat under a tree, watching sunlight filter through the leaves and clouds drift overhead. I thought, "Will I ever remember doing this once my life changes?"

As I write my story, I know the answer is yes.

Skates, Slaps, and Second Chances

When I was twelve years old, I was moved to Hunt Hall. My roommates were girls who had chosen to room with me, and I felt proud to be selected. However, when it came time to move again, I chose to stay in the same room, only to find that the others had chosen to room together without me. It was a humbling realization that I wasn't as popular as I had thought.

In Hunt Hall, there were more privileges. You could play outside anytime you didn't have chores. I received roller skates for Christmas, so I roller-skated often, though we had to follow the rules about which sidewalks we could use.

Other privileges included going to an overnight camp, growing our hair long (unlike in Hardin and Crouch), and enjoying more freedom of movement. We could visit Dallas with an older girl, go to the movies, or roller skate indoors if we had spending money. We could also walk in small groups to the Evans Store, which is about a mile away.

One big change: we were allowed to have a declared boyfriend. We could sit with him during campus sports matches, at Sunday evening church, walk with him after school to the end of the sidewalk, and stand talking for a few minutes.

I became friends with Viola Wright, a girl who left Buckner before graduating, an unusual occurrence, likely because her mother remarried. Viola continued to visit often. One day, some girls from another room said loudly, "We don't like Bobbi Nell." I overheard them and went to see what was going on. One of the girls slapped me. Viola came over, put her arm around me, and apologized for the girl. "She is just showing off," she said. I realized then how unliked I was by some, but also how blessed I was to have a true friend.

Later, I became friends with Mary Louise Turner. We loved skating together. One day, after a long skate, we sat on the curb next to Ms. Brady's car. It had rained, and the car was muddy. For fun, we used a stick to write our initials and our boyfriends' initials on the side of the car.

Ms. Brady was the girls' head matron. Before going to a meeting, she didn't wash her car, where others noticed the markings and commented. Soon, Mary Louise and I were brought before Ms. Brady and reprimanded. We had to wash her car, and after that, we stayed clear of her.

Later, it was discovered that Ms. Brady had been reading our mail and stealing money from letters. She had taken $1 from me once. Eventually, she was asked to leave Buckner.

We rotated work every three months. One of my assignments was ironing in the laundry. I talked too much, so the matron warned I'd have to scrub the floor if I didn't quiet down. I taped my mouth shut and kept ironing.

Visitors arrived that day and thought I was being punished. The administration questioned the laundry matron. Though I had caused trouble, she didn't hold a grudge. I later chose the mangle job, running clean sheets and pillowcases through it with friends. We enjoyed that job and chose it several times.

Another time, I worked at the Sunbeam Home with boys and girls aged birth to five. We did dishes and cleaned the dining room, but the best part was helping feed and comfort the little ones. It reminded me of my love for children, especially my sister Angie, who had been in the Sunbeam Home when we arrived.

That love continues to this day. When a child is dedicated in church, I take the vow seriously and support the family. I often give the child a new $2 bill and pray Luke 2:52 over them: "And Jesus grew in wisdom and stature, and in favor with God and man."

One job was working in Mana Hall, the dining room. Miss Mamie was in charge, strict and no-nonsense. Girls assigned to Mana Hall reported at 5 p.m. sharp. When you finished a task, you stood silently before her until she looked up. Only then could you say, "Miss Mamie, I am through with..." If you forgot to complete the sentence, she wouldn't dismiss you.

48_ Photo: Miss Mamie

Miss Mamie could punish slackers by assigning them to swat flies, count them, and show her the dustpan. If flies were scarce, we cut the ones we caught in half or saved some for the next girl.

Although she grew up at Buckner, she was later dismissed when she was caught taking cakes and pies meant for us. Her son would pick her up, and she loaded the desserts into his car. Afterward, another adult took over her position. Interestingly, Miss Mamie was honored as an alumna at a Buckner reunion, but many didn't know why she had been fired.

Mrs. Dickey, the wife of G. G. Dickey, Buckner's Superintendan, was my sixth-grade math teacher and eighth-grade homeroom teacher. She once told our class, "There is not a student in this class who can't qualify to go to college." That declaration changed my life. It was the first time I thought college might be possible for me.

Before she passed away, Mrs. Dickey left me a cup and saucer as a remembrance. Though I've broken the original over the years, I keep replacing it. Its meaning and message remain unbroken, a symbol of encouragement that changed the direction of my life.

Becoming Who I Was Meant to Be

At 15, I was finally old enough to attend Buhrman Hall, where the girls were seen as the "Big Girls" on campus.

Buhrman Hall came with even more privileges, including all the freedoms of Hunt Hall, plus:

-Eligibility for Student Council: I served by being elected class president, as a reporter, and as a cheerleader.

-Participation on the traveling basketball team in my junior and senior years.
-Col. Buckner introduced Co-ed Saturday recreation.
-Volleyball, which I enjoyed because positions were respected.
-Chaperoned parties hosted by Training Union leaders.
-Saturday movie nights.

49_Photo: Parlor Dating: David Ward, Mary-Beth Cutshall: 1948

-Parlor dating on Sunday evenings, chaperoned and limited to one hour.

I competed in swimming and diving events, using the highest board for dives like the regular dive, jackknife, swan, back layout, and flip. I earned ribbons in all these events.

50_Photo: Swimming and Diving Ribbons

- I don't recall the beginning of my relationship with Vance Horsley, but it was the most enduring boy-girl relationship I had there.

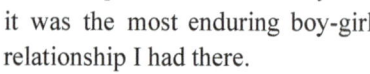

51_Photo: Vance, Bobbi: Texas State Fair (1949)

Twin brothers Vance and Vernon Horsley were accomplished all-around athletes in football, basketball, and track, earning numerous awards.

Vance became my longest-lasting boyfriend during my time at Buckner. My behavior towards Vance was often rude and unappreciative, which didn't reflect my true feelings. I liked Vance, but I didn't want to become so attached that I would marry him. To my knowledge, Vance never married, although I heard he was once close to marrying a woman named Nell, who was not me.

I respect Vance and am glad he enjoyed dating Hazel Brown at Buckner. However, I was firm in my desire to avoid a serious relationship with an orphan. Many of us lacked strong family foundations, and I believed marrying someone who also grew up without a family would decrease the likelihood of a successful marriage.

52_Photo: Vance's athletic awards

At the 2024 Buckner Reunion Committee silent auction, I purchased a plaque displaying some of Vance's awards. After all these years, he still holds a special place in my heart.

Below is picture of Buckner's 1949 Football team (I was 16 years old). Picture includes 3 of the boys I dated at various times: Vance Horsley, Ian Henslee, and Bobby Baker.

BUCKNER FOOTBALL Team - 1949
District Runners-Up [8-2]

BOH	20	W.Wilson	0	BOH	13	W.Point	25	Buckner	32	*Duncanville	6
BOH	45	Crandall	0	BOH	33	*Seagoville	0	Buckner	14	*Lancaster	7
BOH	32	*Forney	0	BOH	25	*Ferris	0	Buckner	31	*W-Hutchins	0
								Buckner	6	*Richardson	7

Buckner outscored their district opponents 173-20

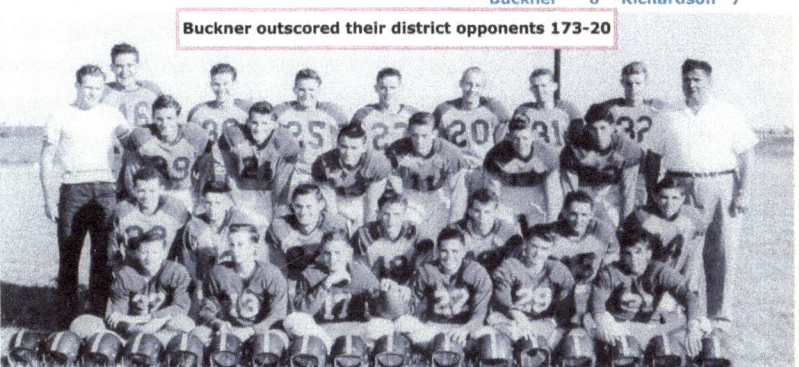

1ST Row: L. Tate, L. Mangum, Jerry Nash, Thurman Shurtleff, C. Bland, W.L. Smith
2nd Row: R. Trantham, J. Lookadoo, I. Henslee, E. Stanley, C. Cutshall, C. May, F. Hardin
3rd Row: R. Stevens, B. Houston, Vance Horsley W. Grayson, J. Taylor, F. Day, B. Baker, M. Alexander
4th Row: H. Campbell, E. Smith, Vernon Horsley, C. Corcoran, R. Bleakley, C. Day, R. McKinney
1st Team All District: Vance Horsley, Bobby Baker, Harold Campbell.
2nd Team All District: Vernon Horsley, Billy Houston

Ira Lee Henslee came to the hospital to see me when I fell in the kitchen and hit my head so hard that I blacked out for a few seconds. The girls I was working with made a pack saddle (two girls made a pack saddle by holding each other's wrists to make a seat). The injured girl would sit on the arms that made the seat. To keep herself steady with the girls walking, the injured put her arms around the necks of the two making the seat. That was the way I was taken to the hospital on campus.
53_Photo: Bobbi, Ira Lee Henslee (1948)

After that visit to the hospital, Ira Lee told everyone that I was his girlfriend. We hung out after school together.

I was a cheerleader and Ira Lee played on the football team. One photo captures a fun moment between us—me in my cheerleading outfit, playfully swapping hats with him, while he fixes the mouthpiece that had come off the top of my megaphone.

Sometimes I would climb out the window at night and meet him in the bushes to receive hugs but no kisses.

Later, I found out that this behavior gave me a bad reputation. I didn't enjoy the way Ira Lee hugged me, or maybe I did like it so well that it was risky. Climbing out the window at night would get you a pass off the campus to never return. I thought, "I don't like that type of adrenaline I am getting when I am around Ira Lee. I want to wait for marriage before having sex."

The night watchman made rounds, and I feared he would tell the administration about boys and girls being out together after curfew. So Ira Lee and I broke up. It didn't phase him. I wished to be back with him, but I knew I had little self-control so I stayed clear of him.

George Dickey was the son of G. G. Dickey, superintendent of Buckner schools. His two older sisters had graduated from Buckner.

Mr. and Mrs. Dickey asked their son, George, to invite me to their house for dinner on my birthday. An adult had never done this before.

54_Photo: George Dickey, Ms. Brady (1948)

I had to get permission not to go to our regular dining hall (Mana Hall) for supper. George thought if he approached Mrs. Brady, she would probably permit me to skip a meal and walk with George to his house for dinner. He made an appointment and went to see Mrs. Brady. She gave him permission.

George walked from his home to Buhrman Hall, where I was waiting to walk across campus to his house for my birthday dinner. I felt exceptional. The dinner was pleasant, and the cake was good.

55_Photo: George Dickey, Bobbi (1948)

To my surprise, the Dickeys excused themselves and made some excuse to leave George and me alone in their living room. We, being friends, had lots to talk about. I thought he would put his arm around me, but nothing happened. Finally, George escorted me back to my dorm, and it was just like friends, with not even hand-holding.

Later, when I was at Howard Payne College, Mr. G. G. Dickey served as registrar. His son, my friend George, went to Juilliard to get a degree in religious organ composition.

56_Photo: Bobbi, George Dickey (1993)

Now I understand why I never received so much as a kiss—or even held his hand. George was gay. Then another realization struck me: the Dickeys had likely arranged that evening hoping I might spark his interest, to encourage him to act like a boy with a girlfriend. Looking back, I suppose I didn't succeed.

Name Changes and Stories

At Buckner, dorms had six to a room until junior high, when we could select our roommates and share rooms with just three others.

In high school, I shared a room with a senior named Dorothy Thedford. Down the hall was a freshman named Dorothy Cline. Cline's brother, Joe, dated Dorothy Thedford. After graduation, Dorothy Thedford became Dorothy Thedford Cline. Later, Dorothy Cline married Joe's brother, becoming Dorothy Cline Thedford. This is a bit confusing but charming in its symmetry.

Another story, Betty Jo Harwood ran away at age twelve with two friends. They encountered a dangerous man in the woods. Betty Jo told the others to run while she stayed behind. She was assaulted. The Home gave her a new name to protect her identity when she was taken into guardianship. Betty Jo had many friends at Buckner, including me. After her name change, most lost contact with her, but I found a way to keep in touch. She never married, and her experience hardened her. I still think of her with sadness and love.

When young boys ran away, they were punished by being made to wear a girl's dress to Mana Hall. The idea was to embarrass them. But that ended when one boy proudly wore the dress, added a ribbon, and made a spectacle. It became clear the punishment was not working as intended.

Sports:

At Buckner, boys were all about football, while girls joined the pep squad

and practiced cheerleading routines with pride.

57_Photo: LR Betty, Bobbi, Roberta (1948-49)

Like every high school girl at Buckner, I started in the pep squad. But in my sophomore year, I became a cheerleader—and I absolutely loved it.

58_Photo: LR Betsy, Bobbi, Roberta (1948-49)

There were three of us—Betty Clark, Roberta Clarkson, and me—and we were close friends, spirited, and yes, a little showy. We knew how to strut our stuff and didn't hold back.

Basketball: Where I Couldn't Cross the Line

And after football, it was time for basketball practice. I played guard on the

girl's team—dribbling and passing, but no shooting. What, no shooting? Isn't this basketball? Yes! But it is Girls Basketball.

59_Photo: Bobbi Basketball clothes(1950)

When the other team had the ball, and the opponent got it, the guard, without crossing the line, had to throw the ball to the other side of the line to get it to their team's shooters.

Our shooters were good. I was fast and competitive. I could maneuver to get the ball from my opponent's shooters. But being short, I could not keep the opponent's tall "forwards" from trying to make a basket. This shortness kept me off the leading team. I was a substitute.

But the coach let me play when we had more points than the other team. He did this because he wanted all team members to receive a jacket for having a certain number of points. Besides, it kept the team congenial and supportive of one another.

60_Photo: Bobbi Basketball Uniform (1950)

The team applauded my tenacity. It made me feel like a worthwhile player. I can truthfully say it was mine once the ball was free on my side of the court.

The only way our team could make points was to get it to the other side of the court without crossing the centerline. Our forwards could only make points by shooting the basket on their end of the court, and no team guard could be on the same side as the same team shooter. That's how "a long time ago" Girls Basketball was played.

Gymnasium

The gym was used for PE classes, school sports (basketball, volleyball, and

wrestling), gymnastic shows, and parties.

The boys prided themselves in just how shiny they could make the floors when they polished them.

61_Photo: Gymnasium

Study Time

Evenings in the dorm were taken seriously. Mandatory study time was held every Monday through Friday. For one full hour, absolute silence was required—not a single voice, whisper, or murmur was allowed. You were expected to study, and there were no exceptions.

If you didn't have homework, you had to read a book. If you hadn't brought one from the parlor bookshelf before quiet hour began, your only option was to read your Bible—which everyone had. No one was permitted to leave the room once study hour started.

The rules were strict, but the rewards for good grades were generous and motivating:

➢ Students who earned A's didn't have to take mid-term exams.
➢ With good grades and no demerits, you could ride the bus to away games.
➢ "A" students got to choose their elective subjects.
➢ They were also given the preferred dorm and Mana Hall assignments—the cleaner, more pleasant jobs.

I went from being a student who once earned F's to one who earned A's. And I can say from experience:

There were a lot more goodies for the "A" group.

Romance with a Matron Present

Sunday evenings were our designated time for dating. After church, the boys would escort the girls to their dorms, where we sat together in pairs around the parlor.

A matron sat nearby, pretending to read the newspaper—sometimes even holding it upside down—just to make sure there was no hugging or kissing. When she finally folded the paper and stood up, we knew it was time. Couples would walk to the door, say their goodbyes, and part ways. The boys returned to their side of the campus, and the girls went back to their rooms.

Still, many of us would linger at the windows, calling out one last farewell—as though we weren't going to see those same boys the very next day at school.

Keeping Buckner Beautiful: Lawns and Flower Beds

The boys took care of both sides of the 60-acre Buckner campus, keeping the grass mowed, trimmed, and watered—even around the buildings on the girls' side. They worked hard to keep the grounds looking neat and orderly.

62_Photo: My brother, Billy Dean (1949)

When it came to flowers, the responsibility shifted. The head matron of each dorm decided what to plant and who would care for it. At Hunt Hall, that job belonged to us girls—and the flower beds always looked beautiful.

Some girls had a real talent for gardening. In fact, Hunt Hall had the best flower beds on campus, thanks in large part to Miss Ratcliff, our matron. She had a green thumb and gladly passed her knowledge on to any girl willing to learn.

I wasn't one of them. But I did enjoy caring for her indoor plants in the outer office. It gave me a small sense of responsibility—and a little quiet time, too. Her inner office and bedroom were strictly off-limits, but tending the plants outside her door felt like a special assignment just for me.

The Calendar of Buckner Life

Life at Buckner was structured in ways that many families might not think twice about. While most children grow up in homes with siblings of different ages, Buckner Orphans Home grouped children strictly by age and gender. I always lived with girls my age from early childhood through high school. We shared dorms, daily routines, holidays, and milestones. The year's rhythm was marked by traditions and seasonal events that made each month unique and memorable.

January: Snowy Lessons and Kind Reminders

On New Year's Day, my classmates and I enjoyed a day off from school due to the snow. We reveled in playing together in the snow, both boys and girls.

I was dating Vance Horsley at the time. While playing, I got a bit rough with Vance. He kindly reminded me that I was taking advantage of his good nature. This experience taught me an important lesson: there's no excuse for mistreating others. "The Lord does not look at the things people look at. People look at the outward appearance, but the Lord looks at the heart." (1 Samuel 16:7). The lesson learned: "Our actions should reflect our true character."

In retrospect, I wanted Vance to force me not to mistreat him by restraining me with his arms around me. That way, I would not have to ask "outright" to be hugged. But I would get the craving to be hugged that I desired.

February: Groundhog Clues and Founder's Day Delights

Groundhog Day was eagerly anticipated. My friends and I believed it held the secret to future weather. We'd sneakily read the matron's newspaper to see if the groundhog saw its shadow. Then, we would be the weather person for our dorm. The paper was always returned in excellent condition to the spot where it was delivered. If kids looked at the matron for confirmation, she would nod yes. She never let on if she knew where we got the information. Did she know we had read her paper, or did she not know? I guess we'll never know which one is true.

Founder's Day (February 3rd) was another special occasion. No school meant a break from routine. At lunch, we received a sack with our plates. It was like a mini picnic! We'd wrap sandwiches, desserts, and other treats in special paper. An apple and an orange completed the meal. Choosing where and with whom to enjoy our sack supper was part of the fun.

One year, an ice storm transformed the landscape.

63_Photo: Ice Storm

We woke up to tree branches glistening with ice—a breathtaking sight! But we had to be cautious—the ice could fall off in large pieces and hit someone within range.

March: Winds of Change and Easter Best

In Dallas, March is known for its blustery winds. My friends and I would take leisurely walks, allowing the wind to sway us. It was a delightful excuse to break from walking in a straight line to the dining hall. We used any excuse to break the routine.

Easter is sometimes in March and sometimes in April. Whichever month it was, it was a special occasion for us. Everyone received new clothes. Boys got new shirts and shoes, while girls received new dresses and shoes.

I fondly remember the matron's care. Sometimes, she chose a dress for me and hung it in my closet, and she did the same for other girls. Other times, dresses were piled up, and each girl could select one. If a dress didn't fit, the matron would alter it, adding or removing details. Feeling noticed and cared for was heartwarming.

April: Tricks and Transitions

April Fools' Day, we played tricks on each other. My friends and I tried to fool each other by telling one something untrue. As the person showed they were fooled, we'd say, "April Fool." One of the best lines would be, "Oh look. There is something on the back of ………….'s dress." We would say this when the third person was within hearing distance. As that person began to look, someone would yell, "April Fool."

On April Fool's Day, one of my roommates took a pair of panties and a bra and ran them up the flagpole. Each morning, Robert Cooke Buckner went to the flag pole and put up the American and Christian flags before 6 AM. This April morning, he allowed the panties and bra to stay up until everyone had seen them on their way to the Mana Hall for breakfast. Then, when everyone was inside, he took them down and put them in the office. I cleaned the office during my three-month duty, so I returned the items to my roommate, Wanda Fay Godsey.

We were delighted when Col. Robert Cooke Buckner returned from military service to take over as manager in place of his father, Brother Hal Buckner. We all thought Col. Cooke was a genuinely good man. Under his leadership, many things that had once earned us punishment were now met with understanding and acceptance.

Each spring in Texas, the weather warmed up. Those who were made to wear long wool stockings, caps that covered our ears, and gloves could take them off and turn them in because the following year, larger ones would most likely replace the ones we had been wearing. I often lost a glove (much to the matron's chagrin), so I would keep one hand in my pocket to avoid a scolding. We received new sweaters in April—either because we'd outgrown last year's or to replace Christmas sweaters. Sometimes my missing glove would turn up in time to be pinned with the other, and other times, I had to turn it in without its mate.

As we outgrew our clothes, they were laundered and passed down to the younger children. It was always a bit surprising to see a little girl wearing a dress, sweater, or coat I once wore—it was hard to believe I'd ever been that small. To confirm ownership when someone recognized a garment, we'd fold down the back of the neckline, where our name had been stamped inside. It was a sweet experience getting to know the younger child now wearing something that had once been mine.

May: We All Had a Sad Story

On May Day, we created colorful flowers from construction paper—simple, handmade blossoms that carried real meaning. These weren't just decorations; they were tokens of friendship. We gave them to our best friends, spreading joy and a sense of belonging. If someone already had a flower, it didn't matter—you just found someone else to share your creation with. By the end of the day, almost everyone had a paper flower pinned to their dress or shirt.

Mother's Day: Honoring Moms

Mother's Day was a tender Sunday at Buckner. The administration would ask each dorm to report: How many of your children have mothers still living? How many have lost theirs?

Each matron was given a mix of red and white flowers to distribute among the children in her care. A red flower symbolized a living mother; a white one, a mother who had passed away. That simple tradition sparked quiet conversations. Children opened up about their mothers—some had died tragically, others were alive but unreachable. Many of us had been declared "orphans," though most still had at least one parent living. We were wards of the Court, placed at Buckner because of situations filled with heartbreak—some involving crime, loss, or abandonment.

Despite our hardships, we found comfort in shared grief. We listened to one another's stories, offering support and understanding. Since nearly all of us had come to Buckner before the age of twelve and stayed through high school, we knew each other's histories well. Every story was hard. If you heard just one, you might think it was the saddest. But after hearing a dozen or more, it became impossible to say whose pain ran deepest.

In the midst of it all, we dreamed of building something better. Many of us were determined to create strong, peaceful marriages—homes far different from what we'd known. I made an early decision: I would not marry someone from the Orphanage. I felt we were all too "needy," too wounded, to truly depend on one another. We had no real experience of family life. Some of us eventually succeeded in building those good marriages. Some did not. But all of us carried the same longing—for stability, for love, and for a home that truly felt like home.

June: Quilts, Campfires, and Cannonballs

One of our favorite summer activities was exploring the woods. Buckner owned two separate areas—one for girls and one for boys—miles apart and geographically separated from the main campus.

Daddy Buck, a kindly cousin of Buckner's founder, lived in the girls' woods and cared for the horses. During the summer, anyone who wanted to learn to ride could take lessons under his watchful eye.

Day trips to the woods were filled with horseback riding, hiking, and wading in the creek. Sometimes, I would sit by myself, just looking up at the trees. If you've ever lived in a dorm full of girls, you know how rare it is to find a moment alone. The woods gave us that chance—to be with others, or to just be still.

On these day trips, we were always greeted with syrup deckers—eight slices of white bread soaked in cane syrup and stacked like a deck of cards. We each got one, and by the time we returned to campus for the 6:00 p.m. supper, our appetites had returned.

As high school girls, we graduated to overnight camping trips—three days and two nights out in the woods. Meals were cooked over open fires. An adult supervised, but we did most of the work: planning, organizing, cooking, and cleaning. We quickly learned how to coordinate so everything was hot and ready at the same time. One group cooked while another scrubbed pots and pans, and we all took turns with every task. It was real teamwork.

Nights around the campfire were our favorite. We'd sing, tell spooky stories, roast marshmallows, and make s'mores—gooey treats of graham crackers, chocolate, and fire-melted marshmallows. As the fire dimmed, someone would usually start a prayer. That was our quiet signal: bedtime under the stars, wrapped in quilts and watched over by God.

The Log Cabin and Quilted Comfort

Deep in the woods stood a rustic log cabin, filled with firewood, cast-iron cookware, and piles of handmade quilts—donated by Texas Baptist women. These quilts were everywhere on campus, but in the woods, they felt like sacred treasures. We'd use as many as we needed to stay warm at night, laying our beds under the open sky before heading to the campfire.

We'd also gather sticks during the day to build that night's fire, and sometimes we pushed the limits, wandering past the boundaries set by our matrons. "Did you make it to the all-white rocks?" we'd whisper. That was the daring line. Further than that, we didn't go.

Diving and Splashing: Ribbons at the Pool

Back on campus, summer meant swimming. Girls had the pool on Mondays, Wednesdays, and Fridays; boys on the other days. We had separate modern bathhouses and a deep end reserved for older girls. I practiced endlessly and began to win ribbons for my sidestroke and various dives—jackknife, swan, front flips, backflips, and of course, the cannonball.

Here's how to do a perfect cannonball: sprint down the diving board, bounce high into the air, tuck your knees to your chest, and explode into the water. The bigger the splash, the better the score. The only rule? Never—oh never—land on your back or face. Ouch! For top marks, sit tall in the air and stay straight. I once earned a perfect ten!

Vacation Bible School: Faith, Character, and Teaching

Every summer included Vacation Bible School. For three weeks, we studied verses, sang hymns, and learned deep lessons about faith and character.

We were challenged with questions that made us think:

- ➢ Was taking a pen or pin without asking really stealing?
- ➢ Was silently nodding when you meant "no" honest?
- ➢ Was singing loudly in church true worship—or just showing off?
- ➢ Was saying, "Take it if you feel that way about it," a form of kindness—or sarcasm?

These weren't just Bible lessons. They were life lessons. We learned to do what was right, even when no one was watching. Saying things from a God-loving heart, not just out of habit, shaped the people we would become.

Even as Academy Seniors, we never outgrew VBS. Instead, we became teachers to the younger children. With the adult teachers on summer break, we stepped up. It was our way of living out Psalm 145:4: "One generation commends your works to another; they tell of your mighty acts."

Watermelons and Spitting Contests

Summers also meant watermelon season. A truck would arrive in front of our dorm once or twice a week, and boys would unload the sweet, heavy melons. Sometimes, we had enough for one melon per two children.

64_Photo: Watermelon Picnic

The boys sliced them open, and we'd eat until we couldn't eat another bite. Then the rinds were hauled away. I remembered how rinds went to the pigs back on the farm. I used to wonder—did Buckner have pigs too? The boys told me about the cows, including one they named "Bobbi Nell," but pigs were a mystery.

After the feast, we'd collect seeds for spitting contests. I wasn't the best, but I had a friend who was. She taught me how to tuck the seed just right on my tongue before launching it. We measured our distances and became proud "spitting friends."

July: A Holiday Made Just for Us

The Fourth of July was a day of grand celebration at Buckner! After a regular breakfast, all trips to Mana Hall were suspended for the day. In their place came a full schedule of games and festivities. For once, we didn't have to prepare our own sack lunches—the commissary treated us to fresh, hot meals, complete with dessert.

Sometimes the day's activities took us off-campus to White Rock Lake in Dallas or to the boys' woods. Other times, we stayed right on the 60-acre Buckner grounds. No matter the location, the day was filled with laughter, games, and the rare joy of boys and girls playing together. No one was left out, and no one looked unhappy.

As evening fell, we gathered on the football field bleachers, buzzing with

anticipation. A professional fireworks company put on a dazzling display just for us.

65a_Photo: Fireworks

As the sky lit up with color and sound, we gasped and cheered with wide-eyed amazement. There were pops, crackles, bursts of light—and even music woven into the show.

We were always reminded: This is just for you.

And in that moment, watching the brilliant sky made just for us, I didn't feel like an orphan. I felt honored. I felt seen. I felt special.

Not once—not ever—was I sad to be at Buckner on the Fourth of July.

August: Birthdays, Blessings, and Bare Feet

My birthday Aug. 24, 1933.

At Buckner, birthdays weren't usually celebrated—unless your roommates took the initiative. Gifts weren't expected and rarely given. But my 15th birthday was different. Somehow, the girls in my room planned a surprise celebration and presented me with thoughtful gifts. I was genuinely amazed—it may have been the first time in my life I had received birthday presents. They "gifted" me beautifully.

I had always enjoyed doing public readings—not impromptu speeches, but reciting poetry or unique devotional pieces from memory. One of their gifts was a reading accompanied by music. I treasured it and used it often as a devotional, reciting it whenever a pianist was available to play the accompanying piece.

After that, I made it a point to give back. I'd save something from the Christmas String or find a small way to give my roommates a gift on their birthdays. Sometimes it was as simple as a 50-cent ice cream from the Campus Mart. But the joy of giving far outweighed the joy of receiving. That truth still holds in my heart today: "It is more blessed to give than to receive."

The Boys' Birthday Tradition

The way the boys celebrated birthdays was—at least to us girls—downright barbaric. After breakfast, they'd gang up on the birthday boy and give him a rough, rowdy birthday beating. Strange as it sounds, my brother Billy Dean always said he loved it. He'd laugh, roll with the punches, and enjoy the friendly chaos of it all. Most of us girls couldn't understand it, but to them, it was a badge of honor.

Back to School in August: Barefoot Summers and Shoe Rules

August meant back-to-school time! We were part of the Dallas Public School System, which had strict guidelines about the number of instructional days required. Because Buckner observed special holidays, our school year had to begin earlier to meet the state's calendar requirements. Our teachers were paid by the district, so the rules applied to us just like any other school.

As soon as the school year ended, the boys kicked off their shoes. Except at church, they went barefoot all summer long. They seemed to love the freedom of it—until the first school bell rang. Then, shoes were mandatory.

Closed classrooms, summer heat, and bare feet didn't mix well. Whether it was hygiene, odor, or simply decorum, society decided boys must wear shoes when school was in session. The reason wasn't clearly explained, and we didn't ask. As I often say, "When there is no answer, don't ask the question."

As for the girls, there were no exceptions. We had to wear socks and shoes—winter, spring, summer, and fall. Even sandals required socks. Not one day went by that we could be barefoot, not even in the heat of summer. Why? We were never told. "When there is no answer, don't ask the question."

September: School, Sports, and Study

September meant School. Our focus shifted from summer play to an hour of quiet study each night, and there were ball sports: Football for the boys and Cheerleading for the girls.

October: Halloween: Matrons' Decisions and Parlor Plays

Halloween at Buckner varied from dorm to dorm, depending entirely on what each matron allowed. In Hardin, we dressed up in costumes and put on little plays in the parlor. Those performances were our celebration—and we enjoyed the creativity and fun.

As for the other dorms, my memories of Halloween begin to blur. Since we moved so often—shifting from one dorm to another nearly every year—it's hard to recall what each matron permitted during Halloween. In total, I spent eleven and a half years at Buckner, and with each move, traditions changed.

My sister Angie remembers going to the attic, which was decorated to be spooky. Apparently, it was set up to scare the girls who dared to enter. That must have been her dorm's idea of Halloween fun. But for me, the clearest memories remain those parlor plays in Hardin—simple, joyful, and uniquely ours.

November: Songs, Nuts, and a Rabbit Joke Gone Wrong

Armistice Day

Armistice Day wasn't a school holiday at Buckner, but it was always remembered—with music. We sang every patriotic song we knew, and even learned new ones. Wherever a group gathered, you could count on someone to break into song. Of course, there was no singing while walking in line to the dining hall. But once we were seated around the tables in Mana Hall, the songs began. We'd sing together, say a prayer, and then eat.

No one left the hall until Miss Mamie, the head of Mana Hall, gave the signal. Sometimes she'd have a girl ring the big bell—one long ring—to quiet the noise of nearly 700 children. She usually waited until the chatter grew into a full roar—especially after school began—just to make the hush more effective. That single bell ring cut through the din like a command from above.

Thanksgiving at Buckner

Thanksgiving was different. We had our big meal—called dinner—in the middle of the day. That evening, there was no supper. Instead, we packed sack meals and brought them back to our dorms.

On Thanksgiving Day, the girls were loaded into cattle trucks and taken to the Boys' Woods, where nut trees grew in abundance. We were each given a paper sack to gather pecans and walnuts. There were no nut trees in the Girls' Woods, so this was our one chance to stock up.

Back in the dorm, we'd mix our nuts with oranges and apples, and create signature blends. Taste tests followed—whose mix was best? When the "winning mix" was declared, its creators were rarely willing to share their recipes. We had to barter for a sample, trying to figure out the secret ingredients so we could copy the best version for ourselves.

The Boys and the Rabbit Hunt

While we were picking pecans, the boys had their own adventure. Armed with batting sticks, they'd head into open fields known to be full of rabbits. They'd chase them down, club them, skin them, and cook the meat over an open fire. Farmers were glad to have help controlling the rabbit population, and the boys were eager for the challenge. Before I arrived at Buckner, there was one legendary day when the boys caught so many rabbits that the cooks prepared a rabbit feast for the entire Home. The photo says it all—it's true what they say: a picture is worth a thousand words.

65b_Photo: Rabbit Hunt (1938)

"No guns were used in the big Rockwall County rabbit hunt in 1938. Using sticks and speed, Buckner Home boys killed 108 rabbits. Miss Mamie, the head cook, and Buckner Home girls prepared them for lunch."

One story stuck with me. A boy sent his girlfriend some cooked rabbit meat. After she ate it, he jokingly told her it was cat. She was horrified—and nearly choked. The relationship ended right then and there. It may have been a joke, but not everyone could take a tease.

I couldn't. And I understand why she broke it off. I later spoke with the girl myself to confirm the story—it really happened.

Sometimes, little things mean a lot.

December: Trees That Turned and Gifts That Tied Us Together

Christmas Eve

On Christmas Eve, the school auditorium became a place of mystery and magic. All day long, the curtains were drawn shut—no one was allowed to peek inside. That evening, when everyone marched into the auditorium, we opened with a prayer, and often the choir sang a carol. Then came the moment we all waited for: the curtains slowly opened to reveal that year's Christmas display.

Each year was different, but the most unforgettable year was when the stage revealed rotating, lighted Christmas trees. A collective roar of applause and amazement erupted. We were so grateful—to the electric company, or to whoever had made that dazzling moment possible.

Beneath the stage display was something for everyone: a Christmas bundle tied to what we called "The String." Each child, from first grade through high school senior, had one bundle. The gifts were tied together along a long piece of

fabric, and when unwrapped, it was like pulling treasure after treasure from a ribbon of joy.

66_Photo: Billy Dean and Bobbi's Christmas "String"

Each bundle usually contained about the same: a stuffed toy, undergarments, a sweater, and a special toy, often matching the item you had wished for back in September. Of course, by December, some of those desires had changed—but that's where the fun began.

When we returned to the dorms, the trading began. Sweaters, toys, even stuffed animals were swapped, making Christmas more personal—and more "blessed" for everyone.

For years after leaving Buckner, many of us continued a holiday tradition. We would greet each other with: "Merry Christmas! I hope you have a good String." I never quite understood why my children preferred wrapped gifts with colorful bows, when to me, there was nothing more wonderful than having all your presents tied together on a string.

Christmas Day: Feasts and Festivities

Christmas Day began with a special church service, a time of reverence and reflection. But what we really looked forward to was the noon meal—a true feast. A family-style meal was served, featuring turkey, cornbread dressing, lumpy potato salad, string beans, and cake, all placed on the table.Somehow, there was always enough for hundreds of students. I remember thinking, "This reminds me of the story of Jesus feeding the five thousand."

At each place setting was a sack lunch for the evening: two slices of bread wrapped in wax paper, an orange, an apple, and more cake. Though we didn't return to Mana Hall for supper, this little bundle served as our final Christmas meal of the day—shared back at the dorm with friends.

Sweaters and Songs

In the final week of December, school was out, and we had time for pure celebration. One tradition we loved was wearing our Christmas sweaters—the ones we had just received in our String bundle.

On the Sunday after Christmas, every student wore their sweater to church. It made for a beautiful sight—hundreds of children, dressed in matching cheer. That year, we were invited to sing for the Texas Baptist Convention, and our sea of sweaters created a memorable picture of unity and joy.began with a special church service, a time of reverence and reflection.

A Year at Buckner in Review

The steady rhythms of weather, tradition, friendship, and faith shaped more than just the calendar year—they shaped me. Looking back, I don't see just childhood memories. I see the roots of resilience, the quiet formation of character, and the gentle grace that has guided my life ever since.

One Voice That Changed a System

It's fascinating how much changed at Buckner during my final year. After more than a decade of following the same routines, something shifted—dramatically. At the time, I didn't know the full story. It wasn't until years later that I learned the cause of that change—straight from the person who sparked it.

Her name was Twila Miller, an English teacher fresh out of Howard Payne College. Early on, she noticed something peculiar about Buckner students she'd encountered in college: they seemed socially awkward. After just a year of teaching at Buckner herself, she pinpointed what was missing in our education. It wasn't the academics—we were well-prepared there—but our social skills were sorely lacking.

Twila did something bold. She went directly to the president of the Buckner board and laid it all out. She told him that, while Buckner students were intellectually sharp, we struggled in social settings. And somehow, she convinced him that for the sake of future students, things needed to change.

And change they did.

As graduation approached, Col. Robert Cook Buckner met with me and several other girls. He encouraged us to stay an additional year, assuring us that the administration would help secure sponsors to support our college education. I was determined to be among those selected.

That year, I became one of the first to experience a completely new approach to life at Buckner. They called us the "Academy Seniors"—a group of ten students: nine girls and one boy who chose to stay a fifth year in high school. We were the test group for this bold experiment.

67_Photo: Academy Seniors
LR: Wanda Mae Polk, Janette Phillips, Frances Fulton, Wanda Faye Godsey, Katherine Henslee, Marie Bailey, Rena Key, Margaret Corcoran, Bobbi (1950)

Because of Twila Miller's courage, we were granted a level of freedom we'd never dreamed of. Suddenly, we could go into town on our own. We could date. We could work campus jobs for real pay. And no more lining up in long rows to walk to Mana Hall for meals. Instead, we dined in a home-like structure—around cloth-covered tables, four to a table, ordering food like any normal teenager might. Our living situation transformed, too. We moved into a new building with updated furniture. Instead of being overseen by matrons, a married couple served more as counselors than rule enforcers; they never interfered—they just quietly supported us.

Even our jobs shifted. Gone were the standard chores like ironing and waiting tables. Now, we hosted at the Visitor Center, staffed the Campus Mart, managed incoming donations from the Dallas Baptist Men's Club, and kept ledgers. Some of us even trained as lifeguards. We learned real-world skills that gave us a sense of responsibility—and dignity.

More and more staff with families began living on campus, and we could earn extra money babysitting their children. Watching how these families lived offered us glimpses of something many of us had missed—normal family life.

And for fun? We were suddenly allowed to go to the movies, live theater, the skating rink, or just off-campus outings with friends. It was a whole new world. In one case, two girls used their three-day vacation—previously only available through approved relatives—to rent a hotel room in Waco. Alone, unsupervised. It was shocking, even to us, but it highlighted just how little freedom we'd ever had.

The changes were profound. Our mail—once routinely opened and read by matrons—was now private. We elected our own dorm leader. We held meetings where we talked things through and made decisions together. No more curfews. No more surprise inspections or being called back to remake a bed. We chatted late into the night, falling asleep when we chose. It felt like freedom. Real freedom. Even though we were still within the boundaries of that 60-acre fenced campus, something inside us changed. We were no longer just orphans—we were Academy Seniors.

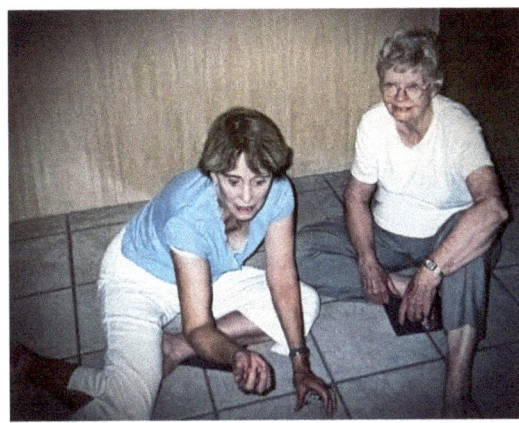

Years later, I met up with Twila Miller. She shared her side of the story, and I shared mine. I thanked her for giving me the chance to think for myself. We laughed, played jacks, and reminisced about that transformative year.
68_Photo: Bobbi, Twila Miller (1963)

I'll never forget the impact the couple who oversaw our dorm in Pender Hall. By giving us space, trust, and room to grow, they helped make that final year unforgettable.

One classmate, Alice Ann Ward, chose not to stay for the extra year. To my surprise, she later wrote to tell me about her new life in college—joining a sorority, becoming a cheerleader, getting her teeth fixed, and quickly gaining popularity.

69_Photo: Alice Ann Ward – 1st row, 1st from right

Alice Ann and I had bonded over hymns and Bible verses. Although we were never in the same classes, we spent countless hours together memorizing scripture and singing hymns. Her friendship—and the thoughtful gifts she sent—helped lift my spirits during that extra, often lonely year. Her kindness reminded me I wasn't forgotten.

Life as an Academy Senior

Guided, Then Guiding

One evening, Col. Buckner called a meeting with the older girls in Buhrman Hall. He informed us that some of the younger girls had been sneaking out at night—meeting boys and swimming after hours. These actions, he warned, put everyone at risk, especially since the night watchman couldn't identify who was involved.

It was a wake-up call. We realized we had a responsibility—not to admire rebellion, but to model integrity. Just as older girls had once mentored us, it was now our turn to lead by example. I thought of Doris Ridge and Barbara Waller, who had guided and encouraged me. Now, it was my time to do the same for those coming after me.

Divine Direction and College Dreams

A group of older girls started a Girls' Auxiliary to learn about mission work in the United States and abroad. I became the president, leading studies about missionaries around the world. I hoped that I might discover how God intended me to serve through this.

Miss Alma Rohm, who came to Buckner in preparation for mission work in Nigeria, became a pivotal mentor.

70_Photo: Alma Rohm (1950)

She taught speech and drama and inspired me to speak boldly for Christ. I wanted to shed my Southern accent and speak with clarity and purpose. Her teaching shaped my desire to pursue full-time Christian service. I dedicated myself to God and asked Him to guide my future. I felt the desire to use every opportunity to serve Him.

What Home Feels Like

We noticed a kind couple at a football game—strangers to Buckner, yet warmly present. Later, we learned they lived nearby and had a habit of opening their home to Buckner girls. Visiting them offered something rare and precious: a glimpse into real family life. For someone raised in a dorm, those moments were a quiet revelation of what home could feel like.

Saw it, Wrote It, Won It, Still Got the Clipping

Since we were scheduled to graduate in 1950, we were considered seniors. As a special gift, The Dallas Morning News treated all Dallas-area graduating seniors—including those of us from Buckner—to a multi-day train trip to San Antonio. It was my first real journey away from the Home, and it felt marvelous.

We toured all the major sights: the Alamo, Brackenridge Park, the Sunken Garden, and other historic landmarks—long before the RiverWalk existed. I was awestruck by the beauty and history that surrounded us.

On the train ride home, an announcement was made: two prizes would be awarded for the best written report of the trip. I had taken notes along the way, partly so I could describe the experience to the younger orphans back at Buckner. I pulled out my class notes on essay writing—we had just studied it in school—and followed the tips our teacher had given us.

I quickly wrote and submitted my essay to the address provided. To my surprise, I was awarded both first and second prizes. I can only assume I may have been the only one who actually submitted a report!

The Dallas Morning News published my piece in May 1951, and it still lives in their archives. I'm proud to say I have a copy.

Dallas Morning Newspaper
Educational Tour
Senior from Buckner Home Thrilled With San Antonio
By Bobbi Nell Richardson
Senior Buckner Home

Ten excited girls from Buckner Home Academy lay wide awake most of one Friday night. We had been told that the General Travel Company was sponsoring a trip to San Antonio Saturday for students, and we were going to get to go. It was the first real train ride that most of us had ever taken. We could hardly wait; the night seemed to drag tediously by, then suddenly it was morning. We had an early breakfast kindly served by Mrs. R. C. Buckner. Then we eagerly hurried to the station, where everyone impressed us with their friendliness.

We anxiously watched the clock until the Katy was ready to leave. Then we were ushered to our places, and excitement grew as the train picked up speed.

We had no idea what we would do after we got tired of staring out of the windows in order to see all the wonderful sights of unfamiliar places and people. However, it did not take us long to think of something, because where there is a group of excited "orphans," you can be sure there will be laughter and singing.

When we couldn't think of any more songs to sing, the people on the train helped us by making requests. After a while, our throats became so dry we could hardly sing, but they did not stay that way long, for a kind man from Highland Park bought us cold drinks. Then we played games. After we had a good box lunch, we sang some more. Then we looked out as the fields began to be covered with mesquite trees. They were pretty green, but the grass below was greener. As we went farther, we saw more and more patches of lovely bluebonnets until there were pastures covered with them. Our eyes shone as we remembered that this was our state flower. No wonder it was chosen above all the others, the beauty of its blossoms made a picture that we could not easily forget.

When we arrived in San Antonio, we were assigned to different buses. It did not take us long to get to our places and start our educational tour of the city. Tommy Fries was our guide and driver. He was very helpful, especially when he tried to keep us cool by telling us about the swimming pools and the little San Antonio River that runs through the city for twenty-one miles and is spanned by forty-two bridges. As it winds its way through the city, it passes through some of the fifty-two parks and plazas and it gave us a refreshed feeling as we watched it flow down a hill and under a bridge. It rose higher than the bridge in one place, so we got to splash through it.

The buildings in the city seemed just like those in any other city until Mr.

Fries singled them out and gave us interesting information about each one. The large department store was quite interesting. Two of its windows were copied from the original Rose Window that stands at the San Jose Mission. These windows were hand-carved by a boy in honor of his sweetheart. Somehow it seemed to portray the loneliness the boy must have felt.

71_Photo: Bobbi at The Rose Window (1951)

After we had gone through the city, we noticed that there were many more trees than we had expected to see. The hackberry trees grow to be ninety feet tall. Upon inquiring about the palm trees, we were told that they had been transplanted in the city.

In Brackenridge Park, which expands over twenty one miles, there are fourteen bridle paths that wind through cedar, and hackberry trees. From the oak trees hang huge pieces of Spanish moss - the first many of us had ever seen.

As we continued our trip through the beautiful park, we came to a bridge that looked just as ordinary as any old wooden bridge but Mr. Fries told us that

it was cement. Sure enough, when we touched it, we found that to be true. (editor's note: trabajo rústico, created by Dionicio Rodriguez in 1926)

72_Photo: Bobbi at trabajo rústico (2023)

Finally, our guide took us up the hill to the beautiful Chinese Sunken Garden. As we looked down into it, we felt we were looking into a crystal ball at a dream world. There were rows of flowers on each side of the walks and at one side stood a large rock house. We would have never guessed that this miraculous garden had once been a pile of rocks, having no value as it was.

Now it stands as a symbol of beauty that made our hearts leap up as we beheld it.

The Alamo is an old mission built in 1718 , but that is not the reason we stopped to see it. For us Texans, it holds a greater significance. Here, men fought and gave their last breath so each of us could have the freedom we now enjoy. As we walked into the main room we were reminded of the historical events that took place under our very feet. There was a hush and the crowd listened attentively as man told us briefly the familiar story of the Alamo. Then we walked through the rooms and saw where great events took place that made a wider step toward victory and independence. We can not praise the heroes enough and as we looked at the wreaths and memorial stones we felt surely there was something we could do.

After a grand supper and a 2-hour parade,we started home. We were ready, because we had learned a lesson of expressing greater love and devotion to our country. Thank God we are free!

Lessons in the Kitchen and at the Sewing Machine

Two classes all female students had to take before graduating were home economics and sewing.

In home economics, we were taught to cook three meals a day, how to use leftovers and cook for a week on a small budget.

Home Economics Class: Bobbi Richardson, Mary Beth Cutshall, Jane McWhorter, Ophelia Isbel, Sarah Ann Crouch, Rosa Lee Woods, Juanita Graves, Margaret Corcoran, Mary Alpha Gilbert, Ruby Taylor, Maxine Newton, Louise Searcy, and Betty Jean Nelson.

73_Photo: Home Economics Class

In sewing class, we learned to make basic garments, an apron, a house dress, a makeover piece, a blouse, and a full suit. We were proud of our work and wore our handmade suits for our graduation photo. 1st row: LR: Rena Key, Margaret Corcoran, Katherine Henslee: 2nd row: LR: Bobbi Nell, Marie Bailey, Wanda Faye Godsey: 3rd row: LR: Wanda May Polk, Willie Hall, Janette Phillips, Frances Fulton

74_Photo: Handmade Suits(1951)

How Would I Pay for College? God Had a Plan

Generosity That Carried Me Forward

How would I pay for college? That question weighed heavily on me, so I began to pray. I asked God to open a door.

Not long after, an opportunity came. At a women's conference where several Buckner girls were invited to share their testimonies, something remarkable happened: each of us

found a sponsor. My sponsor was Mrs. Leta Bateson.

75_Photo: Troy, Leta, and Troy Jr Bateson (1953)

Her husband, Mr. Troy Bateson, owned the Bateson Construction Company. They were a devoted Christian family, and they didn't just want to support a girl financially—they wanted her to become part of their lives.

Even before I graduated, Mrs. Bateson began inviting me into her world. Sometimes she sent a chauffeur to bring me to Dallas for meals or outings. Other times, I rode the bus to meet her. She taught me how to carry myself in polite society—table manners, how to engage in gracious conversation, and the little things a young lady needed to know.

She even bought me beautiful college clothes from Neiman Marcus. Though I hadn't yet seen her home, I was already being welcomed into her care with love and generosity.

Hours Together, One Perfect Score

As Academy Seniors—so named because we had graduated but chose to stay an extra year at Buckner—we still needed to attend classes. That year, a new curriculum was introduced: Bible studies. We took Old and New Testament courses, along with The Harmony of the Gospels, a deep dive into the three years of Christ's public ministry. We were steeped in Scripture, and we loved it.

The goal was ambitious. Every student in the class—boys and girls—was challenged to memorize the major events of Christ's life in chronological order. There were about 300 key items to learn. We practiced with one another, retelling the stories aloud, quizzing each other, and trying to keep everything in perfect order.

My best friend, Rena Key, was remarkable. She memorized all 300 items flawlessly. Though she didn't want to take the qualifying trip herself, she became my tutor. She taught me memory tricks and tested me for fun. We turned studying into something joyful and shared.

When examination time came, we faced both oral and written tests. An adult examiner would take each student aside and listen as they recited their assigned section. Then came the written portion, where we had to describe a selected part of Christ's life from one of the three ministry years.

We anxiously awaited the results. The final lists would be posted, showing how many mistakes each student had made—zero, one, two, or three. Only those with three or fewer combined errors could go on the special trip. The excitement was electric.

When the results were finally posted, there was a mad rush to the bulletin board. I checked the "three mistakes" list—my name wasn't there. Then the "two mistakes" list—still not there. I made my way toward the "no mistakes" list, but there were too many people crowded around it to see clearly. Someone turned to me and said, "You're on it—you didn't miss a single one!" Still, I had to see for myself. I waited, squeezed in, and finally found my name. There it was—proof that all that studying, all those hours with Rena, had paid off..

The Prize, The Tour That Chose My Future

The prize was a multi-day tour of Baptist colleges across West Texas and New Mexico. Boys and girls traveled together in organized groups, though we stayed in separate accommodations each night. We visited several campuses: Baylor, Hardin Simmons, and Howard Payne.

76_Photo: College Tour Group

LR: Mr McBride, Norma Lockadoo, Daisy Morgan, Joyce Thompson, Edith Trantham, Mrs Murdock, Kenneth McKinny, Gregory Buckner, Bobbi, Edward Stanley (sitting) (July 1951)

77_Photo: College Tour Group
LR: Mrs. Murdock, Bobbi Nell, Joyce Thompson, Edith Trantham: New Mexico (July 1951)

It was at Howard Payne that something clicked.

78_Photo: Howard Payne

I felt a deep connection to the place—the spirit, the people, the atmosphere. I fell in love with it instantly. By the end of the tour, I knew: Howard Payne would be my college.

I Graduated, But I Stayed, Lingering in the Known

It was a tiny graduating class. Traditionally, graduates left campus on graduation day—but I found myself wondering, Where will I go until college starts?

At first, I thought I might live with the Batesons, since they had offered to pay my college tuition. But before I made any decisions, Col. Robert Cook Buckner called the graduating class together and offered us a set of options. "If you stay on campus for the summer and choose one of the designated jobs," he said, "you'll be paid $90 before heading off to college."

There were only three positions available:

- One was working with the little children, caring for them during the summer months.
- Another was assisting the new manager of the Campus Mart—a store funded by the Dallas Texas Baptist Men's Association, where children could spend their weekly allowances on candy and ice cream. Each child had an account, and as they made purchases, funds were deducted. The Mart manager needed a capable assistant to help with inventory and keep meticulous financial records.
- The third position involved managing the Maris Visitors' Center. This job included greeting guests, guiding them around the campus, and keeping the center tidy and welcoming.

In addition to earning money, staying on campus came with surprising privileges—ones we'd never had before:

- ➢ We were allowed to date off-campus.
- ➢ We ate separately from the other children, in a small house with specially prepared meals.
- ➢ We had late curfews.
- ➢ We were free to go anywhere on campus without permission.
- ➢ We could use the telephone for off-campus calls.
- ➢ And for the first time, our mail—both incoming and outgoing—was private.

Several of the nine Academy Seniors decided to take advantage of the summer program. Rena Key, Margaret Corcoran, and I chose to work at the Maris Visitors' Center. We thought we had the best job—greeting visitors, maintaining the space, and enjoying each other's company.

I stayed in the newly built girls' dorm, Pender Hall. Each room was furnished like a home—no more institutional furniture, but real beds, dressers, and touches of comfort we'd never known in the dorms before.

That summer brought us even closer, and we pledged to keep in touch after leaving Buckner.

We worked until August, the start of Buckner's next school year, and earned our $90—a satisfying and dignified close to our years at Buckner.

"Welcome, Bobbi. Come in, Dear One": A New Chapter Begins

I lived at Buckner Orphans Home for eleven and a half years, from age six to seventeen. When it was finally time to leave, I picked up the phone and called Leta Bateson—a woman who had mentored and supported me for years.

"Would it be alright if I lived with you until I left for college?" I asked.

Without hesitation, she replied, "Of course. I'll send a car for you tomorrow."

The next day, I packed my belongings and checked out with the house parents at Pender Dorm. They weren't called matrons anymore but were a kind couple who treated us more like family. It was a strange, bittersweet feeling—closing the chapter on a life I had known for so long and stepping toward a future that felt both exciting and unfamiliar.

My new home was on Northwest Highway in Dallas, Texas: a grand Tudor-style mansion that looked like something from a movie.

79_Photo: Bateson's Mansion

When I arrived, the chauffeur opened the limousine door and said, "Welcome, Miss Bobbi. Ms. Bateson is expecting you."

As I walked toward the elegant entrance, I took in the reflection pool, vibrant flower beds, and the graceful European-style architecture. Inside, I heard Leta's warm voice call out, "Welcome, Bobbi. Come in, dear one." The reception area was breathtaking—winding stairs, polished wood, and hidden rooms that whispered of history and mystery. She led me to a bright indoor-outdoor room overlooking a serene pool and a winding path that led to a creek.

Upstairs, I was given my own bedroom—one of three. The others belonged to Troy Charles, the Batesons' ten-year-old adopted son, and a regular guest. A maid gently assured me that my clothes would be unpacked and hung by bedtime. At seventeen, it was almost too much to take in.

When I offered to help with dinner, Leta smiled and said, "Louise has it all under control." Mr. Bateson soon joined us, and we sat down to a meal served with silver utensils and quiet elegance. They kindly laid out expectations: I was to call him Mr. Bateson and call her Leta. Louise was the maid, Fred was the chauffeur and handyman, and a gardening crew came weekly to maintain the grounds.

Troy Charles had been adopted as a baby, thanks to the Batesons' generosity and a timely donation. Now, they were expanding their home to include me—a seventeen-year-old girl about to begin college. It was a quiet, gracious act that I have never forgotten.

The remainder of the summer stretched before me—a calm, generous space in which to adjust. But as life often does, it offered another unexpected turn.

A high school home economics teacher from Collinsville, Texas, contacted me. She had heard about me through her pastor, who remembered me from a Buckner tour. She invited me to help chaperone a senior class trip.

It was a strange, in-between season—no longer a child, not yet truly an adult. On the trip, we visited churches and resorts, appeared on a live radio show in Oklahoma, and shared long, late-night conversations. I was technically in charge once the lead chaperone went to bed, but I still felt like one of the kids. It was a delightful paradox.

When I returned to the Batesons, my Aunt Mattie arrived unexpectedly. She took me shopping and sewed new dresses for me. Between her help, the clothes I had made in Home Ec, the gifts from Buckner, and Leta's generous wardrobe from Neiman Marcus, I felt more than ready for college life at Howard Payne.

Having just had my eighteenth birthday, I was living with the Batesons and preparing to start college when, once again, the pastor from Collinsville reached out. His wife was expecting a baby and needed help. Would I be willing to come to Collinsville to manage the house and cook for a few weeks?

They offered to take me to Howard Payne afterward. Although the Batesons were disappointed they wouldn't be the ones to take me, they understood—I was needed.

So off I went again—playing housekeeper and cook while a pastor fulfilled his calling and his wife rested, awaiting the birth. But the baby didn't come as quickly as expected. Time was slipping away, and college was about to begin. I worried I might arrive late.

Just in time, the baby was born, and I was delivered to Howard Payne College in Brownwood, Texas. There, I was introduced to Dr. Todd, the Bible professor, and settled into a unique living arrangement—the parsonage of the First Baptist Church, which had been converted into a dormitory for the overflow of female students.

And just like that, I stepped out of one world and into another.

College Daze

I was late for a dorm spot, but the substitute housing was suitable. That's how I started my "college daze." Scholarships were supposed to be available for me since my tuition was already halved thanks to my Orphanage status, but I did not know that an application for a work scholarship had been made. I received a job that fit right into my schedule.

The job was to serve the waitresses before they served meals. After they ate with me, they would wait on tables in the dining hall. I served these servers breakfast, lunch, and dinner for nine months. By the end of my first year, an administrator saw no need for that job. The waitresses could eat while they waited on the table.

I don't know how they kept me on scholarship status for the second year. The next job was drying silverware in the kitchen. My drying-silverware partner was my ex-boyfriend from Buckner, Ira Lee Henslee. He was already a year ahead of me at Howard Payne College and was engaged to another student. Still, it was a joy working alongside someone I knew from Buckner.

Ira Lee was the guy I used to sneak out to meet at Buckner for a hug, risking it all until I realized it just wasn't worth getting kicked out over. Ira Lee was the guy who, from the fifth grade through High School, was Salutatorian of the class. This same Ira Lee was my second-year college partner, being all business and drying silverware.

There were 11 of us from Buckner Orphans Home attending Howard Payne, including the Dickeys and Taylors, who were hired as staff members. So, we began meeting as a group. Well, we met at least once to have a Photo taken.

80_Photo:
Buckners at
Howard Payne
LR: Bobbi, Wanda Godsey, Nadine Sikes, Mr/Mrs. Gordon Taylor, Vernon Horsley, Ruth Nevil, Ira Lee Henslee, Mrs/Mr Dickey, Jerre Graves, Eva Nell Turner, Joan Bye, Mary Louise Turner, and David Reynolds (sitting) (1953).

The Picture Changed, But Buckner Was Everywhere

Sadie Hawkins week was a great activity during the first month of college. We got to choose who we wanted to date each night, and I saved my top pick for the weekend. But then my foster mom called, wanting me home that weekend, and I had to cancel on the guy I wanted as a long-term friend. That canceled date stopped whatever was starting between us.

Howard Payne had a tradition of holding schoolwide elections for class favorites, keeping the winners secret until the yearbook came out. The Annual was mailed to us over the summer. When it was time for the freshman photos, I was dating this guy, whom I had canceled on, and we even held hands for our photo.

81_Photo: Bobbi Nell, Durward Rutland (1952)

However, when the yearbook finally arrived in my mailbox that summer, the photo wasn't of me and my hand-holding date but of me and Durward Rutland from Brownwood.

Mary Louise Turner, my skating friend from Buckner, and my hand-holding friend were the runners-up.

When one looked at the pictures, all the other class favorites and runners-up were from Buckner. Sophomore winners were Eva Nell Turner and her boyfriend, with Jerre Graves as the runner-up, and both girls were my roommates at Buckner. Then, there was David Reynolds, another Buckner student, for the senior class favorite. David Reynolds was a Buckner student who created Billie Juanita Graves' new name, Jerre. This same David married Jerre's college friend, and much to his wife and son's surprise, turned out to be gay. There was no Buckner student-favorite in the junior class that year, 1951.

Changing Majors and Dodging Locker Rooms

When I first got to college, I was all set on majoring in Physical Education. In my very first class, there was a substitute teacher. The newly hired professor hadn't started yet because she was finishing up her military service from WWII. We had the teacher's aide instead, and she was always hovering, especially when it was time to change for class. It felt like she was trying to pair up with me, which made me super uncomfortable.

I dropped the class and switched my major to Elementary Education. Still, the mandatory PE requirement was each year for all four years. I satisfied that requirement in the second semester by taking archery and enjoyed it tremendously. There was no changing clothes for Archery.

When I was a sophomore and elected Cheerleader, much to my relief, it exempted me from taking a PE class. "What would I do about PE in my junior year?" It was a relief to learn that "Being married exempts one from PE." There wasn't a Senior year for me. I took enough credits during the summer and correspondence courses to graduate in three years.

170 Miles to Be the Daughter Again

Every weekend, the Batesons were gracious enough to cover my trips back home to Dallas from Brownwood, 170 miles away. I'd always check the campus bulletin board for rides going to Dallas. My regular ride was with two students from Dallas, one guy and the female PE aide from that awkward PE class. They'd sit up front, and I'd be in the back seat. Sometimes, there would be another student going to Dallas. Both in the front seat were from wealthy Dallas families, and they found each other at Howard Payne. The whole setup was that they pretended to be dating when they had other date partners. This ruse kept their parents from knowing they preferred the same sex as partners. It also ensured they stayed in the good graces of their family fortunes. Being "gay" was not acceptable in nice families.

It was clear I wasn't part of their crowd, so I felt okay using my foster parents' money to pay them to get me "home" each weekend. Bateson's home was where I got to be the daughter of my foster parents. It was also an opportunity to show off the Neiman Marcus outfits that lacked acceptance among the farming community students, who were still wearing their mothers' homemade dresses at Howard Payne, Brownwood, TX. Farmers were not making as much money as "city folk."

A Talk That Freed My Mind—and Got Me Grounded

The rules at Howard Payne were something to get used to. One could stay out till 10 pm by signing out. One could date every night. That's not a question. That's a statement. You could even be alone in a car with a guy. It was fine. It was a lot of freedom all at once. I had been given a taste of it a few months before leaving Buckner. I understood then how important it was to provide Buckner Seniors some freedoms they had not had before to prepare them for being on their own.

Once, as a freshman, when I didn't have a date, I signed out to visit, during visiting hours, with a female classmate at her place. She surprised me with the statement that she was not planning on getting married. I said, "Why?" and she told me it was because her dad was in a mental institution, and there was a history of mental illness in her family. That got me thinking about my Daddy and his history of mental health issues. I was starting to worry about my future.

But then she broke it down for me, something I remembered from biology class but didn't thoroughly "soak in" until we discussed it. There are two types of mental illness: one hereditary, and the other due to social conditions. The social condition type doesn't get passed down to kids. That was a huge relief! Suddenly, I felt like I could think about dating, getting married, and having kids without worrying I'd pass on something I had no control over.

Our conversation kept me at her place past curfew. I failed to sign out for an overnighter, so I should have returned before being locked out at 10 p.m. Of course, the student who asked to lock up for the night had to report me. Being called in for the punishment was embarrassing enough. But being "grounded" for a month meant not even a sign-out could get me out of the dorm in the evening. I couldn't even have a date.

A Name Some Hid, and I Spoke Proudly

By the second semester, Buckner had a strong presence at Howard Payne College, with 11 of us there. Even some of the adults who used to work at Buckner were now working at the college. Mr. Dickey handled registrations, Ms. Dickey taught at the local high school, and Mr. Gordon Taylor, helped by his wife, was the dean of boys. Later, after the overnight conversation episode, Nadine "Pinky" Sykes, the dean of women, was my mentor from Buckner. Thanks be to God, she didn't know about the punishment for the "overnighter." We often ate at the same table, and she reprimanded me for my manners. I suppose Leta Bateson's table manners lessons were quickly forgotten. Buckner Habits had become deep-seated.

I let it be known I was from Buckner Orphans Home, which didn't sit well with some. They felt like being associated with Buckner was a mark against one, something they'd rather keep quiet. I was so proud of Buckner and its services that I was pleased to tell everyone about it.

Bobby Baker, I Never Got Your Letter

There was a time when Jerre Graves, who was handling the mail at the girls' dorm, came across a letter for me that looked suspiciously similar to one sent to Eva Nell Turner from Bobby Baker. Jerre decided to rip my letter up, believing it was for the best. She only told me about this years later, after my marriage to

Glenn. To this day, Bobby Baker still says, "I wrote to you, and you never answered." I still say, "Bobby, I never got a letter from you at Howard Payne."

Eva Nell, on her part, felt called to the mission field and wouldn't date anyone who didn't share that calling. Interestingly, the guys she stopped dating became the ones I started showing interest in, which made it seem like I was trying to follow in Eva Nell's dating footsteps.

Gerry and Me: A Cheer Team

Right at the tail end of my freshman year, I struck up a friendship with Gerry Groth. She was all set to marry her high school sweetheart, and they had grand plans of starting a Christian school post-graduation.

82_Photo: Gerry Groth's Wedding
LR: Bobbi Nell, -, Gerry Groth, -

We talked about our sophomore year and realized we both had this cheerleading past from high school. So, why not try out together? We even worked up some stunts to make our demo stand out. The students were to pick three guys and two girls for the squad, so Gerry and I decided to simplify things by teaming up, making it easier for everyone to vote for us as the two females. Gerry was very clever and worked out the routines for us to "stand out" in the tryouts. We did backbends, leaped simultaneously, did the splits, and used our best voices to make the yells the crowd already knew.

Our strategy was successful. Gerry Groth and I received the most votes for the female positions. Among the male cheerleaders elected was my friend's fiancé, Carol Wayne Shaw, who intended to become a missionary in Mexico with Jackie Hall. Another was Charles Bradshaw, who was training to be a pastor. Glenn Parson, whose flips and hand-walking stunts had distinguished him during the tryouts, was also chosen.

83_Photo: Howard Payne
Cheerleaders (1953)
LR: Carol Wayne Shaw, Bobbi,
Glenn Parson,
Gerry Groth, Charles Bradshaw

Glenn received the most votes among the male cheerleaders, so he became the head cheerleader, making us five cheerleaders for the year.

Oh, one more thing. I had recently begun seeing Glenn.

Jerry Graves remained in my college experience as she was in my Buckner life, and we were both fellow speech and drama majors. Jerre was juggling jobs to make her way through college. She had an out-of-school job teaching speech and drama to local kids, and soon, she asked me to teach the fourth and eighth graders. Thanks to the Bateson family's support and tuition discounts, I didn't need the cash, but I took the job for the experience.

A Summer Between Comfort and Calling

My sophomore year at HPC was on the horizon, and I was all set for a summer back in Dallas, living with my foster parents, the Batesons. I planned to get pampered and recharge for the upcoming school year. But again, the Collinsville family called.

The pastor needed help with their Church program since their new baby kept the wife busy. It was a tough call for me and the Batesons. Lounging around in luxury wasn't what I was used to, but I loved feeling like part of a family that cared so much for me.

With the Collinsville folks, I felt more like an employee than family. Still, it felt good to be helpful and earn my keep. It was a mixed bag of feelings. I chose to help out in Collinsville. The choice stemmed from my commitment to Christian Service. At Howard Payne, I joined different groups that set me to dedicate my life to "full-time serving the Lord." Would this Collinsville activity meet this commitment? Certainly not lounging around in luxury when Church activity was needed.

The church building was newly built and dedicated in March 1949. My friend Cherry Ann Graham and Bobby Joe Cannon were the first young people to be baptized in the new church. These two people became my friends while I was in Collinsville. Cherry Ann was the same dress size as I; we exchanged dresses and shoes.

84_Photo: Cherry Ann Graham, Bobbi, 1940 Plymouth (1952)

In June 1951, the church members voted to buy a parsonage. They purchased a house on Silk Stocking Avenue from my friend Cherry Ann's father, W. L. Graham, for $3,500.00. I lived at the parsonage on Silk Stocking Avenue while in Collinsville.

Directing the Summer Vacation Bible School in Collinsville was super rewarding. It was the right choice. Yet, after a while, being the housemaid and babysitter started to wear on me, and I found myself missing the Bateson mansion and having a "mother." As soon as my conscious behavior allowed, I said "goodbye to Collinsville." VBS was over, and I didn't sign up for free babysitting, so I returned to the Batesons.

The Batesons were thrilled to have me back. I made the most of their pool, inviting friends and family to hang out for the summer. It was just the refreshing vacation I needed to prepare for school.

Shortly before classes began mid-September, Dr. Todd from Howard Payne contacted me. He needed assistance caring for his ailing wife, as he was occupied with summer school and their daughter was away. The Todds requested my help, and I agreed to stay with them. Dr. Todd inquired about my enrollment in his advanced Bible class. Since I needed the course and had prior knowledge from Buckner, I became his teaching assistant and easily earned an A on the test. Mrs. Todd's health improved, and their daughter, who was serving in the military, expressed gratitude for my assistance. I developed a close relationship with the Todds, becoming like a surrogate daughter to them.

During this time, I received contact from Glenn Parson, a Howard Payne student working in Portland for the summer. Upon learning I was in Collinsville, he tried to locate me. He eventually reached out to me through Dr. Todd and expressed his intention to pursue a relationship with me during our sophomore year. Dr. Todd, acting protectively, made it clear he would assess whether Glenn was a suitable match for me.

Dr. Todd often received requests from local churches for ministerial recommendations. Glenn, being a student of ministry, was frequently chosen by Dr. Todd for these preaching assignments. However, this was contingent on Glenn demonstrating his suitability for the role. Simultaneously, Dr. Todd and his wife would accompany me to various churches on weekends, where I would share my testimony. Consequently, Glenn and I had limited opportunities to begin a courtship. He would preach at one church, while I would give my testimony at another.

Sophomore Year: When Love Grows and Integrity is Tested

I started going off campus on the weekends with the Mission Band. Being off campus most weekends didn't help my chances of dating. However, participating in Christian service activities felt right rather than looking for interesting dates. After all, "Full-time Christian service" means just that, full-time, all the time!

There was no trip one weekend, so I went to the Training Union program on a Sunday evening. There was a group of eligible single friends. They needed a person to represent the group in some Church-wide activity. I was chosen. When it came time to present myself, I needed a date. By this time, the eligible males had made other arrangements for dates since I was not always present on Sunday evening. I had to go outside the group. I thought of Glenn Parson, who was, in a way, waiting for us both to be free for a date. I called him and asked if he would be my escort, but I called him "Gene," not "Glenn." He overlooked that and became my escort.

Glenn, not Gene, became a "boyfriend" after that escort. There was not much dating during the school year. He went away to work in the Northwest for the summer, as was his usual summer activity. He lived with his aunt, Ella, and uncle, Earl Grant. We kept in touch.

Heading into sophomore year, I had a considerably full plate. I was swamped between my job at the dining hall, cheerleading (which meant no more Dallas weekends), dating Glenn, and teaching speech. Still, I was determined to keep my faith at the center of everything. I learned of a Hispanic girl who had no friends. We started meeting together as prayer partners. We began meeting weekly as prayer partners, sharing our aspirations and setbacks and supporting each other through prayer. We became close friends.

Living in the dorms offered an opportunity to have laundry services provided at no cost. Collecting laundry from the other girls would be a minor task and a good way to connect with them. However, even the small amount of time it took each evening proved overwhelming. I streamlined the process. The girls would leave their laundry and payment with me weekly. I combined it with my own and sent it to the cleaners. Once the laundry was returned, I set up a rack for them to retrieve their items, rather than delivering them individually. This system proved efficient.

Despite dating Glenn, a misunderstanding in 1953 resulted in my attendance at the Howard Payne Coed Athletic Banquet with Bob Cleveland, one of the football team managers. In the banquet photograph, he is prominently featured in a black suit with a white boutonniere. I'm at his right.

85_Photo: Athletic Banquet (1953)

The three women in the front row were employees of the photographer's studio; Mr. Gibbens requested their presence at the forefront for inclusion in the yearbook.

The year zoomed by in a blur, with barely a moment to breathe, let alone study. So when I saw the questions on an English test and realized I was clueless about the answers, I was in shock. I had a feeling of helplessness. Why hadn't I studied more? What am I going to do? As I sat there, heart racing, I spotted my outlet. Taking the class with me were basketball team members, but they weren't there at the time of the test; they were away at a game and would be taking a makeup test. I went to the teaching sub's desk, casually said, " I'll be taking the make-up test," and left the room.

In my room, I used the rest of the class to prepare for the makeup test. I heard this teacher did not use the same questions for those making up the test as she did for the primary test. As a means of studying, I used the questions as an open-book assignment. I answered all the questions from the test and studied them. Then, I wrote the answers and checked them using the book.

The substitute teacher, who happened to be Glenn's best friend and a recent HPC grad, knew me. He decided to delay telling the teacher until he talked to Glenn first. After talking to Glenn, Glenn responded, "She'll work it out."

The next day, the teacher set up a separate room for the group of students who had missed the test to take the makeup test. That group consisted of the members of the basketball team and me. She handed us the questions. We took the test while she made a new reading assignment for those who had taken it the day before, and dismissed them early. The teacher's makeup test, much to my surprise, had the same questions given to the class the day before. I had braced myself for something different. Pulling out my notes, I couldn't help but wonder, "Is this cheating?" I hoped it wasn't. I rewrote the answers I had taken from the book in my study session. I handed in my answers, feeling like I was bending the rules by taking an open-book test. All the while, I silently prayed, "God, please forgive me if this is a falsehood."

It hit me then how 2 Timothy 2:15 talks about studying hard to show ourselves approved by God without any reason to be ashamed. I was getting an A that I felt I didn't earn. My talk with God taught me, "There may be a fine line between right and wrong, but it is best to 'walk on the right side of the fine line.'"

The sub decided not to mention this information to the teacher. Only years later did Glenn tell me about his talk with his friend.

A Proposal, a Calling, and a Plan

As my sophomore year approached its conclusion, my relationship with Glenn intensified. He was about to enter his senior year, and our conversations became more serious. It felt as if we were already engaged. He planned to spend another summer working at an ice plant in Oregon, staying with his Aunt Ella, his mother's sister, and her husband, Earl Grant.

Before leaving, Glenn proposed, "Will you marry me and join me in my ministry?" The ministry aspect resonated deeply; it aligned with my commitment to Christian service. However, the idea of being a "preacher's wife" gave me pause. I questioned how to fulfill such a role. My understanding of marriage was primarily based on books and observing the Bateson family. I even revisited my Home Economics book from Buckner, which included a section on being a good wife. I sought out other resources to gain confidence in this new potential role. If I could learn to navigate speech and drama, I could likely learn to be a wife.

However, the fact that I was a year behind Glenn in college presented a challenge. He was ready to begin his ministry, and I knew I needed to complete my degree at Howard Payne College. Otherwise, this opportunity might not return. I earnestly prayed for guidance regarding my next steps. I would load up on summer classes, take a senior correspondence course during my junior year, and even add a course over spring break. I pleaded with the registrar to allow me to take 20 hours during the school year. Quitting my photo studio job would be necessary, but I'd keep teaching speech to fourth and eighth graders. The Batesons were worried about me taking on wedding plans with a heavy class load, but after prayer and explaining how I'd manage it all, they supported me.

Agreeing to marry Glenn opened up a whole set of problems, planning-wise. Knowing me well, Glenn had one request: "Let's not turn it into a big production." Traditionally, brides go back to their hometown church for their weddings. But picturing my wedding at the Buckner Home Chapel, filled with loads of kids and a choir singing, didn't seem right. Glenn wouldn't have been thrilled, and neither would I. What felt perfect was the idea of getting married at the Batesons' place, which had become home to me. I envisioned descending their grand staircase into a formal living room with about 25 people watching.

Tede and Buster Lyons, from the Sunday School class in Dallas, proposed an alternative wedding ceremony. They had connections to arrange for me to be married on "Bride and Groom," a new television show. I would be given away in New York by Dizzy Dean, the famous baseball player and sports announcer, followed by a honeymoon in Bermuda. The wedding would be broadcast on national television. However, my fiancé firmly rejected this idea. Glenn would not agree to have someone who advertised beer participate in our wedding. He believed that "our testimony in a Christian marriage ceremony with those who have supported us spiritually, socially, and financially would show our gratitude." That was Glenn's conviction, and I agreed that such a television ceremony would be disrespectful to those who had helped us.

Dottie, my older sister, had been like a stand-in parent since our Buckner days, pouring her resources into making sure Billy, Angie, and I never felt like we were taken to an Orphanage to get rid of us. She had been playing the mom role. I thought it only right that she should be the "Mother figure" at the wedding, and Butch, her husband, had been like a father to all three of us. Having him be the "stand-in father" to give me away would be an honor. Angie was to be my maid of honor, and my Buckner best friend, Rena Key, was undoubtedly one to sing. Martha, my roommate from college, and Glenn's sister, Barbara, were bridesmaids. There was one problem. Glenn wanted his good friend to sing as a soloist. This friend was often paired with him in revivals to lead the singing and Glenn to preach. So we solved it by having two soloists.

Troy Charles Bateson, the son of my Foster Parents, would light the candles. My boss would be the photographer, and my professor and friend, Dr. Todd, would officiate. Dr. Todd had met Glenn a year or so earlier and gave us his blessing, which meant a lot.

Teaching Art Without Being an Artist

Returning to Howard Payne for summer classes meant the dorms were closed. The Todds welcomed me into their home. Dr. Todd had agreed to officiate the wedding, and Mrs. Todd even selected and gifted me my going-away outfit. Their kindness made me feel like family.

I dreaded the summer school art class, convinced I would fail. I spoke with the professor about needing a good grade to qualify for correspondence courses and graduate with Glenn. Our conversation was eased by Glenn having recently honored him at an all-school ceremony, conferring a DD degree to celebrate the birth of his **D**arling **D**aughter. Glenn, being a student trustee, had made the announcement. I had skipped an initial test, and an art student, the substitute teacher's wife, had designed the certificate. I presented it to the art professor and confessed my lack of artistic ability. I emphasized the need for an A to take correspondence courses and graduate in three years with Glenn.

The professor reassured me that the summer class focused on art tools and techniques, not masterpieces. He suggested a course on teaching art to elementary students, which would help my teaching credential. It was a perfect fit, allowing me to avoid actual artwork.

It was understood that an instructor of young children wouldn't need to paint like a professional. I decided to present drawings matching those of young children. This worked. While other classmates produced skilled artwork, my stick figures were shown as examples of children's art. I focused on the speaking aspect of art instruction, not the drawing itself.

For one assignment, I demonstrated using chalk in a classroom by doing a devotional chalk talk. I drew Joseph and Mary traveling to Bethlehem on a donkey. Their scarves and garments allowed me to avoid drawing arms, legs, and faces. I only needed to draw the donkey. Another assignment required illustrating literature, so I drew a goat for "The Three Billy Goats Gruff." I depicted only one goat with its head down, showing its horns as it butted the monster under the bridge. I focused on the splash, not the monster. I have never been a skilled artist and never desired to be.

I sometimes wonder if I should have taken the brush technique class. In that class, I would have practiced brush strokes and identified brush types used in paintings, but no artwork would have been required.

Perfect Negatives and a Husband's How-To Guide

A photography studio job occupied my entire summer. Developing negatives was nerve-wracking, and I constantly worried about ruining someone's

wedding photos. Fortunately, I maintained a flawless record in loading and developing negatives. The pay was sufficient to provide some extra funds for the honeymoon.

86_Photo: Bobbi Modeling (1952)

The story of how I obtained the photography job is worth recounting. My curiosity led me into the shop across from the college during my freshman year. At Buckner, I enjoyed taking photographs but understood it wasn't a viable career path. Furthermore, I had dedicated my life to Christian service, so my visit to the photography studio was purely out of curiosity. Following a brief conversation, the photographer suggested I model for some promotional images.

Modeling eventually led to an offer to handle photo negatives, which was a well-paying position. I was introduced to the photographer's wife, who specialized in painting and tinting photographs. My role was to suggest that clients consider having their photos tinted or colored. I held this position until my marriage.

The photographer documented our wedding on film in Dallas. However, I was not required to develop the negatives or print the photographs, as was the practice for some employees getting married. I was taking a vacation and preferred to have the images printed upon my return. My wedding album, filled with the photographer's Photos, became my gift to my husband.

87_Photo: Book, How to be a Minister's Wife & Love it

My husband gave me the book *"How to Be a Minister's Wife and Love It"* as a gift.

The Day I Became Mrs. Glenn Parson

My wedding day was one of the most exciting days of my life. It started with breakfast at the Batesons with my Buckner friend, Rena Key, who had stayed overnight with me. We skipped church but had a devotional, which felt right for the day ahead. We read and talked about Proverbs. Watching from an upstairs window, I saw the guests arriving. I felt a mix of nerves and excitement.

Glenn, my soon-to-be husband, and his parents, Harley and Opal, plus their kids, Barbara, Mickey, and Sue, came first. The male singer who was to sing "I Love You Truly" and the best man, a Howard Payne alumnus with his wives, came next.

My family came. They were my sisters, Angie and Dottie. Dottie and Butch brought my Daddy, Virgil Richardson, from the Veterans' Hospital for the big day. My brothers Ray and Billy Dean, who served in the military, were missing from the wedding.

My father had told me he could not attend my wedding. I had discussed this with him, explaining that Butch would give me away. Mr. Bateson was also available and would have gladly accepted, but he understood he was too recent a figure in my life to hold such a position. Dottie, who had acted as a mother figure over the years, was now assuming that role. It was therefore natural that Butch (R.L. Townzen), Dottie's husband, would be the one to give me away.

As I watched the guests arrive, I was surprised to see my father. I still maintained a distance from him since the night I witnessed my mother lying on the floor, dying from the gunshot wound he had inflicted. I had not yet truly forgiven my father. I desired to and prayed about it, but something held me back. All four of my other siblings had forgiven our father and had enjoyed good relationships with him for years. I also had a relationship with him, but I had not forgiven him at the time of my wedding. Glenn and I were praying about it.

Butch, my sister's husband, was like the dad we kids needed. Dottie and Butch had provided Angie, Billy, and myself with so many things to supplement the clothes, etc. when we were in the Orphanage. After meeting the Batesons, I ended up spending most of my time with the Batesons, but I never forgot the kindness Dottie and Butch had shown me.

From Buckner, there came friends: Pinky Sykes, my teacher; Miss Parks, the administrative office secretary I'd grown close to through my Buckner cleaning job; the Buckner Chapel minister, Bro Hyden, who'd picked me for the Vacation Bible School storytime, and his wife who tutored me in Math, Miss Barnett, now Mrs Hyden. Others present were Ms. McCullough, my math teacher, who made sure I knew the basics and saw that I did understand Algebra. There were Mr. and Mrs. Todd; Mr. Todd was officiating the wedding with the Buckner Pastor, Bro. Hyden.

Tede Lyons, representing a Sunday School class in Dallas, was present at the wedding. This Sunday School Class was a group of women I guided through the Home. They felt the class needed a community project, and I was the recipient. After guiding them through the Home, I sent them a "Thank You note." They, in turn, sent me a gift. When I graduated, they gave me a "Graduation shower." When they heard I was getting married, they gave me another shower. It was good to see representatives from this group of women at my wedding.

When the photographer, who had been my boss, showed up, it was time for

some premarital shots upstairs, pretending to get me wedding-ready, all away from the guests' eyes.

88_Photo: Bridesmaids (1953)
Top: LR: Rena Key, Barbara Parson, Martha Redfern, Dotti Jean Richardson-Townzen
Bottom: LR: Angie Richardson, Bobbi (1953)

Later, I found out the best man, Stewart Allison, and Glenn were getting the same treatment.

The wedding party came from a side room and walked the aisle to the front of the gathering. I made my grand entrance by descending the stairs.

89_Photo: Descending the Stairs (1953)

It was perfectly timed as the music played. The photographer stayed to the side, ensuring not to block the view of my grand staircase walk. It was all happening, and it felt so perfect.

At the foot of the stairs was Butch Townzend, my brother-in-law.

90_Photo: Bobbi and Butch Townzend (1953)

I took his arm and we made our way to the altar, through the middle of our family and friends in the living room.

All the candles stayed lit. Troy Charles did his job perfectly, handing off the rings to the best man.

The Buckner minister started with a prayer, and then Dr. Todd took over the ceremony. After a closing prayer from the Buckner minister, Mr. Hyden, we were officially Mr. and Mrs.Glenn Parson. It took 15 minutes.

Leta Bateson ushered everyone to sign our wedding book. Then, we gathered in the dining room for cake and punch. We cut the cake and fed it to each other without smashing it in the face. The camera seemed to click endlessly as we posed with one guest after another.

My Father at My Wedding

I hadn't invited him to my wedding.

It was my older sister who arranged it, quietly, without telling me. When I saw him standing among the guests, my heart stopped. I hadn't prepared for that moment. I hadn't rehearsed what I'd say, or how I'd feel.

The memories came flooding back all at once: the sound of Mama's scream, the look on his face that day, twisted, unfamiliar, terrifying. I had worked so hard to build a life apart from that pain. And now, there he was.

I hadn't fully forgiven him. The wound was still there, deep, raw, and unhealed. I had prayed, I had wrestled, but the grace to forgive hadn't yet come. Not then.

At one point during the reception, he stepped toward me and leaned in.

I thought to myself, I will not let his violence steal this day from me. This is my wedding. I will walk into it with peace. If I can look him in the eye and not hate him, then I'll know, I'm free.

He was still my father. And I was trying to be whole.

I let him kiss me on my cheek.

It wasn't closeness, it was courtesy.

91_Photo: My daddy (1953)

I couldn't offer forgiveness in that moment, not fully. But I was praying for the strength to get there someday. To lay down the weight I had carried for so long, not for him, but for me. For the peace I was still longing to hold.

After the wedding, I dashed upstairs to slip into my going-away outfit, a suit complete with matching purse and shoes, thanks to Mrs. Todd.

92_Photo: Glenn and Bobbi (1953)

Glenn got the keys to his dad's car, and we exited under a shower of birdseed from the wedding group. We went to a Dallas hotel for our first night as a married couple. The next day, after brief stops in Dallas and our place in Brownwood, we started our mini honeymoon in Brownsville, staying at Glenn's aunt's house. She arranged for us to have the place to ourselves. The local community, composed of Glenn's relatives, welcomed us with open arms and showered us with kitchen goods and gadgets.

Married, Pregnant, Overload, Overjoyed: Graduating as Mrs. Parson

Adapting to life as Mrs. Glenn Parson, or Bobbi Parson, was a significant transition. Glenn was pursuing his ministry studies, and I understood I now had a specific role to fulfill. My husband provided me with a book titled *How to Be a Minister's Wife and Love It*, which I read thoroughly and attempted to implement.

Despite having one year of college remaining, Glenn was invited to pastor a church in Doole, Texas, sixty miles from Brownwood. Glenn arranged to preach in Doole on Wednesday evenings and Sundays for the remainder of his senior year and dedicate a year to assisting the church during a drought from 1954 to the Summer of 1955.

To graduate from Howard Payne College alongside Glenn, I enrolled in an increased course load, completed correspondence courses during holidays, and attended summer school. I was anxious about receiving my diploma. It was not due to being four months pregnant, as my robe concealed that fact. My concern was whether my name had been correctly changed from Bobbi Nell Richardson to Bobbi Nell Parson. What if my name was not called? What if I stood in line on stage and my name was not announced?

The registrar had correctly updated my information. My name was called: "Mrs. Glenn Parson." I felt immense relief. With a smile, I accepted my diploma. Glenn and I were now college graduates.

Doole Days: Faith, Quilts, and Quiet Mornings

Doole was a town situated in a way that allowed access and departure in four different directions. It wasn't a necessary stop for through traffic. The roads leading into Doole were well-maintained, as the Highway Commissioner for the area resided there.

In 1914, Doole had a population of 25, and by the 1940s, the town maintained a steady population of 250 and held within its city limits: a school, a church, and ten businesses, including a diner, a grocery store, and a mechanic's shop. The population was on a decline while we were there in 1954, falling to 40 in the 1960s and, despite a small spike in the 70s, continued to decline until it finally evolved into the ghost town that it is today.

We lived in the parsonage, which was a "Shotgun House" where you could see straight through from the front door to the back. It was a simple setup with the living areas all in a straight line. Notably, our house and the mail clerk's were the only painted ones in town, a detail whose reason I never discovered.

Glenn set up his office at the church, just a brisk walk from the parsonage. The church was the most prominent building in town.

93_Photo: Doole Baptist Church (1978)

At the far end of the street was a general store that also served as a gas station. Doole's downtown consisted of a single block, which included a laundry, another service station, a post office, and an ice house with rental lockers.

One Absence, Many Losses

There was also a school on a hill—larger than the church—but it was no longer in use by the time we arrived. The school had closed due to a decline in the number of school-age children, falling just below the minimum required to keep it open. Ironically, it might have stayed open if one remaining student, lacking parental guidance, had chosen to attend. Because of that single absence, the district decided to bus all the other students to a distant school—a loss for both the student who stayed home and those now facing long commutes. Though the building was still new and in excellent condition, it soon found new purpose as a community center, with the local quilting group happily making it their home. Life in Doole was undoubtedly unique.

I learned to quilt during Vacation Bible School at Buckner. When I moved to Doole, I joined the weekly quilting circle. The welcome was warm, and one of the gifts was a quilt from the congregation. Everyone crafted a square that was then stitched into a quilt for the new Parson's family. I guessed the quilt I was working on would warm someone else in town.

When a person moved into a town, it was customary to give the couple a "pounding." No, hands were not placed on their bodies. It was called a shower or pounding for those who brought a pound of a staple, e.g., butter, sugar, flour, etc. It was a way of welcoming the couple into the community and helping them get started with housekeeping by giving them the groceries they needed to stock their cupboard.

I wasn't the only one in the community with a baby. Just out of high school, a young couple had just had a baby. They were members of the church. Mrs. Brown, another member of the Church, had a baby. We were piecing together the quilt that would be a gift for her growing family. They already had a teenager, so they were all set with a built-in babysitter for the new arrival. She was 15 years old when the baby was born.

My early morning ritual was one of my routines, which had become a part of me. No alarm was needed; I would arise just before dawn. In Doole, I kept it up, taking my Bible and finding a new spot each morning to watch the sunrise, pray, and soak in the countryside's peace. I had never lived in the country before; everything was fascinating, quiet, beautiful, and captivating. God felt so near. I sometimes sang songs like: "God is so near, God is so near, God is so near to me."

While awaiting the baby's arrival, which I initially expected in August, my sister Dottie came to stay with me. Mr. Bateson had offered to have Mrs. Bateson come, but I assured them my sister's help was sufficient. Doole was not a suitable environment for Leta Bateson. I could not envision her leaving her mansion to visit me in the "shotgun" house in Doole.

Dottie was eager to assist and looked forward to the baby's birth. However, it was August, and we did not know that the baby would not arrive until October. It was cotton-picking season. Dottie, accustomed to more activity, picked cotton to help a local farmer. Afterward, she bid me farewell and returned home. It was a helpful visit for everyone.

Our Firstborn: Corinne: Sweet, Still, and Smiling

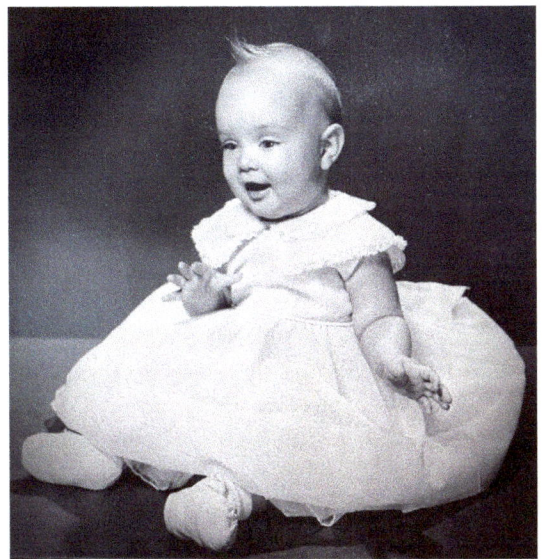

On October 9, 1954, I gave birth to our first child, Corinne.

94_Photo: Corinne (1955)

Corinne's arrival was smooth, leading us to believe all babies were naturally content and self-entertaining upon waking. She was, indeed, a "good" baby.

95_Photo: Corinne Bobbi (1955)

Doole: A Town That Stitched Itself Into Our Hearts

After Corinne's birth, she and Glenn often slept late. I continued my early morning ritual of finding a quiet place in Doole to worship. Sometimes, this meant overlooking the town, and other times, observing cattle grazing.

During holidays, the town practically shut down, and many residents seemed to disappear for days. We adopted this custom, using it as an opportunity to visit relatives. We often returned with family gifts, easing any concerns the church might have had about our modest salary.

Having learned to sew at Buckner and furthered those skills in college, I sewed Corinne's clothes by hand, lacking a sewing machine. My sister Dottie had made my maternity clothes and later altered them into regular dresses for me.

We formed strong friendships in Doole and maintained contact with several church members after leaving. One couple even joined our church in a later pastorate. When a young couple's house caught fire, Glenn, though dressed in his good clothes, rushed to help. He climbed onto the ceiling to knock out the roof, allowing water to extinguish the flames, ruining his suit and shoes.

Each week, a church family would host us for lunch. Ms. Hayworth, a widow, was a particular favorite. She and her husband had adopted twin boys, initially under a trial arrangement. The boys' names had been inadvertently switched, but they preferred to keep the mistaken names, which persisted even after one brother's death. When the surviving brother, Len (originally Glen), visited Ms. Hayworth, Glenn and I enjoyed his company. He and his wife later became missionaries in Africa, and we stayed in touch.

Two years after we left Doole, another family made matching shirts for Glenn and Harley after Harley's birth. A woman who owned hundreds of chickens allowed me to help collect eggs and taught me how to candle them. We remained in contact for years.

Our neighbor's postmistress regularly watered her plants with leftover coffee, a practice I adopted. Mrs. Brown had a baby later in life and had an older daughter who helped care for the infant, creating a unique dynamic. We visited the Turner family after they moved, where Mr. Turner worked as a prison warden, and heard stories about the inmates. Mr. and Mrs. Snowden, a couple who lived eight miles from town, often hosted us for lunch and stayed in touch after our departure.

Many other families made an impression, including the pianist, the service station family, and others just outside the town limits. Doole's only paved road was well-maintained because the highway commissioner lived there. Dan Taylor, a rodeo champion, also lived in Doole, and his wife attended our church. His German hired hand and family rarely attended due to language barriers.

Doole and its residents left a lasting mark. I remember nearly all 250 families in and around Doole, a truly special group.

After my wedding to Glenn, I went to Dottie's to have my wedding dress altered. I wanted it altered so I could wear it for various banquets sponsored by the church where Glenn was the pastor. Dottie agreed to alter. While I was there, Dottie invited my dad over, and Photos were taken.

96_Photo: Me and My Daddy

He Studied Theology, I Taught Kids

Glenn took Corinne and me to his parents' home in Brownsville for the summer of 1955. He planned to work as a longshoreman with his father, Harley Lonnie Parson. Glenn's mother, Opal, cared for Corinne and provided meals for everyone. Glenn's siblings, Barbara, Mickey, and Sue, lived at home, which added to Opal's workload. I sought employment but encountered difficulty due to my lack of Spanish proficiency, a requirement for most available positions.

The Superintendent of Brownsville schools, a church member, learned of my teaching credentials and helped me secure a summer school teaching position in High School English. The job was fulfilling and well-compensated. I recall using specific teaching methods to motivate students to make up failed subjects for graduation.

Glenn diligently loaded boats. His father, as foreman, assigned Glenn less desirable tasks. Glenn was committed to working and earning the longshoreman's substantial wages.

With Opal handling cooking and childcare, Glenn and I earned money for his summer seminary training.

Glenn decided to attend seminary in New Orleans, diverging from the common choice of Fort Worth Seminary.

97_Photo: Seminary

We relocated before the start of the term to find housing and employment.

The seminary housing was infested with roaches, so we purchased a small mobile home and parked it across from the seminary.

I found a teaching position in Metairie, about eight miles from the mobile home. The community was predominantly Jewish, but the school's administration was Southern Baptist. The Superintendent and Principal were both Baptist. I was hired to teach second grade. One of the interviewers mentioned that the librarian lived near me, and we arranged for me to ride with her to school daily.

After about a month in New Orleans, Glenn received an invitation to preach in Houston, Texas. Seminary classes were held Tuesday through Friday at noon, allowing him to travel to Houston on Friday and eturn to New Orleans by Tuesday. After several eeks, the Houston church asked Glenn to become their pastor. He declined, citing his commitment to completing seminary. After deliberation, the church elders offered to fly him from New Orleans to Houston each weekend. With no classes on Friday evening, Glenn could fly to Houston and return to New Orleans on Monday evening, as there were no Monday classes.

I settled into teaching second grade in Metairie. I commuted with the librarian, who also took Corinne to the seminary nursery. We arrived at school in time for the start of the day. Students gathered on the playground with a supervisor until classes began. I began each day with singing and a "sharing time." I taught the class a song each month related to the current holiday. Other teachers heard this and asked me to teach their students the songs. Before students entered their classrooms, I led a 20-minute singing session in a room close to the playground, a positive start to the day.

I did not enjoy teaching and felt I was not performing adequately. Therefore, I was receptive when Glenn suggested moving to Houston. Before leaving New Orleans and Metairie, I resigned and applied to the Houston Public School System. My song time contributed to a positive recommendation from the administration; otherwise, my performance might have resulted in a less favorable one.

Glenn's mother visited for Thanksgiving and offered to take Corinne to live with her until we settled in Houston, which was a tremendous help. During the holidays, while arranging the move, I visited my aunts, Aunt Mattie, who had made clothes for me during college, and Aunt Alta, who informed me that she had assumed guardianship of the three Richardson children after Big Mama and Big Daddy passed away, when we were still underage. These aunts were my mother's sisters. I was glad to see them. Glenn and Corinne were already in Texas. We enjoyed a visit, and they toured New Orleans. Both aunts were widows.

After selling it, Glenn moved into the New Orleans Seminary dorm from our mobile home. He had three years to finish the Seminary and lived in the men's dorm for the rest of his time there.

Harley-Kevin, Aunt Em, and the House That Faith Built

Glenn moved his family into the Church parsonage in Houston. Since it was unfurnished, we had to buy furniture. We purchased what we needed to get by with as little as possible.

98_Photo: Corinne, Bobbi, Glenn (1957)

The Houston Public School System found me a teaching spot quickly. I was placed in a third-grade class. They tried me in a gifted school for second grade, but my teaching skills were not satisfactory. I was placed in a public school in the Spanish part of town. It fit me well, for no Spanish was allowed.

The Houston Public School System was well supplied with specialists and had many resources from the District Office.

99_Photo: Bobbi (1957-58)

It was evident that a new teacher would need extra help teaching Hispanic children, so I was given special help. It certainly was helpful. The teacher next to my classroom was also a good mentor. She taught the same grade, so I could open the door between the two classrooms and hear her teach. Watching her teach contributed to my experience as a beginning teacher.

We had special playground supervisors, so when there was a break and we were in the teacher's room, hearing even more helpful

57-58
FRANKLIN ELEM.

teaching tips was good. I was getting the "hang" of teaching and liked it much better. The teaching supervisor commended me to the principal. The principal's recommendation was "glowing." He told his supervisor he was as pleased with me as a teacher as if I were his daughter.

I taught for three years, then Glenn and I decided I should quit since he was out of the Seminary and the Church was paying a good salary. We still needed some furniture, so I

tutored kids. I was becoming a good teacher and liked it. I used all types of children's games to teach. Games used were: "hopscotch," "true or false questions," "finishing the story," "finding the answer in the reader," and "finishing reading the lesson."

Just before I quit teaching, I became pregnant. In Texas, one could not be pregnant and teach. As soon as one knew they were pregnant, even during the school year, the pregnant person had to resign or go on leave. A substitute teacher took their place. I needed to teach because Glenn was not through the last semester of his seminary term. I said nothing about being pregnant, but one teacher noticed. We met in the teacher's lounge each day. There were multiple grades of one level in the school, from first through sixth. All the teachers had their breaks at the same time.

One day, I received a note from one of the fourth-grade teachers. It read, " I have some larger clothes that would fit you if you want them. Say nothing, and I'll bring them tomorrow." I said nothing. I was given five seasonal outfits (not maternity) the next day. I taught until my seventh month without showing a "big stomach." I resigned at the end of that year.

In the summer of 1958, Steward Allison, Glenn's best man at our wedding, asked if we would like to take a vacation with him and his family. We wanted to go to Boca Chica for vacation. There was nothing there except sand and an old house, unoccupied. Glenn found the owner, and he made it liveable and let us stay there for free. Stewart, his wife, their two children, Corinne, Glenn, and I (seven months pregnant), set up housekeeping in the house. We spent every day, all day, on the beach. Corinne and Allison's oldest daughter was very good friends. They were the same age, about 4 years old.

One day after lunch, we were on the beach, and we all fell asleep. My legs stuck out of the umbrella when the sun moved in the sky. We all received too much sun. But I got the worst sunburn. We decided to go to Brownsville. Glenn's parents lived there. They invited us in, fixed us a good meal, and we rested and visited. Refreshed, we returned to the beach in Boca Chica for the last few days. The whole beach was deserted, except for us.

During our drive with the Allisons, Ruthie, Stewart's wife, suggested a name for the baby that I was carrying. She thought and said, "Why not name him Harley after your Dad?" Glenn said, "That's a great idea. We had planned to name, if it were a boy, Kevin." Ruthie said, "How about Harley-Kevin?" So that is what we named him, born August 18, 1958.

Now, the whole family lived in the church parsonage in Houston, and Glenn no longer needed to commute to New Orleans. I was not teaching with the Houston Public Schools, so I could spend full time with Corinne, getting ready for the baby and learning the role of the preacher's wife.

A family in the Church had been using a "Nanny" when their children were small. They kept the woman after the children were grown. They made Miss Emma their houseguest. But Emma had no income. When the family saw the Parson family's need for a babysitter, they offered Miss Emma. We could not afford much money, but Miss Emma came for much less than she could have received if there had been a need in the area. Miss Emma became a part of our family and moved into the parsonage with us. Glenn led Emma to Christ, and she became a faithful Sunday School attendee and church member. She also took the job of babysitting for the Church. Her testimony of Christ's salvation was very evident in her life. She became more outgoing and assertive in declaring how God showed Himself in her life. She joined our family devotions and prayed the blessing with Corinne when she fed her meals. Emma, Miss Emma, finally became Aunt Em to the Parson family. We loved her like she was kin. She often pulled Corinne from the parsonage in a little red wagon up the sidewalk to the neighborhood park.

Things seemed to progress smoothly until the Texas Highway Department informed Glenn that the church grounds were required for a state highway project. This meant the church would lose its property. It quickly became apparent that membership would decline without a permanent church location until a new site could be secured. Eventually, even the deacons resigned. The only remaining members were the trustees and the Parson family.

The church retained ownership of the parsonage. The compensation received from the Highway Department was sufficient to cover expenses and resulted in a substantial sum being deposited into the church's account. Additionally, the church, named Oldham Memorial, had an endowment. The foundation funds remained intact. Glenn was tasked with finding a new church site. The trustees transferred this authority to Glenn before they departed from the church.

Glenn located a site for the new church and contacted a contractor building homes in a new neighborhood. Glenn negotiated an agreement with the contractor, who donated a prime lot for the church in exchange for being hired to construct it. As the church's foundation was laid, Glenn and I were expecting our second child. A team consisting of the contractor's crew, individuals from the new neighborhood, and Glenn himself constructed the church rapidly. By the time our son Harley was born, they were completing the final details of the church.

My Second Child, Harley, was born August 18, 1958

100_Photo: Bobbi, Corinne, Harley, Glenn (1958)

I was sure there would be "sly comments" about the only red-haired family member. To avoid these, I immediately dyed my hair red. I kept my red hair until Harley was 14 years old.

New Faces, New Voices, and a Congregation in Bloom

The church quickly had full membership, especially since many new homeowners sought a local place to worship. Walking to the church was more convenient than driving to another site. The community lacked a school, making the church a central social point. Early members began hosting gatherings there, inviting both churchgoers and non-churchgoers. These community leaders played a significant role in strengthening the church's membership. They even initiated a door-to-door campaign, visiting people in pairs to invite them to join in worship.

One evening during Visitation, I found myself without a partner, so I went alone. To my surprise, the woman at the first house I visited was not home. The gentleman who answered the door invited me in and asked why I had come. I explained I was visiting for the church. He replied with something akin to, "Well, let's have it." I typically avoided visiting alone with a man in his home. However, I offered a silent prayer and began. I presented the plan of salvation. He immediately accepted Christ and prayed, thanking God for saving him. The entire encounter lasted only a few minutes. I initially doubted his sincerity, wondering if he was mocking the process. But then he said something in all seriousness that convinced me he had genuinely asked Jesus into his life for the first time. Later, men who visited him confirmed his commitment. God works in mysterious ways.

Every week, Glenn met with other local ministers in Houston. The area missionary, who coordinated with all the pastors, ran these meetings. One particular meeting caught Glenn's interest. The churches in Washington, Oregon, and Northern California planned a two-week revival and needed preachers. Glenn immediately signed up and was assigned to a church in a Spokane suburb called Opportunity. While in Spokane, Glenn and the local pastor became good friends. Together, they spent their days inviting community members who did not usually attend church. It was successful, and the church experienced new growth in Washington State, where only 20% of the population participated in any church.

Glenn had been successful in building a youth group in the Houston church. Each Sunday, the young people went to a restaurant to eat. Glenn decided to take his family to the same restaurant. It became a tradition for the young adult males to order the hottest peppers and see who could eat a whole one. The contest escalated with each round, as participants ordered progressively hotter peppers. Fewer people remained in the competition with each round. Finally, Glenn was the only one who could eat the hottest peppers with only one piece of bread without flinching. Glenn explained that growing up in Brownsville, Texas, his family lived next door to a Mexican compound with families who had recently immigrated from Mexico and grew hot peppers. From childhood until he left for college, the Mexican family provided the Parson family with hot peppers. Glenn, being the oldest, started eating them when he was 12. This 6-foot, blond, blue-eyed boy enjoyed eating the hottest peppers he could find.

The Church in Houston continued to grow. Before long, membership in the new congregation swelled to about 400. It became clear that assistance was needed to run the church. Around the same time, a ministerial student and his wife from Howard Payne University came looking for a church job. Being friends of Dr. Todd, the preaching professor at Howard Payne, Robert Schmeltekolp and his wife went to him for assistance. They were short of funds to finish college and needed to work for a while to save money. Dr. Todd, always looking out for the Parson family's interests, knew of the growth at Oldham Memorial Church in Houston and had the couple contact Glenn.

Glenn saw that Robert and Betty could be crucial in the church. The "Hot Pepper" teenagers needed guidance and opportunities to minister. There was no music program, choir, or special music on Sundays. Glenn was tone-deaf but led the congregational singing. He could start the group singing and then mouth the words. There was an excellent pianist who played for congregational singing and special pieces for the Offertory. However, she needed to take time off to have a baby. Robert was a hit in the community with his singing, and Betty played the piano. The Schmeltekopfs quickly became a beloved part of the ministry in Houston.

There had been a revival where Glenn was the preacher and Robert was the music director, so Glenn knew Robert could start a music program in the church.

Robert and Betty, being younger than Glenn and me, would be particularly good with the youth and growing the high school ministry.

It had been about a year since the Schmeltekopfs came to minister at Oldham Memorial Baptist Church. All programs were running smoothly, and every ministry seemed healthy and growing.

As reported in Acts 2:47: "And the Lord added to their number daily those who were being saved."

Building Up or Branching Out? A Pastor's Crossroads

The Church in Spokane, where Glenn held a revival, called. The pastor had resigned due to his wife's illness. They were relocating to Florida to be closer to her mother. The minister had secured a nearby church. The question posed to Glenn was, "Would Glenn accept the pastorate of Pines Baptist Church in Spokane, Washington?" Glenn's answer was, "Yes."

When it came time to announce our family's move, I found it difficult to conceal my disappointment. I had cherished our time with Robert and Betty Schmeltekopf, who now had a baby slightly younger than our Harley. The prospect of moving such a great distance was challenging for me.

The church held a significant farewell banquet, featuring a special guest speaker. Following the event, the speaker stayed overnight at the parsonage. After the children were asleep, the three of us engaged in conversation. I was astonished to learn that this speaker had been a minister in Dawson, Texas, during a difficult period in my life when my siblings and I were living with our grandparents after our mother's passing. He served on the board of Buckner Orphans Home and played a pivotal role in placing the three Richardson children in the orphanage, significantly altering our lives. The evening was filled with unexpected connections and profound reflections. God's ways are indeed mysterious. We were fortunate that He allowed us to gain insight into His work.

Glenn arranged our move with the deacons in Spokane, and they provided reimbursement. Glenn's aunt, from his father's side in Brownsville, had a son

who wanted to go to the Northwest to pick fruit for the summer. He assisted Glenn in driving us and our belongings to Spokane in August 1959.

101_Photo: Harley, Corinne, Bobbi, Glenn (1959)

Harley, Corinne, and I slept most of the journey while Glenn and his cousin took turns driving and resting. We arrived in Spokane at a new parsonage, recently constructed by one of the church members' companies. Fresh milk was on the steps from the local dairy company, whose owner was a deacon in the church.

102_Photo: Pines Baptist Church (2023)

The church's leadership consisted of individuals in business in and around Spokane, including company owners, CEOs, and presidents. The church was located in Opportunity, Washington, a suburb of Spokane. It was situated on one end of five acres, with the parsonage at the other end and open space in between.

When we arrived, Pines Baptist Church in Spokane had about 200 members. Most attendees came from various parts of Spokane, not the neighborhood surrounding the parsonage and church. One of Glenn's goals for the church was to expand attendance beyond the residents living on the hill by the parsonage. Many homes were within walking distance of Pines Baptist Church, but none of the residents attended. We initiated an active visitation program, and in less than two years, the membership grew to 400.

Glenn wanted the church to establish mission churches in the Spokane Valley. However, the deacons did not agree. They preferred to enhance the existing church's prominence and construct a larger building on the land between the church and the parsonage. Glenn attempted to persuade the church deacons to support the establishment of mission churches. Still, it became evident that he would need to relocate to another area to start new churches, as no agreement could be reached.

We developed close friendships with several members during our two years at Opportunity. One member offered to have their older child babysit for a small fee. Their daughter had graduated from high school but did not wish to attend college, so instead of staying at home, she stayed at our house and played with our children.

This situation provided me with an opportunity to substitute teach. I went to the District Office to interview for a position. Coming from Texas, I dressed formally for the interview, wearing a hat, a suit, high-heeled shoes, and carrying a purse. Upon seeing me, the entire office staff erupted in laughter. I joined in, acting like a model showing off my outfit. We all shared a good laugh. I met with the interviewer and was hired as a substitute teacher.

The substitute teaching process worked as follows: The night before the school day, I would receive a call stating which position I would have the next day. I could accept or decline the assignment. Some days, I accepted, and other days, I refused. I did not want to be away from my children for too many consecutive days, so I never accepted a long-term position.

I had heard that younger students generally accepted substitute teachers without issue, but junior high students were inclined to play tricks and ignore instructions. The tricks included tacks in my chair, students humming when I wrote on the board, stopping immediately when I turned around, and frequent restroom requests. There were other typical pranks as well. However, I developed solutions for these situations. For the "tack in chair" issue, I asked a student from the back row to be my ambassador and check my seat at the start of each class. For the humming, I asked them to sing the most popular song of the day at the beginning of each class. I made copies of songs for a class of 30 and had them available when substituting in junior high. We would vote to see which song the class considered the number one hit, and then check if it matched the Hit Parade's selection.

I did not substitute teach frequently, but it was always enjoyable when I did. The principals requested me by name, so I felt welcomed, and student behavior was generally not a problem.

I was happy in Spokane and its outlying City, Opportunity. I had two children, Corinne and Harley, a new parsonage, and a thriving church. I was content, with a reliable babysitter enabling me to engage in church visits and substitute teaching. However, a significant disagreement arose between my husband, Glenn Parson, the pastor of the Spokane Valley church, and the church elders. Glenn envisioned starting new churches in the Spokane Valley, while the elders favored expanding the existing church into a large congregation, reminiscent of those they had known in Texas.

This impasse led Glenn to resign. Seeking divine guidance, he consulted the Area Missionary, asking to be shown where new churches were needed. Glenn felt drawn to Ellensburg, Washington, a college town lacking a church to serve its student population. The Area Missionary connected Glenn with a Baptist minister in Yakima who agreed to sponsor a new church in Ellensburg. Additionally, the Home Mission Board of the Southern Baptist Convention pledged support for a pastor in Ellensburg until the church could become self-sustaining.

Glenn's search for a church planting opportunity involved consulting with area missionaries and prayerfully considering various locations. Ellensburg, geographically central to the state, particularly resonated with him. During a drive to Ellensburg, Glenn and I prayed together about the situation. We learned that Baptist families across Washington were sending their children to Central Washington University for higher education. While some students were later sent to Baptist colleges in Texas, they often remained there, establishing families and careers. This resulted in Baptist students at the university in Ellensburg frequently marrying non-Baptists, causing disappointment among their families. These families hoped that a Baptist church in Ellensburg might encourage their children to maintain their faith during college, marry within the Baptist community, and raise their families in the same tradition.

Ellensburg became a focal point of prayer for Baptist churches throughout the state. It seemed clear that the Holy Spirit was leading Glenn to Ellensburg to fulfill this need.

Ellensburg Washington

I was surprised to learn I was pregnant just as Glenn and the Spokane Valley church were parting ways. Glenn wanted the Pines Baptist Church in Opportunity, Washington, to start missions in the Spokane Valley, while the elders wanted to build a large church in Opportunity. This caused a separation between Church officials and the minister.

Feeling God was directing our lives, we set up housekeeping in Ellensburg in a small two-bedroom house, where Glenn's parents paid the rent. We held services in our living room on Wednesday evenings for the college kids from Baptist homes in and around Washington. Baptist families living in the Northwest had petitioned the area missionary to find a minister to start a church next to the closest University in Ellensburg, Washington. They did not want to send their students back to Texas to Baptist colleges. They wanted a Baptist ministry in connection with Central Washington University in Ellensburg. Glenn felt God calling him to this ministry.

125

When a Home Became a Church

It was time for Glenn and me to establish a church in Ellensburg. We prayed, "Oh Lord, how will this be done?" God knew we had two children and were expecting a third. Glenn would have to earn a living if I stayed home to care for the children. He wanted to spend his time building a church, so when the new baby was born, we decided he would care for it, and I would get a job. Our day-to-day living needs were numerous. We had no stove or refrigerator. We had no friends except three college students from Baptist families, who went home on the weekend. Most of all, we had no church members. Glenn tried to be a public school teacher but didn't want a secular job. I enjoyed my work, so I was willing to take a job outside the home.

Here's how it worked out. With our kids, Corinne and Harley-Kevin, Glenn and I moved from Spokane, where Glenn had been pastoring a church in Opportunity, Washington. Glenn was passionate about starting churches in places that needed them, and Ellensburg, with its university, seemed like the perfect spot for a new Baptist church to help keep students connected to their faith while they were away from home.

We didn't know anyone in Ellensburg who desired a church. The families of a few students, excited about Glenn becoming the local parson, did not live in Ellensburg but wanted to send their students there. Since those students typically went home on weekends, Glenn started meeting with them in our living room on Wednesday evenings for prayer services. For the first few Sundays, when Glenn didn't have anyone to preach to, we went to a church in Yakima, the sponsoring church for the work in Ellensburg.

The First Baptist Church in Yakima was our nearest neighbor and sponsored our efforts to start the church in Ellensburg. Our families and the family of Yakima's pastor grew quite close. His kids were a bit older than ours, so his daughter's outgrown clothes ended up with Corinne and his son's with Harley-Kevin. When it became apparent that I was expecting again, the Yakima church threw me a lovely baby shower. There was no older baby in that family from which we could expect "hand-me-downs" for our new offspring.

Growing the Church in Ellensburg

As we embarked on this church-planting adventure in Ellensburg, things were tight. The Home Mission Board of the Southern Baptist Convention recognized Glenn's dedication to establishing new churches and provided a monthly stipend. On top of that, my dear foster parents, the Batesons, continued to be a lifeline. They generously helped with our finances, covering the doctor's bills for Corinne and Harley, and even promising to do the same for our new baby. It was a huge relief knowing we had that support.

Glenn's parents were also incredibly supportive. They paid the rent on our modest two-bedroom house, which was a tremendous help. Glenn, ever resourceful, got permission from the landlord to convert the basement into two extra bedrooms. His carpentry skills, honed while building the church in Houston, came in handy as he transformed the space. This gave us more room and allowed us to have a separate laundry area.

Moving day itself was quite an adventure! We let Corinne, eager to make new friends, go next door to play, while Harley was supposed to stay in the yard. But suddenly, our two-year-old vanished! We were frantic, dropping everything to search for him. We finally found him across the street at the police station. The officers were giving him candy and chatting away, though Harley wasn't a conversationalist at that age. It was a funny, if not slightly terrifying, moment. Years later, I was amazed to see some of those policemen join our Ellensburg congregation. It felt like a full-circle moment.

Starting a new church from scratch required a lot of creative thinking. We knew some resources were available, but any borrowed money had to be repaid, and with another baby on the way, we needed to be smart about our finances. It felt prudent that Glenn would be the primary breadwinner for now. He tried selling cars for a while, which covered the cost of babysitters for Corinne and Harley. I also took on a substitute teaching job from September to Thanksgiving. Thankfully, Ellensburg's school district didn't have the same restrictions as Spokane, and I could teach while pregnant. In 1960, my substitute position turned into a long-term role, a blessing. The baby was due around Thanksgiving, so the timing worked out. Glenn had previously tried student teaching but didn't enjoy it, so car sales and leading revivals became his primary income sources.

So Much for Hypnosis!
My Third Child: Joni (born December 3, 1960)

I had meticulously planned for Joni's birth to be a serene and empowering experience using hypnosis. My doctor had previously used this technique with me and discovered I was particularly receptive to it. However, as my due date neared, Glenn, my husband, was leading a revival in another city.

In his absence, one of the three original college students who had been part

of our church's early days graciously offered to stay with me that weekend. When my water broke unexpectedly, she swiftly drove me to the hospital, ensuring that a neighbor was available to care for my other children, Corinne and Harley, until her return.

103_Photo: Bobbi, Joni (1961)

The labor progressed with such astonishing speed that the doctor didn't have the opportunity to induce hypnosis. The hospital staff had a challenging time getting me into the delivery room before the baby's head began to emerge. In that moment, I gratefully welcomed the administration of a spinal block for pain relief.

Photo: Bobbi, Special Ed Teacher (1962)

After the baby was born, we decided that I would get a full-time teaching job, and Glenn would take on primary childcare duties. Breastfeeding the baby was a practical choice, as it was less expensive than bottles and formula.

When I eventually started working as a special education teacher, I made it clear from the beginning that I would need my lunchtime to nurse the baby.

There wasn't a formal teacher training program for special education at the time. Hence, the university contracted with the public school system to provide a university professor as a resource for us teachers. This arrangement was to continue until the college could develop a proper Special Education Certificate program, which was a unique and fortunate situation for me.

We Bought a House—and Built a Church

We began holding Sunday services in a small upstairs room—just enough space for a dozen members and our children. But it quickly became clear that this setup wouldn't allow our congregation to grow. Without more space, we couldn't welcome new members or raise the funds needed to construct a proper church building. What we truly needed was a larger home on a sizable lot—something that could serve as both a temporary worship space and a foundation for the church we hoped to build.

To find it, our family would pile into the car and drive around Ellensburg, scouting possible locations. During the week, while I was teaching, Glenn devoted his time to the search, determined to find a place that could become the heart of our new church community.

One day after school, Glenn surprised me. He took me to a familiar hillside overlooking the town—a place we had often visited to pray. Time and again, we had stood there together, lifting up heartfelt prayers for the salvation of the people of Ellensburg.

But this visit was different. As we pulled up in front of a three-acre lot with a large, stately house, Glenn didn't stop to pray. Instead, he turned to me and said quietly, "This property is for sale. I believe, deep in my heart, that God is calling us to plant the church here." In my heart, I had always imagined it as the perfect spot for a church.

We stood together on that ground and prayed, asking for guidance and a way to make it possible. The Sunday offerings weren't nearly enough to cover the cost, but Glenn felt confident he could borrow from the bank. We called a business meeting and shared the vision with our small congregation. To our joy, they voted unanimously to move forward with the purchase.

To raise the down payment, we sold church bonds to members of Baptist churches in Texas. My dear foster parents, the Batesons, generously purchased the largest portion—making the dream a reality.

The house itself was like a gift from above. It had six bedrooms and six bathrooms. The large living room became our sanctuary for Sunday services. The dining room, den, and upstairs bedrooms were transformed into Sunday School rooms. We even rented out some of those rooms to male students, agreeing that they would keep them clean and ready for Sunday School in exchange for reduced rent. There was even an old "ice room" with thick walls, a relic from another time. We put a heater in there, and it became another Sunday

School classroom. The one-bedroom on the first floor was the only room we didn't use on Sundays. The spacious kitchen became our nursery, and we set up a changing table in the adjoining bathroom.

Everything was falling into place except for one thing: We didn't have a piano for the church services. Glenn temporarily bought a record player until someone mentioned an upright piano for sale. Every penny we had was tied up in the property, so Glenn and I bought the piano, paying for it monthly.

The church pianist had a job, so she couldn't give lessons. With all our money committed, I ended up teaching the children piano myself, even though I wasn't a pianist.

The church, the parsonage, and the student housing were all under one roof, and life was becoming incredibly hectic. But we held onto the verse from 1 Peter 5:7, "Casting all your cares upon Him, for He cares for you," and we trusted that God would guide us through it all.

Relocating the church to our recently purchased six-bedroom house truly transformed our lives, the Parson family's lives, and breathed a remarkable energy into our growing congregation. I remember it so vividly. We found ourselves in this prime spot in Ellensburg.

Imagine, just a stone's throw away, literally one street over, was the bustling entrance to Central Washington University. And right across from us, on the other side, lay the park and stadium, the heart of the renowned Ellensburg Rodeo. It was, and still is, quite the event, held every Labor Day. That park was also alive all summer with activities, especially for the kids, including a popular swimming program. All of this meant a steady stream of people passing by, and some of them, thankfully, felt drawn to join our church family.

Our initial arrangement, holding Sunday School and services in our house, was becoming increasingly impractical. We desperately needed a dedicated church space. Separating our living quarters from the church was essential, and Glenn, the visionary, had a plan. He decided we would build the first unit of the church right next door to our house. I watched as he meticulously sketched the plans, ordered all the necessary equipment, and then got to work, physically building. It was quite something to witness. We were using the new space, even in its unfinished state.

I remember the construction phase so clearly. The roof of the first unit was going up, and each night, we'd cover the exposed part with a large tarp. Every Saturday night, after the children were tucked into bed, we'd carefully place the songbooks on the chairs, ready for Sunday's service. Then, one Saturday, late into the night, we were jolted awake by the sound of heavy rain. A windstorm had blown in, bringing a downpour. Glenn immediately sprang out of bed, and I followed close behind. Thankfully, the rain had stopped, and the tarp was still mostly in place. But, oh my, the songbooks and chairs were soaked! We frantically started wiping everything down, every single book and seat. When we were finally done, exhausted but relieved, we sat down and sighed. We laughed a little, saying, "Will we ever forget this fretful wiping frenzy?"

Thinking back, it strikes me that this is the first time I've recalled that particular night in such detail. At the time, we were so busy juggling so many things that we rarely had a moment to pause and reflect. There just wasn't time for reminiscing. It's surprising how those memories can fade. Glenn and I had a ritual of praying together before each service. After that frantic wiping session, we needed to pray. And after that, we went to bed and slept soundly. We were so grateful to have dry songbooks ready for our Lord's Day service on Sunday morning.

Mother, Teacher, Scholar: All in a Day's Work
What Polly Taught Me

As a special education teacher, I was incredibly fortunate to work alongside a dedicated university professor, Dr. Ted Theodore Naumanan from Germany. He became a mentor, introducing me to various innovative teaching tools designed to meet my educable students' diverse needs. I eagerly absorbed everything he shared, like a sponge soaking up knowledge. I was particularly drawn to programmed learning, using machines for instruction, Montessori Education, teaching by objectives, and individualized learning plans. Dr. Naumanan generously loaned me books, articles, and films, expanding my understanding and sparking new ideas. I always focused on finding the best way for each of my eight students to learn and thrive.

I remember one school day so clearly. We were gathered in a circle for a group meeting, and I was about to introduce a new technique. But before I could begin, one of my students spoke up. He said something like, "Wait, teacher. Polly has a problem. She's not happy." He went over to Polly, put his arm around her, and listened as she shared what was troubling her. We all talked about ways to solve the problem, and only then, when Polly felt heard and supported, could we move forward with the lesson. Mark Schlenbaker even checked in with Polly afterward to ensure she was truly okay. That moment was a powerful reminder to me. From then on, I became much more conscious of ensuring all eight students were comfortable and ready before proceeding with any instruction. Some days, we would have a sharing session, which is the day's lesson. It was all about meeting them where they were.

Mastering More Than Education

How I earned my Washington credentials, raised a family, and stepped into university teaching

I needed to obtain a Washington Teaching Credential to continue teaching in Washington, as my Texas Certification wasn't accepted out of the State of Texas. Since I was going to the University for a Washington Credential it was easy to take other classes to get a Master's Degree in Special Education. This led me to

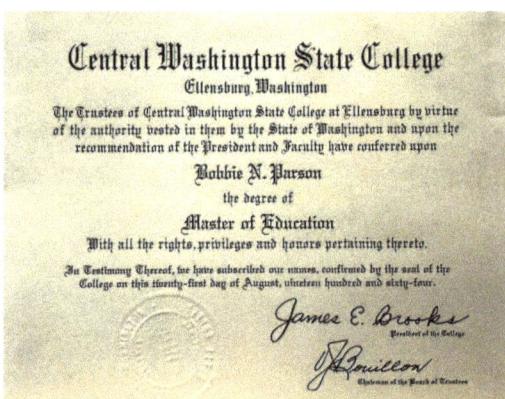

pursue a Master's Degree in Special Education, which fulfilled the credential requirement and opened doors to a teaching position as an Assistant Professor at the University.

104_Photo: Master's Degree (1964)

I received my Master of Education from Washington State College in Ellensburg, Washington, on August 21, 1964.

A BB, a Hug, and a Man Ashamed

The first unit of the church was complete, and the auditorium was nearly finished. Glenn received a full salary, and the University paid me well, too. The first member of the church, aside from the Parson family, was a single man who lived in the house church as a tenant. We used his room for a Sunday School class until the church building beside the house was ready. He was an auto mechanic, a Sunday School teacher, and a great asset to our little church. Later, he married and moved away once the church had grown enough.

One evening, when Glenn was away at a revival, and the three kids were asleep, I was ironing near an open window. Suddenly, a bullet shot through the glass, passed right over the ironing board, and landed on the floor. I screamed and ran into a large closet we used as part of the nursery on Sundays. Our single tenant, Virgil, still lived there and barely heard my scream. Knowing Glenn was gone, he rushed to see what had happened. He found me hiding in the closet, terrified. We embraced, simply out of fear and relief. When we came to our senses, he left immediately. The next day, he arranged to move out. When Glenn returned from the revival, Virgil apologized profusely. "I have asked God's forgiveness, your wife's forgiveness, and I am so ashamed," he said. Honestly, I didn't think it was all that serious. The hug was just what I needed then, and I was mostly just grateful I hadn't been hurt. Later, we found out the bullet was just a BB pellet, shot by a boy trying to get Corinne's attention.

Special Ed Teacher to University Assistant Professor

Meanwhile, my teaching career was taking a new turn. My job teaching mentally challenged students in the Ellensburg Public Schools ended when I was offered a position as an Assistant Professor at Central Washington University. We hired a housekeeper to help care for the children as I spent more and more time advancing my career.

Around this time, a couple with Master's Degrees in Education moved to Ellensburg. The husband became Corinne's sixth-grade teacher in a university demonstration class, and Harley entered first grade in the same program.

I was recruited to teach an experimental Montessori class for five-year-olds and older Special Ed students who were considered "educable." Joni was one of my students.
105_Photo: Joni (1964)

I taught using the Montessori method in the mornings and Special Ed students in the afternoons. At school, Joni didn't call me "Mother"; she called me "Teacher."

With the University's Support: My Path Into Montessori

The University supported me wholeheartedly, even sponsoring my summer studies at the renowned St. Nicholas Montessori Training School in London. There, I met a diverse group of students, including several from East India, and formed close friendships with two international Montessori instructors. One of the most meaningful connections I made was with an exceptional Montessori teacher from Belmont, California. Through her, I was introduced to Sister Christina Marie, the director of the Montessori School at Belmont College. This introduction would prove significant, as I later share in the story of how Sister Christina Marie offered me a pivotal professional opportunity.

When the Cow Didn't Know the Difference

With all the children out of the house during the mornings, our housekeeper's workload became lighter. Her husband worked as a livestock inseminator, and one memorable day, our whole family took a holiday to watch him at work. We observed as he inseminated a cow—a fascinating experience for the kids, Glenn, and me alike. What struck us most was the cow's complete lack of awareness about whether the process was artificial or natural. It was an unforgettable and oddly amusing moment we all talked about for years.

Montessori Mastery: Teaching the Teachers

Meanwhile, Glenn's brother Mickey and his wife Paula had settled in Yakima. Mickey traveled back and forth to Ellensburg to finish his final semester at the University, pursuing a Master's in German. Paula had already graduated and taken a job elsewhere. As a psychology major, Mickey needed a practicum supervisor, and I filled that role. He conducted a study on my Montessori students to compare their outcomes with students taught by traditional methods. His results confirmed that Montessori methods were more effective academically, but he also noted that my students, including Joni, showed fewer spontaneous behaviors, "like hothouse plants," he said.

As my direct work with children wound down, I shifted to teaching university students, using Mickey's films of my Montessori classes. I even had the students role-play as pupils, using the Montessori materials themselves, a much more satisfying approach than passive observation.

Glenn was often away, preaching revivals and speaking at church conferences, while I traveled to present Montessori workshops. Eventually, the question arose: Could I, as a professor and Montessori-certified teacher, certify others? The American Montessori Society told me no unless I earned their credentials. They agreed to send evaluators to watch me teach both children and teachers. After their observation, I was awarded certificates to teach students and to train teachers, certificates I still hold and treasure.

Country Music in Heaven?

After Mickey graduated, I had Corinne look after Harley and Joni during the day. I hired responsible university students to babysit if Glenn and I were away in the evening.

One winter evening, I set out alone for Wenatchee, Washington, to speak at a meeting. It was clear when I left, but as the sun set, I knew the roads would soon ice over. Approaching a curve, I slowed to a crawl. A car was coming toward me. I faced a choice: If I moved to the side, I'd hit ice. If I stayed in the center, we'd collide head-on. I chose the ice. My car flipped and landed upside down in a ditch. As it happened, I said aloud, "Lord, I'm coming Home." Strapped in by my seatbelt, I hung there for a moment, unsure if I was alive or dead. But then two things struck me: First, I wasn't hurting. Didn't dying hurt? Second, I heard country music playing. Was there country music in heaven? Before I could figure it out, a knock came at my window. A kind stranger helped me out. We drove to a roadside phone, called a towing service in Ellensburg, and notified the Highway Department about my car.

In Wenatchee, the driver dropped me at my meeting, and he went on to his appointment across town. I said nothing during my presentation about the accident. Afterward, as I lingered answering questions, a few women noticed I wasn't rushing off. I finally explained I was waiting for someone to pick me up because of the accident. We prayed together in gratitude for my safety. I only realized later: I didn't have a scratch, only a run in my hose. God had truly protected me.

Seven Years in Ellensburg: A Ministry Blossoms

By our seventh year in Ellensburg, the Parson family had become well known throughout the town. Our home, nestled near the University, sat right in the heart of the community. What had started as a church with no members had blossomed into a congregation of nearly 400 people. Among them were prominent city residents and many Baptists who had deliberately moved to Ellensburg to support the ministry near the University.

Most of these new members had been Summer Missionaries who were now starting families but still wanted to be involved in planting churches in areas where they were needed. Frank Johnson and his family were among the first to come, and their help was instrumental in establishing the church.

The community warmly rallied around us, offering their friendship and support. But not everything went smoothly. One day, someone stole our car and the children's wheel toys, which they had placed on top of the car to take to school for a special play day. Thankfully, a compassionate radio announcer, who knew Glenn from his daily morning broadcasts, urged the thief to return the car and the toys. Miraculously, they were promptly returned. Glenn's voice on the radio had made people feel as if they knew him personally, and it helped in ways we never anticipated.

The ministry flourished under Glenn's leadership and was guided by the Holy Spirit. A young couple soon joined our team, drawn by the church's remarkable growth. The husband's passion and energy made him an immediate asset, especially in reaching university students. Before long, many young people became active members of the church community.

Each Child, A Unique Journey, A Mother's Humbling Moments

Each member of our family found their niche in Ellensburg:
- Corinne, the horse lover, often walked her horse to the boarding stable, saddled up, and rode through town.
- Harley thrived in the city's parks and recreation activities.
- Joni, ever the social butterfly, had friends over to play almost every day.

During school days, Joni was also in my Montessori class, serving as a model student and demonstrating her mastery of the Montessori materials. She learned to use every piece of teaching apparatus with skill and confidence. However, she had one persistent habit, thumb-sucking. It was a visible "slap" against my teaching and parenting skills, especially when college students wrote observation reports about her. I tried everything in private to persuade Joni to stop, but nothing worked.

Harley was old enough to attend the park programs alone, but Joni was still too young. Wanting her to feel comfortable around water, I took her to the public pool to practice putting her face in the water before she started swimming lessons. One day, as she was practicing, she didn't lift her face out of the water. I quickly called for help, and someone lifted her out. Thankfully, she began breathing again almost immediately. From then on, my care for Joni became even more motherly, tender, and protective. It was a humbling reminder of how precious and fragile those early years were.

Aunt Em's Visit: A Gift of Love and Memory

One summer, while we were busy growing the church in Ellensburg, Aunt Em asked if she could visit. We were delighted to extend the invitation.

When she arrived, she had the chance to meet the grown-up Corinne and see that Harley-Kevin was no longer a baby. Even little Joni, now four years old, was full of life and energy. It was like reconnecting a piece of the past with our present.

We made special memories together. We showed Aunt Em and the children the breathtaking view of the Grand Canyon, and near Ellensburg, the remarkable sight where you could see five majestic mountains all at once. Aunt Em could attend worship with us at our church on Sunday, which made the visit even more meaningful. It was a joyous time for us all.

Dear Aunt Em was doing well. She was retired and living with her brother, the two of them looking after one another. Before she left, she used some of her own saved money to buy groceries and cook a fabulous meal for our family. What a treasure she was, a true jewel of a friend and relative. Aunt Em would never be forgotten.

Determined to Achieve Full Professorship

To achieve full professorship at the University, I needed to meet three requirements: lecture at the University for three consecutive years, publish a book, and maintain active membership in a professional organization by paying annual dues. It was a demanding path, but one I was determined to complete.

Called to Follow, Strong Enough to Yield

Everything was going smoothly in Ellensburg. The church was thriving, solid leadership was in place in every department, the building provided plenty of space, and our visitation program brought in new members weekly. Glenn's schedule was hectic, and mine was just as full. I often spent two or three days away from home giving lectures. Eventually, I found ways to travel less, but I was balancing a lot during that season.

Then, in 1968, when I least expected it, Glenn said, "We're leaving. I want to hear what they teach at the California Seminary."

I didn't need to protest. We had made wonderful friends and built a strong, vibrant church. Even though part of me still hoped to meet the final requirements to become a full professor at the University, I must admit that we had accomplished what we set out to do in Ellensburg. The goal we came to achieve was complete.

I accepted that it was time for a new chapter. I would work to support our family while Glenn pursued his studies. The seminary may need me in some capacity, but my applications were not accepted, nor did I pursue a position in the public school system. It was clear that it was time to call in some divine intervention.

We moved to California, and Glenn enrolled at the Golden Gate Baptist Theological Seminary in Mill Valley, California, a graduate theological school of the Southern Baptist Convention, on Seminary Drive. Known as one of the most multicultural seminaries in the world, Glenn wanted to learn firsthand what Baptists were being taught to preach, particularly regarding social issues that weighed heavily on his heart. Glenn was especially passionate about integrating races within local congregations, a vision he carried with conviction and hope.

Montessori in the Public Schools—My Renewed Mission

I interviewed for a position in the Larkspur School District, 6 miles from Glen's seminary in Mill Valley. Since the regular district interviewer was on vacation, a district principal conducted my interview instead. The meeting went well. During the conversation, he asked if my husband was with me, so I brought Glenn into the room. Then, somewhat unexpectedly, the principal shared a concern: my file lacked strong recommendations that matched the experience I had described during the interview.

Wanting to help, he invited Glenn and me, along with his wife, to dinner at the Officers' Dining Club on Treasure Island. Over the meal, we discovered we had a special connection; he and his wife were graduates of Howard Payne College in Brownwood, Texas, the very same college where Glenn and I had studied. We had much in common, and he wanted to support me. After dinner, we returned to his office, where he tore up my incomplete file.

When I returned to Ellensburg and Central Washington University, I found that those who had previously failed to provide recommendations had now completed them. I also took the opportunity to remove an outdated evaluation from my file, which read, "I hope she becomes a good teacher," written long before I became a university professor. It was time to ensure my file reflected the teacher and professional I had become.

With an updated, fully-supported file, I reapplied. The new materials were sent to the principal in Larkspur, and new interviews soon followed. One of those opportunities came from the Franklin McKinley School District in San Jose. They interviewed me with great interest: the district wanted to be the first public school system to introduce Montessori into its classrooms, and they were looking for someone to "spearhead" the effort. That opportunity kept me firmly rooted in my specialty, working as a Montessori education specialist, bringing the method into a broader public school setting.

Our First Home—Dedicated to the Lord

Glenn attended seminary classes in Mill Valley during the week while I continued teaching Montessori in San Jose. At the time, we lived in Cupertino, and the children attended school there. Glenn had the hardest commute, an hour each way. He often caught rides with others traveling in that direction, and on some days, he stayed overnight near the seminary ready for morning classes.

After nine months, Glenn completed his seminary training in 1968 and accepted a call to pastor a Southern Baptist church in San Mateo. I directed the Montessori program in the Franklin McKinley School District during the school year. In the summer, I returned to Ellensburg for a summer teaching job, taking our three children with me. Glenn stayed behind to get acquainted with the new church community.

With both our salaries combined, we finally had enough to buy our first home, priced at $20,000. Homeownership had been a long-standing goal for us. To make it possible, the church provided a housing allowance as part of Glenn's salary, and we rented out the church parsonage to help offset the cost. Our new home in San Mateo, located at 4004 Martin Drive in a neighborhood off Hillsdale Boulevard called The Village, was one of the nicest on the block.

We had a corner lot with a large backyard and a charming playhouse for the children.

106_Photo: Home in San Mateo, California

It was our first real home; until then, we had always lived in parsonages. Grateful for this blessing, we dedicated the house to the Lord's service. I still remember us standing together in our living room, singing, "Bless This House, O Lord, We Pray," as we committed our new home and family to His care. Here is a link to the song sung by Perry Como (https://tinyurl.com/yz44zzd9).

New Chapter: Living in California

Always thinking about planting new churches, Glenn successfully led the church to purchase property across from San Mateo College; however, by 1969, construction on a new building had not yet begun.

Glenn requested that I stay with him in San Mateo for the summer of 1969, rather than returning to Ellensburg to teach.

Tears on Earth, Held by Community, Joy in Heaven

During the Christmas holidays in 1968, to see Mickey and Paula in Walla Walla, where Mickey was serving as pastor, Glenn told me that he felt the knot growing under his arm was cancerous. When we returned from the trip, Glenn resigned from the Southern Baptist church in San Mateo and had the church bring in a supply pastor to take his place. We became members of Pilgrim Baptist Church in San Mateo and joined their black congregation.

The children found places in the Sunday School program, and I began teaching fourth-grade mixed boys and girls classes. Glenn helped the pastor lead the service on Sunday. Even though Glenn had surgery to remove the knot under his arm, he kept attending Pilgrim Baptist church until he began to run a very high fever and was hospitalized. The doctor pulled me aside and said, "I am going on vacation for two weeks. Another doctor will take my place. I don't expect Glenn to be alive when I return. Perhaps you'd better be prepared for his passing."

Of course, this broke my heart. In February of 1969, I took my kids to see Glenn in the hospital. He asked his full-time nurse to take them to the reception room. That is when he told me not to bring the children to see him anymore, and not to come. He said, "You are among the living. I'm among the dying." I felt he was divorcing me. I could not keep from crying day and night.

One evening after work, the grief over missing Glenn became overwhelming. Not seeing him, not being by his side, was almost more than I could bear. I drove to the parking lot of Redwood City Hospital, sat alone in my car, and wept. As I cried, I noticed a familiar figure approaching, one of the men from the church we had once pastored. He was a United Airlines pilot. Without hesitation, he got into the car and sat beside me. Together, we prayed. Afterward, he said he would speak with Glenn about letting me visit.

He invited me to his home, where his wife welcomed me and prayed earnestly for our family. As he left to talk to Glenn, he said, "I left my wife praying for you and your children. She will comfort you while I speak with him."

By God's grace, the effort bore fruit. Glenn agreed to see me.

When I arrived at the hospital, I found many from our former church already there. They had set up a schedule to ensure someone was always with Glenn. Their presence, their love, reminded me of God's promise: "So do not fear, for I am with you; do not be dismayed, for I am your God. I will strengthen you and help you; I will uphold you with my righteous right hand.", Isaiah 41:10

I rejoiced to know Glenn was surrounded by people who loved him, had sat under his teaching for two years at the Southern Baptist church in San Mateo, and now offered their comfort, prayers, and time. Members of Pilgrim Baptist Church also visited faithfully, ensuring an elder served him Communion each week. Glenn was not alone.

Meanwhile, I continued working at the County Office of Education, and the children settled in school and made friends in the neighborhood. But how could I tell them what lay ahead? I waited until early April, when Joni and Harley were away on playdates with two different families, leaving Corinne and me alone at home.

I asked Corinne to come into my room. We sat together on the bed, read from the Bible, and prepared to nap. Silently, I prayed, "Dear Lord, please help me accept that Glenn will be with You soon, not with us. Give me the strength to know how to tell our children." Finally, I told Corinne, fourteen years old and so brave, that her daddy was not expected to live. I also shared that a minister from another denomination had offered to visit and pray with us. She quietly responded, "It's okay for him to come, Mom, but it's unnecessary."

It's hard to put into words what I felt on the day the hospital called and said, "We are sorry to tell you your husband has passed." No tears were left, only a deep, soul-aching sorrow that filled every part of my body.

A Widow's Prayer, A Mother's Strength

What about our ministry? What about my life's calling? At sixteen years old, I had given my life to the service of the Lord. And even amid such profound loss, that commitment had not wavered.

How was I supposed to raise three children on my own after Glenn passed away, when I had never been solely responsible for them or even felt capable of it? I was overwhelmed. Where could I look for solace? God was still the God of Comfort, who knew me and how to guide me through this difficult time. I put my whole heart into asking, "Help me, Dear God, in my time of need."

Although I was a new member of the Pilgrim Baptist Church, I knew comfort from these members could help me. But would they? Pilgrim Baptist Church, mainly an all-Black membership, rallied around me and the children and brought comfort. In addition, members from several families of the church Glenn had pastored came to my rescue, providing hospitality in thoughtful and efficient ways. Someone purchased my clothes for the funeral; another listened when grief overtook me. Most crucial was the church treasurer, because Glenn's resignation had never been formally recorded or voted on, Southern Baptist benefits continued after his passing. As a result, my monthly benefits continued and still do.

Burial, Blessings, and a New Beginning

Glenn's father and mother arranged to have Glenn's body buried in Combs, TX. Glenn's siblings, Barbara Ridley and her family, Mickey and Paula Parson, Sue and Paul Prator, each offered assistance to me as Glenn's family. As a single parent, the Bateson family knew I needed support and help. They offered money and told me their home was my home as needed. Somehow, Mr. Bateson knew I needed a car, so he and Leta sent me money to buy one. The kids and I bought a Volkswagen.

Corinne, Harley, Joni, and I arranged to go to Texas for Glenn's burial. A pastor of Antioch Church, Charles Bradshaw, who cheered with Glenn and me in college at Howard Payne University in Brownwood, TX, thought it prudent for him to escort the family to Texas for the burial. This was a great comfort and so thoughtful.

When we returned from Brownsville, the children and I stopped at the Batesons. We stayed for several days, maybe longer, until Leta Bateson, with much care, said, "Honey, don't you think you had better go home and get on with life? " This woke me up to my responsibilities, so Corinne, Harley, Joni, and I flew to California and resumed our lives on Martin Drive in San Mateo.

Life as a Single Parent

Work, Worship, and the Will to Continue

The job at the County Office of Education provided me with a way forward, a path out of mourning and back into the rhythms of everyday life. Work and Pilgrim Baptist Church became my anchors. Each day, I worked, the children attended school, and in the evenings, I ensured they had dinner and adult supervision while I continued my studies. I had enrolled at San Francisco State to earn a California teaching credential, since my Washington State certification wasn't recognized in California, just as Washington had once refused to recognize my Texas credentials.

Sundays remained sacred. We all went to Pilgrim Baptist Church, where the congregation's support continued to lift us.

This pattern of working, studying, caring for the children, and worshiping carried us steadily from April through June 1969.

Speaking for Him, Worrying for Them

Glenn had been scheduled to speak at the Sixth Army's Educational Conference in May. When I informed the conference planners that he would not be able to fulfill the commitment, they surprised me by asking if I would take his place. I saw no reason why I couldn't. After all, I had been a university professor and was currently serving as Director of Education at the San Mateo County Office of Education. I answered confidently, "Yes, I can do it."

The assignment with the Sixth Army was set to begin during my summer break from work, which was a blessing. However, because it was summer, it also meant I needed to find care for my three children while I traveled for the conference work. The assignment stretched over six months. Sometimes, I took the children with me; other times, Corinne, still so young, stepped up and acted as caregiver for Harley and Joni. Occasionally, I left them in the care of trusted friends or wherever I could find someone willing to help. It wasn't always easy, and I often worried, but somehow we managed.

I was relieved and grateful when the six months finally ended.

The Gift of Connection and a Deepening Love for Montessori

As mentioned earlier, while I was a student at the Montessori training school in London around 1960, a fellow student introduced me to Sister Christina Marie, the director of the Montessori School at Belmont College.

107_Photo: Sister Marie London (1971)

Fortunately, I had kept in touch with this student, and she was aware that I had moved to San Mateo, California—just a few miles from Belmont. When Sister Christina Marie needed someone to evaluate Belmont's graduates who were teaching the Montessori method in various towns across California, she thought of me, reached out, and offered me the position.

My responsibilities included traveling to each school, observing the teachers in action, and writing detailed reports for Sister Christina Marie.

In 1971, I joined Sister Marie and a group she organized to tour Montessori schools throughout Europe. It was fascinating to see the Montessori method applied in early education and the upper grades, particularly in Italy, where Dr. Maria Montessori's work had its deepest roots.

These experiences, both my summer in London and my time working alongside the Nuns at Belmont College, profoundly shaped my understanding and

143

application of Montessori principles. They expanded my vision of how Montessori education could grow beyond the early childhood years. They gave me a lasting appreciation for the global reach and adaptability of the Montessori approach.

Breadwinner, Mother Filled with Regret, Searching for a Father

During summer breaks from my regular job, I worked part-time with the State Department in Sacramento. Even though I wasn't at my usual workplace, juggling work duties and childcare was a daily challenge. I realized how much I was neglecting my children. To make it up to them, I took them camping, enrolled them in special programs like the YMCA, arranged music lessons, and tried to give them whatever money could buy.

At the same time, I was frantically searching for a husband, but in truth, I was searching for a father for my three children. I felt so inadequate as a parent.

Their father had been both mother and father while I focused on making a living. Now, without him, I was trying to fill both roles and feeling like I was failing. I had no clear model to follow. Having spent my childhood at Buckner Orphans Home from the ages of six to seventeen, I didn't have the experience of being parented myself. But even that, I knew, was a poor excuse. After all, my sister Angie had grown up under the same circumstances, and her three children proudly called her a "great mother." I had no excuses, only deep regret for my falling short.

My Children Needed a Father More Than I Needed Applause

I was at a crossroads in my life. I could see what it would take to move to the next level in my career, but I didn't have the energy or drive to pursue it. A couple approached me, offering to sponsor my candidacy for San Mateo Superintendent of Schools. They even asked permission to post an announcement on a highway bulletin board to promote my campaign. But in my heart, I felt torn. My lifelong commitment to a spiritual life, my responsibility to my children, and my desire to be a successful professional seemed to pull me in different directions. After much reflection, I concluded that I needed not an elected office but a husband, a partner, and a father figure for my children. Marriage became my priority.

A New Chapter Began Beside the Pool

Before school started that year, Joni, Kevin, and Corinne asked to take a trip to Yosemite, and I agreed. Once there, they each picked out bicycles to ride around the park, with a deadline to return for dinner. While they explored, I headed to the pool for my daily swim. As I finished a lap and reached the pool's edge, a man approached and knelt beside me. He asked if I would sit and talk with him. I agreed, got dressed, and we introduced ourselves. His name was Peter Dranius. He was born in Greece but now lives in South Africa and visits his uncle in San Francisco.

I excused myself when I saw my children returning from their bike ride. As I was leaving, Peter asked if I would meet him later. I agreed to meet him at the Lodge lounge after dinner. That night, Peter and I had our first date. He told me his uncle was George Christopher, the former mayor of San Francisco. Before the children and I left Yosemite, I gave Peter my phone number.

Back in the Bay Area, Peter and I continued to date, meeting halfway between San Mateo and San Francisco. We spent several evenings together for about a month. Eventually, Peter left for New York, preparing to return to South Africa.

One day, I received an unexpected call from Peter. He asked, "Would you come to New York?" I initially declined, explaining that I needed to stay with my children. Then Peter suggested, "Bring the kids with you." And so, Kevin, Joni, and I boarded a plane to New York. Peter met us when we arrived and took the children to all the places they wanted to see. After visiting the Statue of Liberty, Kevin said, "I'd like to see the Smithsonian." Without hesitation, Peter bought us tickets for the fast train to Washington, D.C., so that we could visit the Smithsonian.

He Offered a Life Abroad—I Needed One at Home

During the train ride, Peter surprised me by asking me to marry him. I hadn't seen it coming. Caught off guard, I asked, "What on earth would we do with the kids?" Peter quickly responded, "There are excellent schools in Switzerland. They could go to boarding schools."

I couldn't imagine anything more misaligned with my goals. Marrying Peter and moving to South Africa sounded adventurous, but sending my children away to boarding school? That was unimaginable. Peter must have sensed my hesitation. He said gently, "Don't give me an answer yet. Let's wait. I'll write to you every day, and then you can come to South Africa and see how you feel."

Time passed, and true to his word, I received letters or some form of correspondence from Peter daily. Eventually, he sent me an invitation and a plane ticket to Johannesburg for a month-long visit, including a return ticket. Once again, I arranged for the children to stay with relatives or friends while I traveled.

In London, I Met the Fruit of My Labor

Having booked a flight to London with a stopover, I decided to take the opportunity to visit the St. Nicholas Montessori Training Centre, where I had

previously received my education. There I met Phoebe Child, co-founder of Montessori Training.

108_Photo: Bobbi, Phoebe Child (1971)

While there, I encountered an American woman and asked her casually, "What brings you to study Montessori here?" Her answer caught me by surprise. "I attended a demonstration class taught by Mrs. Bobbi Parson in Ellensburg. Her teaching impressed me, so I knew I had to come here for training."

She had no idea she was speaking to Mrs. Bobbi Parson until I introduced myself. We both laughed and enjoyed a wonderful visit together.

The Journey Was Real, But the Answer Was No

Before embarking on the trip to South Africa, I had hired Doug DeBouchamp, a personal and professional growth consultant. Together, we developed a set of objectives and activities to meet my spiritual and career goals. However, traveling to South Africa was not on that list. I asked myself, What was I doing, going to South Africa?

Despite my doubts, I pressed on. I was prepared to return to California after London when Peter called. "You weren't on the plane," he said. "Where are you? I'm waiting for you in Johannesburg!" I assured him I would be on the next flight, and I was.

When I arrived, Peter and I set off on a whirlwind tour: we visited Swaziland, Kruger National Park, Durban, Cape Town, and Pretoria, the capital. We even attended a soccer match, sitting among the locals and eating oranges like everyone else. I was having a grand time, caught up in a dazzling adventure far from the life I had left behind.

Eight days into our whirlwind tour, Peter turned to me and said, "You aren't going to marry me, are you?" In that moment, I knew my vacation and the pretending were over. I had to be honest. "No," I admitted quietly, "I'm not going to marry you."

Peter took it with grace. "I would always like to be your friend," he said. "There's no reason we can't stay in touch, even if we marry someone else." I agreed.

Meeting Friends and Touring Kenya

Generously, Peter encouraged me to continue traveling in South Africa while he returned to his work in Estcourt.

I immediately thought of friends I had made from Kenya while at the Montessori Training School in London. On a whim, I bought a ticket to Mombasa, where one of the women I had studied with lived. Her relatives welcomed me and even took me to a Montessori supply store, where I arranged to have some teaching materials shipped back to my home.

After visiting for a time, I left Mombasa and traveled toward Nairobi. Along the way, I had an unusual encounter, a man carrying a boa constrictor around his neck. Feeling adventurous, I asked if I could try it. He placed the heavy, slimy snake around my neck. The sensation was far less thrilling than I imagined, and I quickly asked him to remove it. I was relieved to have it off!

I checked into an American hotel when I arrived in Nairobi on a Saturday night. On Sunday morning, I attended a local Baptist church. I had long been praying for a missionary couple I had heard about, even though we had never met, and to my amazement, I met them there that very morning. We visited for a while, and they invited me to join them on a missionary trip the following day. As I was preparing for the journey, there was a knock at my hotel room door. Standing there was the brother of another woman I had met during my Montessori training in London.

"Please," he said warmly, "don't stay in this hotel. Come be our guest at my home with my wife and children." I promised I would, just as soon as I returned from the missionary trip.

One Month, A Thousand Realities

I then visited friends from Montessori training in Mombasa and Nairobi, Kenya. I joined missionaries on a trip to a Masai tribe, witnessing the profound cultural differences. Before I left, I stayed with the family of a Montessori friend.

The missionary trip was to dispense medicine, check the Masai tribe members, and minister to their health needs.

109_Photo: Masai

The people with health problems lined up to see the medical missionary. I was there as a friendly visitor to interact with the women and children. I found the flies, odor, and filth were almost more than I could take. The women and many young girls had babies. The red cloth was wrapped around the mother and the naked baby with no diapers. When there was a mess, it was wrapped in the fabric and turned over, and another part became the baby's clothes.

I was most impressed by their hair. I didn't know what they used to put on their heads, but it looked like they used dung. Flies were everywhere around the mouths and eyes of both mother and baby. The women were curious and wanted to touch my long, straight hair. They smiled and showed me their babies, who smiled and cooed like American babies. Later, the Masi men came with jugs of cow's blood in drinking containers around their waists. Their herds stayed at a distance. The doctor checked the men to see if there were any new health needs among the tribal men.

The Missionaries spoke the tribe's language, and we had a devotional with scripture and prayer. This was my first and only tribal missionary experience.

Back at the hotel, the brother of my East African friend's brother came, and indeed, I went to stay the rest of the month with him and his family. I toured his large acres of peas and saw workers working in his fields. Years later, when I visited his sister, she told me the workers had boycotted him and killed him. They would have slain his family as well, but he had heard word of the uprising coming and sent them to Canada, thus sparing his family the fate he suffered.

Their Turn for Adventure

After being away for a month, my first task upon returning to California was to gather my children from the various places they had stayed. But it didn't take long for them to express their feelings. The three Parsons, Corinne, Kevin, and Joni, felt they'd missed a vacation. "We didn't go anywhere!" they protested, practically begging to go to Yosemite. Wanting to make it up to them, these dear ones who sometimes acted like forsaken children, I readily agreed. I wanted to bring some joy back into their lives, and Yosemite felt like the right place to start.

Yosemite had always been a vacation destination I wanted to explore more fully. My three children, Corinne, Joni, and Harley, had been there before and were eager to return before the school year began. I had just returned from nearly a month in South Africa and Kenya, and I welcomed the chance to spend uninterrupted time with them before returning to work. We made a few stops along the way to let the kids stretch and play, arriving at Yosemite late in the evening. We checked into a cozy cabin serviced by the Lodge, which was conveniently located just across from the dining area, shops, and outdoor meeting space. Tired from the drive, we went straight to bed.

Everything Aligned—Except the Tennis

The next morning, the children first requested to visit the shop next to the Lodge office. While they browsed, I made breakfast reservations and waited on a nearby bench. I noticed a man sitting a few feet away, reading a book. He looked up and smiled—not just any smile—this was the kind of smile that said, "I'm single." I nodded in return.

Soon, the kids came out, and we headed to breakfast. On the way out of the dining area, I saw him again, still reading. I called out playfully, "Do you do anything other than read? What's the name of your book?" "If I remember right," he said, "War and Peace." Sitting beside him was a much younger girl. Oh great, I thought, he likes them young. Before the conversation could go further, Joni tugged at me. "Mother, you promised we'd play tennis." I turned to him and said, "Goodbye." He replied, "See you around." As we walked away, I tossed over my shoulder, "How can you? You don't even know my name."

Joni and I made our way to the tennis courts near the Ahwahnee Hotel with our brand-new rackets, ready to play. But both courts were occupied. Not wanting to let disappointment spoil the moment, Joni spotted the nearby nine-hole golf course and suggested we try it. We had no real golf experience but played plenty of miniature golf. Close enough. We were trying our best to take it seriously when I noticed someone walking past. The guy. He didn't look right or left, just headed toward the tennis courts.

Later that evening, we had dinner reservations at the Ahwahnee dining hall. I had a tradition of using formal meals to teach the children proper etiquette. We dressed up, and once seated, I guided them through every step, napkins in laps, polite conversation, and Harley offering the prayer at the table. It was a delicious meal, shared with intention and grace.

Afterward, we returned to the Lodge, where table games were set up in the lounge. The kids immediately dove into a card game, and he was again reading. When he looked up and saw me this time, he gestured for me to join him. He was on the couch, and I pulled up a chair across from him.

He looked at me and said, "Let's tell our story right now." He began:

Bill: My name is William Batchelder, but I go by Bill.

Bobbi: My name is Bobbi Nell, but I go by Bobbi.

Bill: I'm a widower.

Bobbi: I'm a widow.

Bill: My wife died in 1969 of cancer.

Bobbi: My husband died in 1969 of cancer.

Bill: I've been dating for four years, hoping to meet someone serious about marriage.

Bobbi: I've been dating for four years and hope to meet someone serious about marriage.

Bill: I live on the Peninsula.

Bobbi: I live on the Peninsula.

Bill (laughing): Are you making fun of me?

Bobbi: Everything I've said is true. Is yours?

Bill: I have three children, two girls and a boy.

Bobbi: I have three children, two girls and a boy.

I can't recall much else from that conversation, except that I told him we were leaving Yosemite on a specific day. He replied that he would be leaving that same day. We said goodnight and went our separate ways.

On the day of our departure, we were checking out when Bill showed up. He told me he'd forgotten to get my contact information, so we exchanged phone numbers and addresses. I could barely remember how to pronounce his last name, Batchelder. When I saw it written, I broke it down to remember it: "Bill," easy. "Batch," like a batch of cookies. "Elder," like an elder in the church. Batchelder.

It was unforgettable now.

The telephone rang, and it was Bill. He wanted to meet at a tennis court in Burlingame. Naturally, I grabbed my new tennis racket, which I had only used for lessons, and headed over. He was pleased that I was on time.

Tennis, however, did not go quite so smoothly. We warmed up, or at least tried to. I spent most of the time chasing stray balls. We never even made it to an actual game to keep score, which was a blessing, considering how badly I was doing just warming up. Without a word, I could see Bill's frustration rising. Finally, he walked over, zipped up his racket, and said bluntly, "You don't know how to play tennis." I admitted I had never played. He shook his head in exasperation. I zipped up my racket and quietly left.

Well, I thought, *that ends that.* Driving home, a little dejected, I told myself it was better to find out early, before we invested more time.

As I walked in the door, the phone rang. It was Bill again. "Did you get the can of balls?" he asked. I hadn't. Somehow, he didn't believe me. That sealed it in my mind, there would be no dating relationship with Bill. Our short encounter would be the end of it.

Dating Again—with Coke and a Bird Named Bobbi

A babysitter told me about a singles dinner event on the Peninsula. You signed up, paid a set price, and were given a date, time, and location for dinner with other singles. Curious, I decided to try it. The dinner was held in Palo Alto.

I was surprised that the only drinks offered were water, unless you requested something else. I didn't drink alcohol or coffee, and all I knew how to order was iced tea or hot tea. Neither was available. I hesitated when asked what I wanted and finally asked for a soft drink. "Which kind?" the server asked. The only ones I knew were Doctor Pepper and Coke, so Coke it was.

While ordering, a man approached and asked if I would join him at his table. I agreed. I don't remember his name, but he was a doctor with Kaiser Permanente. I asked him about Kaiser, and by the end of the evening, I decided to join. I have been a Kaiser member ever since.

After dinner, the doctor walked me to my car. As he left, another man introduced himself and asked if I would date him the following Saturday. We exchanged phone numbers, and I sang all the way home to San Mateo, feeling almost as giddy as if I'd had a strong drink!

When I got home, my babysitter was asleep, so I couldn't immediately thank her for introducing me to the singles club that opened up a whole new world.

Word got around quickly that I was single. The phone started ringing regularly, and I realized I had to teach my kids how to answer and take messages properly. There would be no more answering with "Sorry, she's not here!" and hanging up. Instead, they practiced saying, "Hello," or "Good evening," or "Good day," and then, "My mother is not available right now. May I take your name and number?" Practice, practice, until they finally groaned, "Mother!" and sighed heavily. To encourage them, I promised a prize to the best "good responder." I was serious about dating and didn't want to miss a single opportunity to meet a potential husband.

The man who had approached me at the singles event, the "last-minute guy", called to confirm our Saturday date. "Remember, we have a date. I expect you to keep it," he said firmly. I wish he hadn't phrased it that way. Around the same time, a friend told me about a man from Hillsborough, wealthy, single, and looking for a blind date. Woe is me! I was locked into a commitment with the last-minute guy and would miss the chance to meet a man "of means."

Still, I honored my commitment, and I was glad I did.

He turned out to be a delightful friend for several dates. He gave wonderful hugs and kisses, and although we didn't take things further (our lives soon became too busy), we parted fondly. Later, I learned he sweetly honored me, naming his bird "Bobbi."

No Longer Just Surviving—Now Leading

The death of my husband thrust me into educational circles for which, at first, I felt ill-prepared. That was my thinking, at least. But over time, as I became accustomed to being asked to speak, write, and demonstrate teaching techniques, I realized I had already been doing all those things, and more, while serving as the family breadwinner during Glenn's church-planting years.

110_ Photo: Bobbi (1971)

I had to remind myself that I had earned my status as a professor of education at Ellensburg State University and had traveled across Washington State speaking as a paid consultant. The foundation had already been laid; I simply needed to step fully into the professional woman I had become. It was time to let go of outdated images of myself and embrace the new reality.

Significant challenges awaited. One was working with the Sixth Army, teaching religious education instructors how to apply educational methods in their training programs. Another was collaborating with consultants from the California State Department of Education in Sacramento, helping them develop mission statements, set goals, outline objectives and activities, and design methods for evaluating their work.

I also taught the fundamentals of the Montessori method, bringing what I had learned to broader audiences. At the same time, I worked hard to keep my position at the San Mateo County Office of Education, serving as a Coordinator of Projects across the county's 23 school districts.

At every turn, I faced steep learning curves. But I kept telling myself, "I can do this." Little by little, experience by experience, I proved that I could indeed succeed as an educator, a leader, and a professional woman.

Same God, New Church Home

After Glen's passing, the Parson family transitioned from Pilgrim Baptist Church to the Presbyterian Church on 25th Avenue in San Mateo, California. For different reasons, all family members supported the move.

Harley chose to discontinue playing in the children's Sunday band at Pilgrim Baptist Church after recognizing the exceptional musical abilities of the other members.

Joni experienced feelings of isolation at Pilgrim Baptist because none of the children her age from the church's predominantly Black community attended her predominantly white public school.

For me, the shift to the Presbyterian Church offered greater convenience. The children's schools were located near the Presbyterian Church, providing after-school activities with transportation. This setup enabled me to work knowing my children were looked after, making it feel right to support the Presbyterian Church. As a result, I became their 4th-grade Sunday School teacher.

The move was easy because, as I learned during the pastor's membership explanation, Presbyterians and Baptists share fundamental beliefs but differ primarily in their practices. Baptists traditionally abstain from drinking, smoking, and dancing—hence the saying, "Baptists are the 'Shall Not' people," humorously adding that they even avoid making love standing up to prevent any appearance of dancing. Presbyterians, in contrast, enjoy greater social freedoms.

Reflecting on the saying, "Where your treasure is, that is where your heart is also," it became clear that my commitment to giving to God through a church now resided with the Presbyterian denomination.

He Called Back—And So Did Hope

Working in education after Glenn's death was a very different experience from when he was alive. Between my professional responsibilities and the demands of dating, I was now solely responsible for raising three children. It was no small burden. As a woman, I wanted to earn as much as possible to give my children a good life. At the same time, I longed to find a suitable partner, someone who could share family life with me.

I was both surprised and excited when Bill Batchelder called. I had assumed he had crossed me and my tennis racket off his list long ago. We had exchanged addresses, and I had even driven by his property once. His well-kept gardens and large home left a lasting impression. I could see myself living there, I thought.

Bill invited me on a date, which encouraged me. I wanted to make the most of the opportunity. He typically called on Saturday mornings for dates that night, a habit that initially left me wondering if I had missed something, but I quickly learned that spontaneity was just Bill's way. Recognizing this, I stopped dating anyone else. I wanted to be available for Bill, not just on Saturdays and holidays, but always. Although I did meet a friend for coffee after teaching a class at San Francisco State University, and once had an unplanned coffee meeting with someone I had dated previously, otherwise, I gave up dating altogether. I had a clear goal: to be ready if something serious developed with Bill. Deep down, I realized that part of my motivation was a longing for security. I wanted that beautiful home, and what it represented.

As I continued to date Bill, I recognized that I had started focusing more on material comforts than my original commitments. I remembered my prayer at sixteen: "Lord, I commit my whole life to serve Your Kingdom. Whatever you ask me to do, I will do it with all my heart, soul, and resources." I asked Bill if he would pray with me after our dates to re-center myself. He agreed, and from that point on, we prayed together each time we met.

On one of our dates, I asked Bill when he had become a Christian. He spoke about his confirmation, his wife's church membership, and attending services with their children at the Lutheran Church. His answers were sincere, but looking back, I sensed something was missing. Still, I thought, Who am I to judge?

We continued dating every Saturday or holiday that didn't fall on a Sunday—nearly six months had passed since we first met. I began to realize Bill might never propose, and I didn't want to spend the rest of my life still searching for a husband as I edged closer to forty.

From 'You're Not Going to Marry Me, Are You?' to 'Set the Date'

One evening, during a date, I finally asked, "You aren't going to marry me, are you?" Bill seemed startled. "Oh! Do you want to get married? We can do that!" "Yes," I said firmly. "I do want to marry." Then I added, "Are you going to ask me?" He smiled and said, "Well, when would you like to get married? Set the date." It wasn't the most traditional proposal, but I took it as the best he could offer, and I gladly accepted it.

<u>With Our Children at Our Sides, We Said 'I Do'</u>

A dear friend from Howard Payne University, whose last name was Pettigrew and who lived in California, offered to plan my wedding. I gladly accepted. Together, we chose the date: during Easter vacation in 1973. I was pleased to be marrying at 39 years old, on April 7, 1973, just months before my 40th birthday on August 24.

Although I had joined a Presbyterian Church, I continued to attend Pilgrim Baptist Church on some occasions and maintained friendships there. Several friends from Pilgrim were invited to our wedding. I chose Pilgrim's organist and soloist to perform the ceremony's music.

Among those participating in the ceremony:
- Mary Ruth and Patsy Batchelder served as ushers.
- Chris Batchelder stood as the best man.
- Corinne served as matron of honor.
- Joni was our flower girl.
- Harley lit the candles.

Attending were the Pilgrim Baptist Church minister, his wife, and family, several Caucasian friends from the congregation, my attorney and a book author, Ann Alexander. (Corinne was reading her novel "The Pink Dress".)

111_Photo: Church for Our Wedding

And yes, I was the bride, and William Patrick Batchelder was the groom.

The ceremony was performed by the Associate Pastor of the Presbyterian Church on 25th Avenue in San Mateo.

Described, Not Judged—And Finally Seen

Immediately after the wedding, Bill and I headed to North Shore Lake Tahoe for a skiing honeymoon. We mostly dined at modest restaurants, but one night we treated ourselves to a lovely dinner with a pre-fixed menu, a small but memorable indulgence.

One evening, as we sat across from each other in our room, Bill began describing my face, piece by piece. He said, "Your eyes are set back deeply into the sockets. One eyelid seems normal; the other comes down lower. Your eyebrows are wide and long. You have a long nose. Your hair is red, though that's not your natural color." At first, I felt hurt and was on the verge of tears. But then I realized, he hadn't judged any of these features as good or bad. He simply observed them. For the first time, I saw myself as others might, giving me a strange new perspective. Bill reassured me, saying, "Marriage is forever. We can make it what we want it to be."

Blending Wasn't Easy—But We Chose to Try

My children

Four years following Glenn's passing, my children had matured. Corinne(19) had graduated from Hillsdale High School, experienced London, and enrolled in a Design and Merchandising program in San Francisco. Harley-Kevin(15) was a freshman who transferred to the nearby Woodside High School. Joni(13) was now in seventh grade, having moved on from elementary school (typically K-5) to junior high (usually 6-8).

Bill's children

Chris(20) had graduated and was at home, considering his next educational step after trying two different colleges. Patsy(19)was also a graduate, deciding on her college plans. Mary Ruth(17) was still a sophomore at Woodside High School.

Bill worked hard to help our two families blend into one. Six children and two adults, under one roof, learning to live and love together. It wasn't always easy, but it was the beginning of a new and hopeful chapter in all our lives.

112a_ Photo: Blended Family

1st row: Harley-Kevin 2nd row: Mary Ruth, Joni - 3rd row: Chris, Corinne - Top: Bill, Patsy, and Bobbi (1973)

I Married for a Home—And Found a Husband I Loved

To accommodate the Parson family of four, Bill built an additional bedroom. He also added a spacious family room off the kitchen, with a tile floor at one end and sliding doors opening onto a covered deck. A hot tub awaited at the far end of the deck, and stairs led down to a large patio.

The patio was well thought out and featured an outdoor kitchen perfect for gatherings. On one side of the patio stood a tree with a charming playhouse nestled among its branches; on the other, a neatly kept vegetable garden stretched out.

The carport provided room for tools and could fit one or two cars, provided we didn't fill it up with too much "stuff," which was always a temptation.

The yard was full of life: fruit trees produced seasonal bounty, and a rose garden bloomed beautifully in the front. A birdbath stood in the middle of the front yard, adding a touch of charm. A semi-circular driveway made entry and exit easy.

The house itself had a red-tiled roof and white-painted walls. Along the sides, ornaments and flower beds added color and warmth beneath the windows.

We almost always entered the house through the back. The entrance opened into a long room, once a covered porch, now enclosed and functional, with a small bathroom off to the side.

From this room, a door at one end led to a narrow hallway lined with three bedrooms. At one end was the large main bedroom with a full private bath, generous closets, and large windows welcoming the sunlight. Down the hall, the first bedroom was spacious enough for two beds. The next bedroom was smaller and had a door leading directly outside. Across from it, another small room mirrored it, with a bathroom conveniently nearby. A third door from the hallway opened into what had once been another porch, now converted into a livable room.

At the far end of the hall was a door leading into the kitchen, the heart of the home. Off the kitchen, another hallway led to a bathroom, a bedroom with a closet, and a stairway down to the full basement. The basement was brightened by above-ground windows, featuring a laundry area, a full-sized walk-in storage room, and another door leading outside. It was practical and full of potential for all the storage and space a growing family needed.

By Thanksgiving of 1974, we had fully moved in and settled.

That year, I prepared and served our first Thanksgiving dinner in our new home, a moment that truly made the house on Stockbridge feel like home.

112b_ Photo: Bobbi Thanksgiving (1974)

Though I had originally married Bill with practical hopes, dreaming of home security, I soon realized I had grown to love him truly.

Sword Dancing, Christmas Socks, and a New Life Together

Bill didn't smoke or drink during the week. But on weekends, when he did drink, he usually just went straight to bed. One Saturday afternoon, after he had had quite a bit to drink and turned in early, Patsy came into the room and gave him a firm talking-to. She told him that this was no way to treat a new bride. Her words stuck with both him and me.

Right after our honeymoon, we celebrated Bill's birthday (b. May 9, 1927). I planned a party and invited a colleague from the County Office who was also a professional belly dancer. She was fantastic. At one point during her performance, she balanced a sword on her head, made it spin, and even lit it on fire, all while dancing. She was so skilled that none of us were the least bit worried about her setting herself or the house on fire.

A year or so later, we were all stunned when Corinne surprised us with her own belly dance performance at Thanksgiving. I don't know who was more shocked, her siblings or mother. All I could think was that Glenn, her father, "would have turned over in his grave." That old Southern expression summed it up perfectly.

As our first Christmas together approached, with the whole family living under one roof, Bill kept saying, "I don't want anything for Christmas. No gifts for me." He repeated it so many times, I knew there had to be a story behind it. Eventually, he admitted that growing up, the only gifts he ever received were clothes, socks, ties, and shirts. He had plenty of those now and didn't want anything more of the same. So I gave him something unexpected: a family membership to the Alpine Tennis Club, which cost over $400. He was surprised and genuinely pleased.

We settled into a shared routine. We were assigned tasks to help keep the house and yard in order. I supervised cleaning inside on Saturdays, and Bill took charge of the yard. Bill would head to the Alpine Tennis Club on Sundays to play tennis and unwind.

For our spiritual life, the Parson family transitioned from the Presbyterian Church on 25th Street in San Mateo to Menlo Church on Santa Cruz Avenue. Corinne, Harley, Joni, and I attended services there regularly, and the rest of the extended family joined us on holidays.

A Mother's Navigation: Work, Schools, and Street Divides

Before my marriage to Bill, balancing my work schedule with my children's schooling had become increasingly complicated. They could no longer walk to or from school on their own.

When one of their former teachers from George Hall School, known affectionately as "L.N.R." (Eleanor), started a private school, Joni and Harley asked to transfer there. Eleanor personally picked them up and returned them home each day, providing an excellent bridge during that transitional period, at least until I married Bill.

During Easter vacation, the children left Eleanor's school and returned to regular public school.

As a County Office employee for the San Mateo County Schools, I understood how difficult it could be to transfer students between districts. Approval from both districts was rare without a strong reason.

Living at Bill's residence added complexity. Our street served as the boundary between Woodside and Atherton and divided the Redwood City and Los Lomitas school districts. Despite our home being in Woodside, it was zoned for the Redwood City School District, which had a lower rating than the adjacent Los Lomitas District in Atherton.

To give Joni better educational opportunities, it was suggested, and I agreed, to use an Atherton address so she could attend La Entrada School, a short bus ride away.

To ensure Joni could attend the better-regarded La Entrada School in Menlo Park, a neighbor of Bill's, for whom she babysat, permitted her to use their Atherton address for enrollment. Another kind neighbor, whose horses the Batchelder children frequently visited, also offered assistance. This generosity allowed Joni to avoid the lengthy bus journey to the less desirable Redwood City Schools.

Bikes in the family

Bill owned a well-maintained bicycle that he used frequently. On weekends, he cycled from our house to the Club to play tennis before biking back.

Harley and Patsy, who were in Sun Valley, Idaho, believed I should also have a bike. Although I had never owned or ridden one, they assumed a gift would enable me to "get on and ride." This was far from the truth. I feared the bicycle and eventually sold it because it felt too large and unmanageable.

113_Photo: Patsy, Harley, Bobbi (Idaho, 1983)

Peninsula Professional Women's Network

I joined PPWN, founded by Nancy Collins, who later authored several books, including one on mentoring. I was chosen as the group's president and authored portions of its newsletter. The PPWN provided a networking space for women, and my interest in tennis blossomed through the friendships formed there.

Inspired by friends from PPWN, I decided to learn tennis. The opportunity arose when Bill mentioned he was considering giving up his Alpine Swimming and Tennis Club membership due to lack of use. Joni and I immediately offered to take it over. We started taking lessons and soon learned to play. Eager to improve, I began organizing practice matches to play complete sets against opponents.

114_Photo: Bobbi tennis (1989)

After playing for some years, I established a club team. Incredible as it may sound, we achieved victory at the USA League national championship in 1999, a story I will elaborate on later.

A Joyful Union: My Daughter Joni Marries David Cropper

David and Joni met in a banking class Joni was teaching in Los Angeles, where David was a student. Following the class, David received an assignment in

Northern California. Joni also offered her a choice of location for her banking career, and she similarly selected Northern California. After some time living together, they decided to marry. Their wedding took place at Menlo Presbyterian Church in 1990.

115_Photo: Joni, David's Wedding Party
(1st Row LR): Corinne, Bill, Joni, David, and Bobbi
 (2nd Row LR): Dave Pleger, Patsy, Chris, and Harley.

Visiting Glenn's Niece in Texas

For many years, I've made it a point to attend the yearly Buckner reunion in Dallas, Texas. This tradition allows me to connect with Glenn's family, particularly his sister Barbara's daughter, Pam. Pam and her husband, Hank Hood, have a daughter named Jordan, and they reside close to Dallas. My visits with Pam, Hank, and Jordan are a regular part of my time at the Buckner reunion.

116_Photo: Bobbi, Jordan Hood (Texas 1992)

Another branch of my family in the Dallas area is Sue and Terrell Landry. Sue is my niece, the daughter of my older brother, Ray Richardson. Like my visits with Pam's family, I see Sue and Terrell whenever I'm in town for the Buckner Reunion. Sue's parents were Ray and Vernice Richardson, who have passed away since this book was written.

Grandchildren

In 1995, my family had grown to include Corinne's Husband, Dave Pleger, and her son Evan; and Joni and David's children: Brian, Adam, and Haley.

In May 1995, Haley's dedication was held at Menlo Presbyterian Church, the family's church. Joni and David celebrated the occasion with the entire blended family.

117_Photo: Family Picture (1995)

1st Row: LR: Corinne, Bobbi, Joni(with Haley), Bill
2nd Row: LR: Evan, Brian, Adam
3rd Row: LR: Dave Pleger, Harley, David Cropper

118_Photo: Haley, Bobbi, and Joni (1995)

162

Telling My Faith Story at Menlo Church

The Parson children, Corinne, Harley, Joni, and I joined Menlo Church in 1973, shortly after my marriage to Bill Batchelder. Joni and her children actively participated, often performing in services, which I always enjoyed attending. Years later, I felt a desire for greater involvement in the church. Volunteers were encouraged to get involved in some new activities sponsored by the Church. I became interested in the Faith Story group.

At the initial meeting for the Faith Story group, the facilitator, Margie Barkhau, asked for a volunteer to open with prayer. When no one responded, I offered. Margie then explained that the group aimed to collect and edit personal stories of faith journeys from congregants to compile into a book for distribution. This description differed from my initial understanding of the group's purpose, and I immediately wanted to withdraw. Margie suggested I could be their "prayer warrior."

Subsequently, the group began the process of collecting faith stories. Each member was to write their own story for the book. Another member offered to write mine, knowing my reluctance. I shared my story with her, and she submitted it. However, she then moved away and became inactive in the group. I hesitated to use her version as it contained inaccuracies.

During a church retreat, I mistakenly entered the "Writing Your Story" workshop while moving between small group meetings. The leader shared story-writing tips, giving us time to write and share short pieces. Afterward, at a larger group meeting, I was chosen to read my story, which was well-received. I felt a sense of accomplishment and gratitude. Later, during a visit with Meriam and Wayne Oler, I couldn't sleep. Feeling inspired, I wrote my Faith Story without revision, and it was published in the Menlo booklet.

To inform the congregation about the booklet, Margie Barkhau spoke at each Saturday and Sunday service, recounting the creation process and then introducing me to share my story. Over one weekend, I told my story five times across five services. The positive reception was surprising, even from the minister, John Ortberg, though his enthusiasm seemed to wane after multiple retellings. I was relieved that most congregants only heard it once. Below is a copy of my faith story.

Princess

By Bobbi Batchelder

2005

Born to a sharecropper father and a mother who birthed nine children before she was thirty-two, I was the seventh child. The parents buried twin girls and two boys, who died soon after birth.

The effects of World War I and the depression were still visiting in the back woods of central Texas in 1933-1939. As a result of this and a gunshot witnessed by the household, the mother was dead, and the father was hospitalized. The five children were left homeless.

In December 1939, three of us (see picture) were placed in an orphanage.

119_Photo: Angie, Billy, Bobbi (1939)

The other two siblings were separated to be brought up by relatives. When realization dawned on this six-year-old, she felt she had been lifted from the outhouse to a big southern plantation home. The orphanage had running water, electricity, three meals a day, magic flushing, and "What was that roll of white stuff?"

A lot had to be taught: brushing teeth, bathing, combing hair, which clothes to wear when. There was a whole set of clothes for play, another for school, and still others for Sunday and special occasions. When someone said, "We have to wear shoes and socks," I thought, "You mean we actually HAVE shoes and socks to wear?" There were hats, coats, gloves, shoes, and overshoes. What a concept!

Everyone had his or her own bed. No more two or three to a bed. Now they could tell who put that water in the bed at night - no more pushing me into the puddle. Thirty little six-years-olds to a matron, six beds all in a row. And it was this way for five rooms at one end of a long hall with terrazzo floors. Each child had a set of sheets, a pillow, and a stuffed animal. So many quilts were available here that there was no more need for heated bricks under the covers.

Facilities never known before were a hospital, a fully equipped dental office, an elementary school, and a separate high school. A church and religious educational building were at the center of the 25 buildings on this 60-acre campus. They cared for the physical and educational needs of seven hundred fifty children, ages 1 month to eighteen years. This was Buckner Orphans Home in Dallas, Texas. Who could ask for anything more?

But where was Mother? Where was Father? Where were kin? Who loved me? Who could love me among so many? Where did I fit in this marvelous place that I had no idea existed? This was lacking: a feeling of belonging, being wanted, and being loved.

Then, one day, many of us girls were playing in the big playroom with toys from our own toy chest. I could not do the same. I just sat on top of mine, thinking. There is someone who loves me - Jesus, God's son who died so that I might live. Oh, how He loves me! Oh, how I love Him. Then, just like a flash, this person came face-to-face with me in my mind's eye. He knew me. I knew Him. Then I knew who I was: a child of a king, royalty. I was a princess at age eight, and if I live to be 80 (now 71), I will still be a princess. My father is the King.

From Childhood to Adulthood: Stories of Our Sons and Daughters

After Bill and I married, our household grew to eight: Bill's children (Chris, Patsy, and Mary Ruth), my children from my marriage with Glenn Parson (Corinne, Harley, and Joni), Bill, and me. The number of people living at home varied; sometimes there were just seven, and sometimes there were just Bill and me. Regardless of the number or whether they were Batchelder's or Parson's children, I grew to love all six.

120_Photo: Bill, Me, and Our Kids (1995)
1st Row LR : Patsy, Chris, Mary Ruth, Corinne,
2nd Row LR: Bill, Bobbi, Harley, Joni

165

Bill's Children: Their Journeys

When Bill and I exchanged vows, he was already a father to three children.

121_Photo: Mary-Ruth, Patsy, Chris (1977)

This meant that our marriage immediately encompassed the joys and responsibilities of a family, blending our lives and experiences from the beginning. His children became an integral part of my life, and I embraced the role of stepmother with an open heart, eager to build meaningful relationships with them. Our early years together were defined by the dynamics of this pre-existing family unit, navigating the intricacies of blending households and fostering a sense of unity and belonging for everyone.

Chris's Journey

Chris, Bill's oldest child, born February 18, 1953, maintained excellent health through exercise and healthy eating. After completing his master's degree in business, he became our financial planner.

122_Photo: Chris Batchelder

We anticipated him starting his own family, but his path shifted when he met Damaris Moore at a religious meeting, and they became partners. Now retired, Chris, a former financial planner, and Damaris, a retired librarian, reside in Oakland and vacation in Bodega Bay.

Courage in Every Step: Remembering Patsy

Patsy, the second oldest in the Batchelder/Parson family, (b. March 9, 1954) possessed a remarkable athletic spirit. Her adventurous nature once led to a speeding ticket for cycling at 50 mph down a steep, narrow road off Highway 84. A skilled rock climber, Patsy also served as a Yosemite Rescuer, aiding climbers in challenging situations. Her passion for the outdoors extended to running, climbing, and long-distance hiking.

←123_Photo: Patsy

Patsy found a kindred spirit in Andy Wiessner, who shared her deep respect for nature.

124_Photo: Patsy and Andy →

Andy owned extensive land near wilderness areas and dedicated himself to land conservation through private-government exchanges. Their commitment to environmentalism was a strong bond.

←125_Photo: Patsy and Andy's wedding (1997)
Eric, Mary-Ruth, Patsy, Andy, Bobbi, and Bill

We were very close to Patsy and Andy, going on vacation trips

126_Photo: England
LR Patsy, Bobbi, Andy, Bill

And Birthday partys.
127_Photo: Bobbi at Patsy's birthday party

Courage Beyond Words

Patsy received a diagnosis of Amyotrophic Lateral Sclerosis (ALS), also known as Lou Gehrig's disease. This progressive neurodegenerative disease affects nerve cells in the brain and spinal cord. The news was devastating, not only for Patsy but for our entire family. ALS progressively robs individuals of their ability to walk, talk, eat, and eventually breathe. Witnessing Patsy face this cruel disease was incredibly difficult. The initial symptoms were subtle, perhaps a slight weakness in her hand or a slur in her speech, easily dismissed initially. However, these signs gradually became more pronounced, leading us on a path of doctor's visits and tests that ultimately confirmed the heartbreaking diagnosis.

Years into their marriage, Patsy faced the devastating diagnosis of ALS. For two courageous years, she lived with the inability to speak or swallow. Despite these profound challenges, Patsy remained determined to live actively, even hiking challenging trails with braces. Eventually, she required constant oxygen and, as her hands became less functional, relied on a feeding tube. Confronted with the relentless progression of ALS and the absence of a cure, Patsy made a profound decision. Believing that life on earth with incurable ALS was far less appealing than eternal life with God in heaven, free from the disease, she chose to "Be with God."

On February 9, 2019, Patsy peacefully passed away at home. Her siblings, Chris and Mary Ruth, deeply mourned her loss, as did her step-siblings, Joni Cropper and Harley Parson. Joni, who shared a close bond with Patsy, thoughtfully provided the family with private time to grieve. This gesture was especially comforting for me, her stepmother, who loved her dearly as a daughter.

Mary Ruth: From Challenge to Cherished

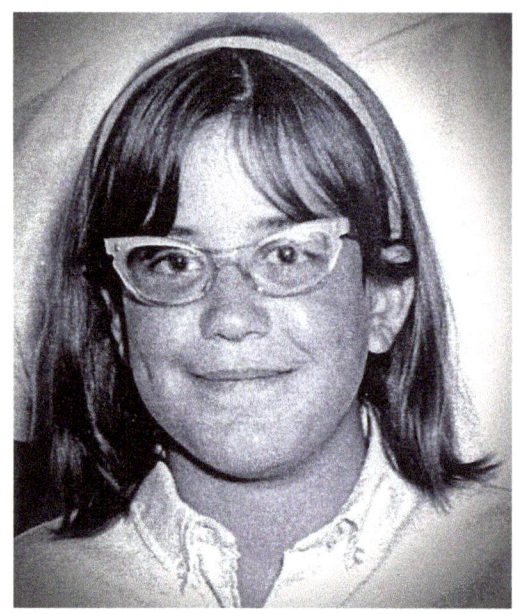

Mary Ruth (b.Feb 1, 1954) was given both her grandmothers' names, Mary Murphy and Ruth Curry, and her family made a pact to always call her by both. Some people shortened her name to MR as a compromise, keeping the combined identity intact.

128_Photo: Mary Ruth (circa 1966)

When I joined the Batchelder/Parson family, Mary Ruth was a junior at Woodside High School. She was active in the school's theater program and showed real talent for acting. She also dabbled in sewing, starting several projects that Corinne kindly helped her finish. Though Mary Ruth didn't wish to pursue sewing further, all the fabric that Jeanette Curry Batchelder—Bill's late wife—had purchased for dresses for Patsy and Mary Ruth was passed along to Corinne, where it found new life.

Before my marriage to Bill, Mary Ruth had taken on the responsibility of managing the household while her father worked and her older siblings, Chris and Patsy, were away. When I stepped into that role, it allowed her to step back and enjoy a more typical high school experience during her final high school years. This shift in our family dynamics required patience and adjustment from both of us.

After high school, Mary Ruth went on to attend college in San Luis Obispo, got married to Erasmo Garcia, and had a son, Eric

129_Photo: Mary-Ruth, Eric, Erasmo (2004)

I will never forget Mary Ruth's kindness and attentiveness during times when I was ill or simply not feeling well. She always made me feel cared for and valued.

130_Photo: Mary Ruth Bobbi (2005)

Our relationship was not without its challenges, but over time, Mary Ruth found a place in my heart. I came to love her deeply, not just as a stepdaughter, but as my own child. Today, we share a wonderful friendship—at least from my perspective—and I cherish her presence in my life. I truly consider her my daughter, and I hope she knows how much I love her.

My Own Three: Corinne, Harley, and Joni

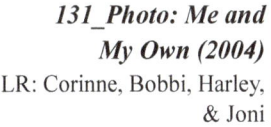

131_Photo: Me and My Own (2004)
LR: Corinne, Bobbi, Harley, & Joni

Corinne: Her Hands Made Magic, Her Absence Still Felt

Corinne, my firstborn child, (b.October 9, 1954) returned from studying Montessori in London before my marriage to Bill. Despite her student teaching in England, she realized teaching wasn't her path, declaring her independence by saying, "I'm my father's daughter. I can do what I think is right for me". Back from London, Corinne enrolled in The Design and Merchandising School in San Francisco, completing the design portion by the time Bill and I wed. For her practicum (1973), she secured a sponsorship from Bill's uncle at Macy's in San Francisco, working as a buyer and eventually becoming a vice president in purchasing.

At home, Corinne contributed by helping with daily dinner preparations and cooking Sunday evening meals. It was a joy to see her develop into a skilled cook of healthy and delicious food, which our family of eight greatly enjoyed. After her Macy practicum, Corinne moved to LA (1974) to do the merchandising part of her course. While she was grateful for winning the Merchandising Award, she admitted she had wished for the Design Award.

Corinne wanted to get a university degree, and while awaiting university admission, she worked as a window designer for a clothing store, creating outfits and making garments for mannequins. For leisure, she joined a local recreational dance class. Her rapid progress as a beginner led her instructor to offer free advanced lessons in exchange for teaching the beginner class. Later, the instructor connected her with a dance group, and she was chosen as one of eight "Beverly Hills Dancers," performing around LA and raising money for elaborate costumes that Corinne designed but didn't sew.

Following her university training at Northridge University in Los Angeles and CPA certification, she became a partner in an accounting firm. Subsequently, she and another female partner established their own CPA business. I was very pleased with her business achievements.

Corinne phoned to arrange a meeting with me and her fiancé, Dave Pleger, cautioning me beforehand about his dislike for mothers. I questioned her desire to marry someone with such feelings, but she insisted I meet him and reserve judgment. Upon meeting them, it became clear that this was her wish, and I respected her decision.

131_Photo: Dave Pleger, Corinne, Bobbi, Bill (1989)

Corinne and Dave Pleger had their first and only child, Evan, on October 14, 1991.

133_Photo: Corinne, Dave Pleger, & Evan (2004)

Corinne possessed an extraordinary gift for designing and crafting historically inspired garments—Victorian gowns, Regency dresses, Renaissance ensembles, and other period attire that beautifully captured the elegance and craftsmanship of bygone eras. During her marriage, she created more than 100 of these intricate costumes for herself, her husband, her son, and friends. Corinne proudly wore many of them to themed events and celebrations, several of which are shown in the photos below.

The 2003 Buckner Orphans Home Reunion, celebrating the Alumni Association's centennial, asked members to wear costumes representing their chosen period. Corinne crafted eight of the worn outfits.

133_Photo: Bucker Orphans Reunion (2003)

That's me sitting on the ground in front in a light blue dress with a red ribbon pendant.

The following are some more examples of Corinne's incredible accomplishments

135_Photo: Evan at Renaissance Fair (2010) ↓

136_Photo: Dave Pleger, Corinne (2010)

137_Photo: Corinne and friends →

Losing Corinne: A Mother's Grief

Bill and I often cared for Corinne's young son, Evan, and later joined Corinne and Dave for holidays.

Every year, we travel to LA for either Christmas or Thanksgiving with the Plegers. In 2011, Corinne invited me to Thanksgiving weekend. Harley and his wife, Helene, were also there. We enjoyed a pleasant Thanksgiving, spending time watching TV after dinner. On Friday, we saw a movie, and on Saturday, we prepared for a ballroom dance. Corinne had a Victorian dress for Helene and one for me, helping us dress and offering advice on wearing such attire.

Feeling unwell, Corinne decided to rest and skipped the evening's ball. Harley kindly escorted Helene and me. When we returned, Evan quietly told us that his father had taken Corinne to the hospital.

The next morning, Harley came to the hotel where I was staying, with heartbreaking news—Corinne had passed away. The initial report listed "heart failure" as the cause, but knowing her history of good health, I struggled to accept it. I asked Harley about it several times, hoping for clarity.

Later, Dave described what had happened in the emergency room. Her heart monitor began showing irregular patterns, and despite immediate efforts—both by a nurse and by Dave himself—to perform CPR, she could not be revived.

Corinne's passing left us reeling. At 57, she was vibrant—healthy in every visible way. Her sudden collapse and the diagnosis of "heart failure" never sat easily with me, or with her doctor. Corinne had no known heart problems. There were warning signs: —uncontrollable coughing, and fatigue.

In time, the autopsy revealed a tumor on her adrenal gland. A quiet intruder, long unnoticed. The medical term was pheochromocytoma—a rare condition, so easily missed, and so often silent until it turns deadly. It releases surges of hormones that can spike blood pressure, strain the heart, and tragically trigger fatal arrhythmias.

We will never know for certain. But perhaps, had the signs been clearer or the right test ordered, the course might have changed. These "what ifs" are part of grief's shadow.

And yet, I find some comfort in knowing this: her passing was not due to weakness or neglect, but to a hidden storm no one discovered. It reminds me just how fragile even our strongest can be—and how precious every moment truly is.

Corinne's ashes were placed in a vault. In the days leading to the memorial, Angie's quiet presence became a great source of comfort to me—a gentle expression of God's grace in the midst of sorrow.

Grief touched every corner of our family. Dave and Evan were devastated. Joni, though grieving deeply, stepped in with great care and resolve, managing Corinne's affairs and helping Dave navigate the many details of memorial planning. Harley's grief took an unexpected turn, alarming those around him enough that he was hospitalized for observation, and sadly, he was unable to attend his sister's service.

During those tender days, I found strength through Angie, my extended family, and two dear Buckner Alumni couples who lived nearby. Their kindness held me up.

On the day of the memorial, my two grandsons walked quietly beside me into the theater. As we descended the steps, a sacred hush fell over us. The service was stunning—loving, elegant, and heartfelt. It captured the radiant spirit of my daughter, Corinne, a woman of great grace and beauty, both inside and out. She was taken too soon, and though her life was full, her absence echoes in the memories stitched deep into our hearts.

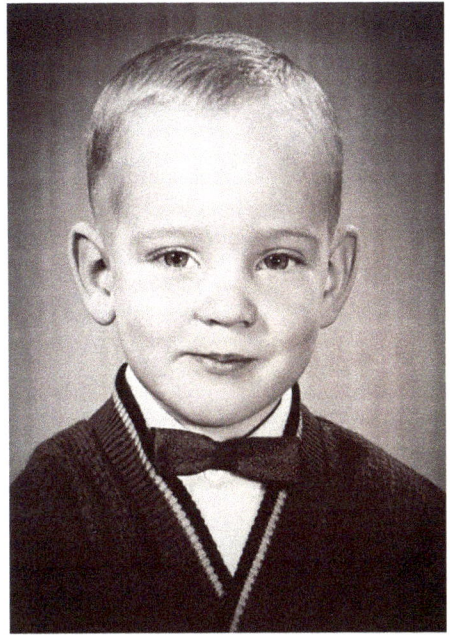

Born on August 18, 1958, Harley-Kevin Parson, my biological son, was known as Harley from the start.

138_Photo: Harley

He spent some time living with his grandfather, also named Harley, which led to some confusion on the phone.

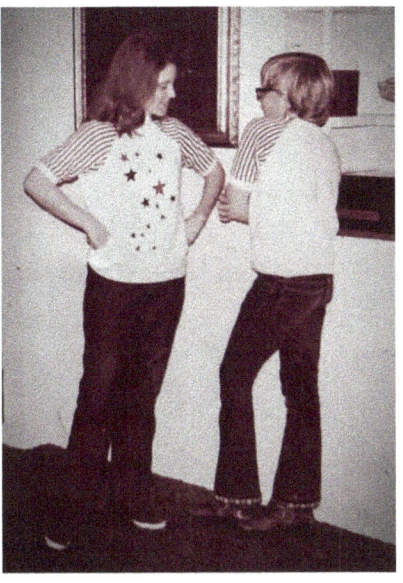

139_Photo: Bobbi, Harley-Kevin (circa 1971)

Harley adopted the name Kevin at his insistence and consistently used it in all interactions.

140_ Photo: Harley-Kevin, Bobbi

This became clear during his ear surgery when the nurse didn't recognize the name Harley. Consequently, I addressed him as Harley-Kevin, but soon transitioned to calling him Kevin exclusively.

When I married Bill, everyone knew him as Kevin. After leaving for college, Kevin reverted to calling himself Harley. He found that too many people named Kevin were at school and in his wider social circles.

Living with Bill taught Kevin respect and alignment with Bill's expectations. Bill's demands were structured and transparent, leaving no room for negotiation. Kevin learned to comply with Bill's directives as it was easier.

Following a period of youthful experimentation, Harley decided to settle down. He resided at our home in Redwood City and used his homemade skateboard for transportation. After an extended stay at home, he enrolled at San Francisco State University and earned a degree in Recreational Therapy. His practical experience included organizing a summer camp for students with physical disabilities.

Harley married Helene, an exchange student from France, in 1999.

141_Photo: Helene, Harley (1999)
Despite Helene's emotional difficulties that prevented her from working, Harley loved her deeply. They were together for 20 years. Harley worked from home, while Helene was also home frequently. The demands of Helene's needs often interrupted Harley's work. Eventually, Helene believed divorce was the only path to a peaceful existence.

Their divorce left Harley in debt. His close friend and stepbrother, Chris Batchelder, offered financial help for the settlement. However, a misunderstanding regarding the nature of this assistance caused a prolonged strain in their relationship. Fortunately, they have recently reconciled, and Chris has offered further financial support. Harley's jobs did not provide a sustainable income for his lifestyle, and his inexperience in managing his primary job resulted in a problematic relationship with his employer. He was ultimately terminated, and a lawsuit is currently pending.

Harley is Joni's cherished brother and my beloved son. They know me as Bobbi, Mimi, or Mom, though Harley prefers to address me as Mother.

Joni Jean: A Daughter's Strength and Spirit

Born December 3, 1960, I was asleep when the nurse came to record Joni's birth details. Having returned briefly from a revival meeting where he was preaching, Glenn wrote down the baby's name as "Joni Nell" Parson. Upon his return to the revival, he discovered I had changed it on the birth certificate to "Joni Jean." I felt "Joni Jean" would lend itself to the nickname "JJ," with more women entering professions, as I was, JJ seemed more suitable than Joni Nell. Glenn agreed with the name Joni Jean.

142_Photo: Harley, Joni, Caregiver (1961)

Joni developed into a delightful and lively person who was well-liked. She possessed a strong will and would not be persuaded to do anything against her preference, choosing to stand alone rather than follow the crowd. I don't recall her ever using the name JJ.

Having a working mother from birth made Joni susceptible to teasing from her siblings, though this ceased as she matured and formed friendships quickly.

143_Photo: Joni, Bobbi (1976)

Initially, I was also Joni's teacher. Joni became an exemplary student, often observed by university students.

One observation likened her to a "hot house plant," suggesting she was performing for the observers, a behavior I seemed to encourage, much to my later regret.

Following her father's death and what felt like four years without consistent parental presence due to my work and dating life, Joni was raised by various "caregivers," some of whom I suspect were not ideal.

144_Photo: LR: Joni, Bobbi, Corinne (1990)

David Cropper and Joni met in a Los Angeles banking class, where Joni was the instructor and David was a student. Following the class, David received an assignment in Northern California. Joni also opted for a banking position in

the same region. After living together for some time, they decided to marry. Their wedding ceremony took place at the Menlo Presbyterian Church in 1990.

145_Photo: Joni, David's Wedding
1st row: LR: Corinne, Bill, Joni, David Cropper, Bobbi;
2nd row: LR: Dave Pleger, Patsy, Chris, Harley, MaryRuth,

Joni and David have three children: Brian, Adam, and Haley.

146_Photo:LR: Haley, Brian, Bobbi, Adam (1997)

While Joni pursued her career, I had the joy of helping care for her children. They lovingly call me "Mimi," a name that still warms my heart.

147_Photo: David, Brian, Haley, Adam, Joni (2021)

Brian married Rachel, and together they have a son named Beck—my first great-grandchild. Adam is married to Chelsea.

My marriage to Bill introduced trauma into Joni's life, which might have been lessened with better handling on my part. Joni experienced a challenging time from her teenage years until the arrival of her first child. She sought resolution by revealing Bill's inappropriate conduct and my lack of intervention. Despite a turbulent childhood and young adulthood, she eventually forgave me.

Our relationship has since stabilized. I am grateful for the person Joni has become: a devoted wife to David Cropper, a wonderful mother of three and a new grandson, a gifted spiritual leader, a forgiving individual, and a loving daughter.

When Womanhood Felt Diminished

In 1979, I was hospitalized with a punctured uterus caused by a malfunctioning IUD, a complication that ultimately required a hysterectomy. I remained in the hospital for ten days following the operation.

Although I wished the surgery hadn't been necessary, the emotional aftermath proved even more difficult. During my hospital stay, I fell into a deep depression. I didn't want to see anyone—I just wanted to die. Joni, however, insisted on visiting, bringing friends with her. Their presence, along with Bill's unwavering support, became a lifeline. Paradoxically, being discharged and returning home marked a turning point. Somehow, I emerged from the ordeal not just healed—but stronger than before.

Bill suggested we file a lawsuit against the manufacturer. Though I was initially hesitant, he assured me he would take care of everything—and he did. Reaching a favorable settlement through legal action brought a measure of consolation. Through it all, Bill's steady support, Joni, my friends and my faith helped carry me through.

Downsizing our Home

During my hospital stay, Bill gently suggested that we consider a more relaxed lifestyle. Our children were grown, and with his retirement approaching, the upkeep of our large 1927 home—built on what had once been a chicken farm—was becoming increasingly burdensome. I could sense his desire to simplify our lives.

I had always loved that house on Stockbridge Avenue. In fact, one of the reasons I had wanted to marry Bill was because of that beautiful, spacious home with its charm and character. But I also understood that life brings seasons of

change. Though I felt attached to the house, I told him, "Okay, it's fine with me if you want to move." I was willing to go along with Bill—just as I had with my first husband, Glenn—trusting the path we were taking together.

148_Photo: Condo (2023)

Shortly afterward, Bill found a condo at 50 Horgan Avenue, Unit #52, in Redwood City. He told me about it and mentioned that it had originally been listed at $130,000 but had already risen to $150,000 by the time he spoke with me. Not wanting to miss out or risk another price increase, he moved quickly to make the purchase.

A Woman's Path Through Shifting Leadership

After marrying Bill, I continued working at the San Mateo County Office of Education. Dr. Barnes, the female director, significantly supported my career advancement during her tenure there. Her belief in promoting women to management was crucial to my growth.

The arrival of a male director following Ms. Barnes's retirement marked a turning point. The new head of the Department favored men for leadership positions over women. Consequently, my duties diminished, ultimately leading to my termination. I suspected his Mormon faith contributed to his bias against female administrators. Despite this, he did help me secure a position within the Cabrillo Unified School District in Half Moon Bay in 1983.

They Called Me Doctor B

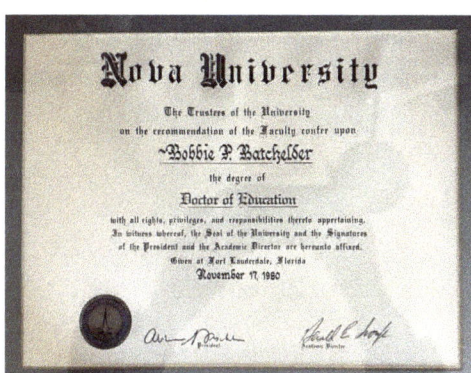

While working under the new supervisor, a positive development occurred: I pursued a Doctor's Degree in Education Administration at Nova University and earned it in 1980, leading to a higher salary.

149_Photo: Bobbi's Doctor of Education Diploma (1980)

With this degree came a name change. The students called me "Doctor B".

Assistant Vice Principal: Leadership with a Mission

Appointed initially as a temporary Assistant Vice Principal at Half Moon Bay High School for two months, while permanent candidates were interviewed, I decided to apply for the full-time position with a clear purpose. My motivation was to champion the academic achievement of the Cabrillo School District's only Black student, whom I knew from my Sunday school class at Pilgrim Baptist Church. Obtaining this position felt like a God-sent opportunity.

My responsibilities as Assistant Vice Principal included:
- Student supervision
- Establishing and managing student disciplinary procedures
- Overseeing graduation ceremonies
- Directing Student Body activities, including the athletic program

- Conducting evaluations for half of the teaching staff
- Supervising and evaluating adult ground monitors and office personnel
- Monitoring the lunch program
- Maintaining order in the Faculty lounge
- Ensuring the functionality of vending machines and managing the associated finances.

Excited about expanding my responsibilities, I accepted the position of Principal for the Half Moon Bay High School Summer School. This new role would make me the only administrator on campus throughout the summer.

For four years, my assignment in Half Moon Bay as an assistant vice principal involved a 19-minute commute from San Mateo. My schedule was demanding: 7:30 a.m. to 5:00 p.m. on weekdays and 7:30 a.m. to 12:00 p.m. on Saturdays. I took a much-needed vacation each summer break, playing tennis until the school year resumed in late summer.

During my tenure at Half Moon Bay High School, numerous achievements brought me pride, but one particularly resonated. The black student, whom I had previously taught in Sunday School, harbored aspirations of attending military school directly after graduation. I worked with two government senators to help secure his admission following his high school career. This student was

exceptional, having served as Student Body President and consistently achieved honor roll status, demonstrating excellence in academics and athletics. His success was a source of profound fulfillment for me.

150_Photo: Bobbi Half Moon Bay High School (1989)

Although ready to retire and dedicate my time to tennis, the newly appointed superintendent of the Cabrillo Unified School District approached me with a compelling proposition. She asked me to postpone my retirement, offering an incentive I couldn't decline. If I agreed to stay and support her for one more year, she would authorize adding two additional years to my retirement. This was advantageous, allowing me to retire with 27 years of service instead of 25.

Leadership in Turbulent Times: The Realities of School Administration

Classroom management became increasingly complicated. Several issues arose that disrupted the educational environment during my final year as Assistant Vice Principal:

- Students previously considered well-behaved began to disrupt the regular school day.
- Substitute teachers faced greater difficulty maintaining control in the classroom.
- Campus monitors required assistance because students were in unauthorized locations before, during, and after classes.
- Some students were consistently absent from their classes.
- Student behavior became increasingly defiant.

As Assistant Vice Principal last year, I addressed numerous noteworthy situations as part of my responsibilities. Here are some examples:

The Day the Books Dropped

A substitute teacher abandoned a class, reporting to the office that they could not manage the students. Upon entering the classroom, I sought to understand the situation by asking the students to explain what had occurred, using raised hands to manage responses.

One student recounted that they had been instructed to reread an assignment already completed for homework, intended for class discussion, as per their understanding of the lesson plan. Frustrated by the inaction, they devised a plan to gain the teacher's attention: the entire class would drop their books simultaneously at a signal. This occurred, prompting the teacher to flee the room.

While acknowledging the creativity of their attention-getting tactic, did they want to show me how that looked and sounded to the substitute? They did. I was impressed by how organized it was. They were in perfect timing. Subsequently, I guided the class to consider the teacher's potential feelings upon hearing the sudden loud noise, which elicited thoughtful responses.

I then informed them of the teacher's statement that she would not return to the classroom and asked, "What would be the results of her action?" They seemed unaware of the consequences, so I explained the likely loss of her substitute teaching status. To shift towards a favorable resolution, I asked, "How can we make this a win/win situation?" The students offered various solutions, some humorous. After a moment of shared laughter, we decided to "ask her back into the classroom and apologize." Ultimately, the substitute teacher expressed her gratitude after class. The anticipation of the regular teacher's return the following day brought relief.

The Librarian and the Results of Sex Behavior

Our librarian came to me and said, "I have a situation that I need help reporting." He mentioned hearing a commotion from the next room connected to the library. It was part of the Non-Educable Special Education Class held on campus but administered by the District Special Education Director.

The librarian heard the noise during the noon session when no students would be in any classroom. When the Librarian opened the door, to his amazement, he saw "the results of sex behavior." This embarrassing situation was brought to my attention. However, my "out" was that I was not in charge of that educational program, so the incident was reported to the Director of Special Education at the District Office.

When No One Was Home to Say "Go to School"

There were more jobs for adults on the "bay side" of the San Francisco Peninsula than on the "coast side". As a result, many parents working on the "bay side" left their children to care for themselves. This meant that more students had to manage getting to school, deciding what to have for lunch, and figuring out how to entertain themselves after school.

In my last year, as the assistant vice principal, I observed an increase in non-graduates. We held a staff meeting to brainstorm solutions in response to this issue. As a result, we hired a dedicated teacher to conduct classes specifically for students who were struggling or had inconsistent attendance. This exceptional teacher taught a different subject each period of the school day, targeting students who were behind in those areas. The regular teachers assessed each student's current level in their subject, and the special teacher tailored the instruction to meet the individual needs of those students. Once students caught up with the curriculum, they returned to their regular classroom. This program proved highly successful, and the number of non-attending students significantly decreased.

Some students who enrolled during the registration session had never attended class. One particular student refused to go to school. The school contacted his single mother to see if she had any suggestions on addressing her son's non-attendance. She explained that she worked "over the hill" and couldn't monitor when he left for school or returned home. She felt helpless in getting him to attend classes. After consulting with the District Office, it was decided to warn the mother that her son would be dropped from school and no longer allowed to attend any school in the District. The superintendent supported the school's decision regarding the boy's attendance. A registered letter outlining this decision was hand-delivered to the home, requiring the parents' signature. As a result, the student was expelled.

Wait... *Your* Mom Got Me Expelled?

Several months after I resigned as Assistant Vice Principal at Half Moon Bay High School, my son, Harley, traveled across Europe. During his travels, he connected with a group of boys who were hiking together. One evening, while sitting around a campfire, each boy shared his story about how he came to join the group. One boy recounted, "Dr. B from Half Moon Bay High School got me expelled." Harley then informed him that the Dr. B he was referring to was his mother.

Retirement and Tennis

My last school year at Half Moon Bay High School had ended, and I was eager to move on; play more tennis.

One Widow's Vacation, Another Woman's Beachfront Bonanza

Before I could organize any tennis games, I was asked to house-sit for a month at a home on the coast. The house belonged to a widow who wanted to travel to England. It was located on the coastal side of Highway 1, past San Gregory Road.

151_Photo: Bobbi, House Sitting

The large home had most of its windows facing the ocean and featured several paths leading down to the beach. There were two types of kitchens: one electric and another with gas. The house also included multiple bedrooms and a couple of living rooms.

I was already familiar with the area because Bill's son, Chris, had rented a house a few doors from where I was house-sitting. The widow's home was perfect for entertaining, so I took every opportunity to invite friends, close relatives, and visitors to enjoy the ambiance. I rarely spent any days alone there. However, being alone was wonderful at night once the guests had left. I loved watching the ships pass by and the moon and stars reflecting on the water. The view from every window in the house was stunning, creating a lovely picture. Overall, it was a very relaxing month.

Trading Tennis Time for a Future Theologian

At the end of the month, I thought, "Okay, I'm going to start playing serious tennis." I was a beginner aspiring to become an advanced player, but I remained at the beginner level because I hadn't yet committed to seriously playing.

My daughter, Joni, needed a babysitter as she wanted to return to her banking job after the first four months of maternity leave. I was excited about looking after my first grandchild, baby Brian, who was just four months old. When he was placed in my arms shortly after his birth, I felt God telling me, "This baby has been chosen for exceptional religious service."

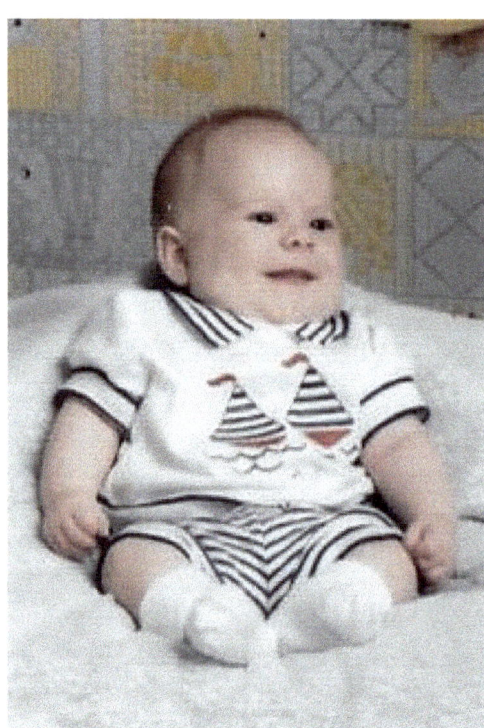

152_Photo: Brian Cropper (1991)

Joni proposed that I engage Bobbie, a local sitter operating a babysitting service from her residence, to care for Brian. This suggestion came after several months of limited participation in Saturday drop-in tennis. Utilizing Bobbie's service enabled me to conveniently leave Brian for short periods, finally allowing me to take tennis lessons at the Alpine Hills Tennis Club.

When my full-time Brian-sitting ended and Joni's second son, Adam, was born, Joni quit her full-time job and traded babysitting with her friend, who had two girls whose ages were similar to her two boys. She would work part-time and sometimes play tennis as well.

(note: Brian graduated from Harvard Divinity School, then taught religious studies at various high schools in the SF Bay Area. He's become a gifted minister who has preached from the pulpit as a guest pastor at my church in Portola Valley.)

Serving the Lord On and Off the Court

Joni and I often played together on mixed-level doubles teams. We were both committed to tennis and serving the Lord.

153_Photo: Joni and Bobbi

Regularly attending church and participating in various groups, we strived to grow our faith in Christ. I was deeply interested in having the Lord help me maintain my commitment to serve Him. I engaged in church activities while playing tennis, often feeling obsessed with the sport and trying to view it as a way to "serve the Lord." One of my partners accepted Christ, and another player and I prayed together, which helped strengthen our faith and resolve to share the message of Christ's saving power.

Leading My Team to a National Tennis Championship

Chris Bradley, the tennis director at Alpine Hills Tennis Club, organized matches for beginning players, which benefited me and others who wanted to improve their tennis skills. After dedicating many hours to practice, some of us reached a 3.5 player rating and formed Alpine's 3.5 competitive team. We also

played on a team of mixed-level doubles, which included Joni.

154_Photo: My Tennis Team (1998)
1st: LR M Crosby, B Ward, Chris Bradley, Bobbi
2nd: M Hamner, R Fisher, S Scott, A Stasiack, S Thomas

Playing tennis in tournaments and putting teams together for competitive play and practice was very fulfilling. As a team, we could finally enter competitions, which led us to try for the National Tennis Award at our age and level.

My Alpine 3.5 Senior Women's double team won first place in the district, the county, and the state and went to the national competition in Palm Desert and won; we were national champions.

155_Photo: USA League National Tennis Champion Trophy : (1999)

Each of my nine team players received their own personalized trophy .

I Couldn't Stay—Until Grace Made Us One

Bill and I found ourselves on diverging paths within our relationship. My faith and involvement in religious activities deepened, while Bill's actions increasingly contradicted his Christian profession. When I addressed this with him, he confessed, "I said I accepted Jesus as my Savior, but I didn't. I believe Jesus was just a prophet."

Despite being in separate counseling, I concluded that remaining with a non-believer exhibiting questionable behavior was detrimental to myself and our family. My therapist and I explored two possibilities: divorce or separation. Honoring our commitment against divorce, we decided to live apart. I secured a room for rent through a member of Menlo Church and made arrangements to move, as did Bill.

However, we quickly recognized the significant financial burden of maintaining separate residences. We then agreed to continue living in the condo temporarily while we finalized the logistics of establishing separate addresses. Bill discussed the impending move with his therapist, who discerned that Bill did not want either of us to move out. With this understanding, Bill's therapist firmly stated that I, as a Christian believer, should not be the one to leave the unbeliever.

1 Corinthians 7 New King James Version:

Verse 13: *"And the woman which hath a husband that believeth not, and if he be pleased to dwell with her, let her not leave him."*

Verse 14: " For the unbelieving husband is sanctified by the wife, and the unbelieving wife is sanctified by the husband: else were your children unclean; but now are they holy."

Bill's attitude had not changed. He acted as though I were compelled to live with him, so there was no need for counseling. We should just keep on as we had been. He would go to church, but no counseling was needed.

After some discussion without emotion, just a casual conversation, Bill asked what he should do. "Perhaps you should ask the minister what you should do?" I said. He made an appointment with Menlo Church's minister. The minister called a group of men together and presented Bill's problem. One of the three men the minister spoke with said he would like to meet with Bill.

Bill followed the counselor's suggestions and decided to believe in Jesus, the son of God, whom he had never seen. Believing was already a part of Bill's knowledge. He believed the chair would hold him when he sat in it, so Bill guessed he could believe that a son of God named Jesus came to earth and died for his sins.

One morning, I said, "Bill, now you know too much about Jesus not to accept him. This knowledge puts you in a dangerous position. Every day you refuse to profess your knowledge of Christ, you are rejecting Him." Bill responded, "What should I do?" I quoted:

Romans 10:10:

"For with your heart you believe and are justified, and with your mouth you confess and are saved."

Then I said, "You should make that confession right now in a prayer to God."

Bill put out his hand and said, "Dear Lord, I am sorry for my sins, and they are many. Please forgive me and save me. Amen." He said, "Is that all?"

I said, "At the first opportunity, you should publicly profess what you have just done, be baptized, and join the church. Your behavior should be a testimony of what you believe. "

I may not have said all that, but over the next day or two, we discussed "What Bill should do." Our anniversary was coming up on April 7th. At the same time, the Menlo Church was holding a two-day study session. We signed up to go. It was there that Bill made his public profession of faith.

A group that wanted to join the church met for a long session with the pastor. After the session, the names of those who had accepted Christ for the first time were asked to stand at church, and they professed their salvation and their intent to join Menlo Church.

What a great day in our 31-year marriage! Bill spent a great deal of time confessing his sins. He wanted everyone he had sinned against to know he was sorry and to make things right. After his conversion, we had a much happier life.

Bill Takes Up Painting

Bill's move from a house in Woodside to a Redwood City condo freed up his time to pursue painting as a hobby.

156_Photo: Bill's Paintings

Despite creating many high-quality pieces, he had no interest in selling or exhibiting his artwork. As he painted, I requested a painting from him as a gift for each holiday, birthday, and anniversary. Over time, this resulted in my collection of his art.

Spending Time with My My Girls and Grandkids

Patsy treated me, Joni, and Mary Ruth to a trip to the wine country.

157_Photo: Patsy, Bobbi, Joni, MaryRuth (2001)

158_Photo: Eric, Brian, Bobbi, Adam, Haley (2001)

Trusting God Through Another Loss

Bill and I enjoyed friendships with individuals from the Alpine Hills Tennis Club for several years. We participated in a dinner group, regularly attended church on Sundays, and participated in a prayer group. During one prayer group meeting, a member shared his Parkinson's disease diagnosis and described his symptoms in some detail. Upon hearing these symptoms, Bill became concerned

that he might also have Parkinson's.

159_Photo: Bobbi, Bill (2004)

Bill seemed to develop the adverse effects of the disease slowly. His everyday life was slowly ebbing away, and it was inevitable that he would need some in-home care. A delightful and strong woman came each morning to handle his bathing and dressing. She had a great sense of humor, and Bill depended on her for total care. I also relied on her for housework. She cleaned the house while Bill slept and even started dishes for our evening meal.

By noon, I had played tennis, shopped, done the laundry, and handled the mail. So, the afternoons and early evenings were spent interacting with Bill. It was a delightful time. We talked about spiritual things, our trips, and what the kids and friends were doing. It was a good time in our marriage, and I cherish it.

Our Sundays Church groups were praying for Bill. His hospice and "in-house" care was caring for his physical comfort.

I joined Valley Presbyterian Church in Portola Valley because I could care

for him until Mary Ruth or Eric could relieve me at 10:00 a.m.

160_Photo: *Valley Presbyterian Church*

Valley Church began at 10:30 A.m. and needed deacons. I had been a deacon at Menlo Church, so I was accepted as a member at Valley, but I had to abandon my membership at Menlo Church.

One morning, Bill got up to go to the bathroom. He usually sat on the side of the bed until I could come around and walk with him. However, that morning, he did not wait for me. He fell and broke his leg. His leg healed quickly, but he was still in rehab when he decided he did not wish to go through any more falls. His balance was getting unpredictable. Falling was always going to be a problem.

Bill's children came to listen to his plea to accept his decision to die. They needed to know that I had no input into his decision; it was his idea and decision. The Menlo Church minister, Frank VanderZwan, could not persuade Bill to try to live.

Bill was dismissed from the hospital to enter hospice care in a home close to the condo.

In 1979, Bill decided to give us a more leisurely lifestyle. We had no children at home, and Bill was close to retirement. Looking back on that decision to sell and live in a condominium, it was paying off. He would leave me in a good situation without much house maintenance. Thirty-seven years later, in 2016, Bill was ready to "cash in on life." He knew his new life would be in "heaven."

Bill chose not to eat. We did not tell him any negative things that were going on. Someone saw him daily: his daughter, Mary Ruth, son, Chris, me, or a friend. After the first couple of weeks, it was too painful to see him. He slept most of the time. It seemed a burden on him to have visitors. I saw very little of him during the last week of his life.

Church groups were praying for Bill. Because Bill was not home, I could go to Menlo Church's early service, greet my friends after worship, and then go to Valley Presbyterian Church at 10:30. It was so comforting to have such good Christians walking with me through this trying time. The Women's group meetings led by Reborn were beneficial to me. I was meeting with this group on July 10, 2016, when I felt the desire to see Bill. I left the group praying for him.

I entered Bill's room, got in bed with him, and said, "Bill, if you want to be with God, go with my blessing. I love you and want you with me, but I will be with you in Heaven just a few minutes after you get there." I kissed him and left the room. He seemed to hear me.

I talked to those who had cared for him for the next three weeks. I asked them, "What is keeping Bill alive? He has not eaten in three weeks." They gave me an answer, but it came from the spirit: "It is time now for Bill to come home."

I left where Bill was and went directly to see an ex-neighbor living at the Retirement Home down the street from the Condo. As soon as I arrived in the parking lot, my cell phone rang, and the hospice told me that when I left Bill, they went in to check on him, and he breathed his last breath then.

Immediately, the process was undertaken to get Bill's brain analyzed and his body parts taken to study.

I went ahead and visited my friend, and we prayed together. The notifications went out about William Patrick Batchelder's death on July 16, 2016. The funeral was set for August 24, 2016, my 83rd birthday, at Menlo Church, Santa Cruz Ave, Menlo Park.

No Marriages in Heaven, But We Will Know Each Other

Program for William (Bill) Batchelder Memorial Service, August 24, 2016, included:

-Introduction by Frank Vanderzwan,
-Congregational singing,
-Solo prayers, and
-Speeches by
-Harley Parson,
-Dave Peterson
-Bobbi Batchelder.

-Reception followed the service with
-Photos of Bill's family were placed around the room, and a
-Video of Bill's art and activities, which included
-Football as a high school kid
-Children with his first wife, Jeanette: Mary Ruth, Patsy, and Chris
-Bill's Art

Bill's burial ceremony was held sometime after the Church Memorial Service. This happened because of where Bill was to be buried and the work necessary to obtain parts of his body preserved for science. Bill's daughter, Mary Ruth, her son, Eric, and I picked up Bill's ashes. We arranged to put the ashes in the reserved space for Bill in Golden Gate National Cemetery. The Military Memorial service was held at the main building inside the cemetery grounds. Mary Ruth Batchelder was handed the flag as part of the military ceremony.

We were pleased that we had considered military service. It was impressive. After the military part, the audience introduced themselves to the group. The small chapel held about 20 people. Mostly, the family was present. However, some military people were there, and at least one man from the Condo came. He had read about it in the paper, dressed in his uniform, and was in the audience. What nice support these people provided for Eric, Mary Ruth, Harley, and me.

After the chapel service, Mary Ruth, Eric, and others went to the grave site. The hole had been opened for the urn. Margie Barkhau had come to the Chapel, picked me up in her car, and taken me to the grave. I watched from the car as the ashes were buried.

This was William (Bill) Batchelder's earthly burial, concluding 43 years of marriage. I thought, "Bill and I will be together when we meet again. There will be no marriages where we go, but we will know each other. Oh, blessed day."

Living Alone
Making My Home My Own

I looked around my condo at #52, 50 Horgan Avenue, and realized that although we had upgraded a few finishes before moving in, very little had changed since Bill and I first settled there decades ago. The space still reflected a life that had passed—and I was ready for something new. The condo needed a facelift, and so did the way I lived in it. I didn't want to preserve it as a shrine to the past; I wanted to fully embrace the life ahead.

I hired a contractor and welcomed his design ideas, approving most of them without hesitation.

161_Photo: New Kitchen

Over several months, the transformation took shape. Closets in all three bedrooms were modernized, and sleek new cabinets were added around the garage. I stepped aside and gave the team full access—playing tennis in the mornings and occasionally spending the night at Barbara Sequoia's condo across the way.

When the renovation was complete, I furnished the space entirely on my own terms. I bought new pieces that felt fresh, functional, and reflective of who I was becoming—not who I had been.

162_Photo: New Furniture

The extra bedroom became a proper guest room. Every closet was redone. Even the toilet had a heated seat. I opened my home to friends for visits and meals, delighted to host in a space that was now fully mine. It wasn't just a remodeled condo—it was a renewed life, lived forward.

Cultivating Community and Family

I remained an active member of the Dinner Group and continued sharing meals with Peter and Leslie. At the same time, I deepened my involvement at both Menlo Church and Valley Presbyterian, finding strength and purpose in those communities. With Joni's move to Woodside, she began hosting family holidays and birthdays, which gave me even more joyful opportunities to stay connected with those I love. My circle of faith, family, and friendship was strong—and growing.

The Gift That Cost Me

I had made a clear decision: I would use funds from my investments for my daily living expenses, and preserve the condo as part of the inheritance for my children and Bill's children. Still, while I was alive, I wanted to offer something more personal and meaningful—my hope was to help each sibling own a home of their own.

When I shared this intention, my step son, Christian—who was managing my finances—strongly disagreed. He believed it was a poor financial choice and warned that if I proceeded with my plan to purchase a condo for one of his siblings, he would resign from managing my finances. I told him I understood, and I accepted his resignation.

Unfortunately, the fallout went deeper than financial. My relationship with Chris was broken, and regular contact was lost. The emotional toll was far heavier than I had anticipated. Adding to the pain, the sibling I had hoped to help, declined the gift. In a heartfelt attempt to restore the relationship, I later offered to reinstate Chris as my financial manager—but he declined.

In the end, I was left with a deep sadness. My desire to give was sincere, but the cost turned out to be far greater than I imagined. I had meant to bless my family—and instead, I lost part of it.

Overdoing to Overcome

Becoming swamped was most likely due to trying to overcompensate for the losses I was having. Here are some of the activities in which I was involved:

- Remaining active in the Dinner Group.
- Working with two Stephen Ministers in the Stephen Ministry program.
- Participating in two churches.
- Caring for my friend Patti Harvey, who had cancer.
  163_Photo: Patti Harvey

Caring for the Body God Gave Me

I became more intentional about caring for my body. As a Kaiser member, I kept up with regular checkups and followed my doctors' recommendations. Hearing aids helped with my declining hearing, and cataract surgery improved my vision. When Kaiser added dental coverage, I even had my teeth straightened with braces.

She Left His Side to Stand by Mine

I had developed a bunionette—a bony growth on the outside of my right foot. Although it wasn't painful, it distorted the shape of my shoe. My doctor advised against surgery due to my age, but I felt strong, capable, and determined. I insisted on going forward with the procedure. Knowing I'd need help during recovery, I called my sister, Angie. She immediately offered to come to California from Amarillo, arranging for her daughters to check in on her husband, Troy, at the senior center.

The surgery went smoothly, and I returned home the same day. Angie, a trained nurse, took wonderful care of me. I experienced no pain and wore a walking cast for ten weeks. Not wanting her to feel cooped up while helping me recover, I arranged for ten friends to each take her on a small outing—one for each week she was with me.

Over the course of her stay, Angie enjoyed:

- Dinners at the homes of three couples from my Dinner Group
- Attending Menlo Church and meeting Diane Julian, Jim, and Patty Harvey
- Viewing Stanford's campus from the top of Hoover Tower
- Visiting a Half Moon Bay winery and making me a candle holder bowl at a glass-blowing shop
- Exploring Golden Gate Park and the Natural History Museum
- A duck pond picnic in Palo Alto
- Lunch by the ocean along the coast
- Shopping in Pescadero and buying fresh bread
- Easter services at Valley Presbyterian Church
- Family luncheons at the Alpine Tennis Club

During our quiet time together, she taught me to play Mahjong—a game I had only dabbled in before. We passed the days playing cards, watching the Kansas Jayhawks, and sharing endless laughter.

One Kaiser checkup included an MRI, scheduled while I was still in my cast. Angie helped me navigate the long hallways on a knee scooter. That trip turned into a comedy: I pushed off the walls to stay straight while Angie ran behind, laughing, trying to catch up. We raced through the hospital corridors like two mischievous kids—and just barely made it to the appointment on time.

Back home, we toasted our victory with champagne while we waited for results. A little too much celebrating resulted in a misstep—I fell and gave myself a black eye that proved difficult to explain!

When the cast came off, Angie saw how well I was doing. I no longer needed help, and she knew it. With Troy's health declining rapidly, she returned to Amarillo to be by his side, visiting him daily until his passing in 2017.

I'll always treasure those ten weeks—filled with sisterhood, silliness, healing, and love.

At Peace With Two Years More to Live

Sometime later, the doctor called. The MRI tests that I had when I was recovering from my foot surgery, pointed to the need for additional tests—not in Redwood City, but at Kaiser Santa Clara.

When the doctor told me there were two dark spots on one lung and a confirmed cancerous spot on the other, I felt a quiet stillness settle over me. While many might expect panic or despair, what I felt most deeply was trust—trust in the God who had carried me through every season of my life.

Kaiser recommended a biopsy and chemotherapy, but after prayer and reflection, I knew in my spirit that I would not pursue aggressive treatment. I didn't feel called to fight death, but rather to embrace life—however long it would be—with grace and purpose. I signed the document declining extraordinary life-saving measures, not out of fear or resignation, but from a place of surrender.

I placed my future entirely in God's hands. I believed He had numbered my days, and no scan or prognosis could alter that sacred timeline. I wanted to live whatever time remained fully present—with peace in my heart, my faith unshaken, and my eyes fixed on eternity. Whether I had two years or two days, I belonged to Him—and that was enough.

I called Angie.

She Left Everything—for Me

She had already heard about my diagnosis and, without hesitation, offered to come stay with me for the two years I was expected to live. She had just buried her husband and thoughtfully downsized her life in Amarillo—selling everything she didn't wish to keep. It was a season of letting go for both of us. Angie returned to be with me as I made preparations to die.

Preparing a Place—Body, Home, and Soul

Back at the condo in Redwood City, Angie and I reflected on the time she had come to care for me after my hammer toe and bunion surgery. When she arrived, we immediately reorganized the living and sleeping spaces to give her privacy and a sense of comfort—doing our best to recreate the space and independence she had known in Texas.

But this wasn't just about physical arrangements. From the very beginning, one of our shared priorities was to find a spiritual home together. As we settled into this unexpected new chapter—two sisters under one roof—we began the process of establishing church membership, side by side, anchoring ourselves not just in routine, but in faith.

What Do Presbyterians Believe? A Sister's Search

Angie was unfamiliar with the idea of being a Presbyterian. She said, "I don't know what Presbyterians believe." I said, "Here's a brochure for the 30th Presbyterian Women's Gathering in Louisville, Kentucky, on August 2-5, 2018. We could go to the Women's Gathering, and you can find out about it."

Angie was very interested, so we signed up to go to the Presbyterian Women's Gathering in Louisville, Kentucky. Anticipating a short life, I booked the finest room available at the conference hotel, opting to travel "first class."

When Angie and I arrived in Louisville and waited for the bus to take us from the airport to our hotel, we saw two women waiting. These two women,

Michael Walters and Joyce Summers, were from San Jose and had booked a room close to ours. We became instant friends.

Here is Angie's report of that time in Louisville:

"As a new attendee of the Portola Valley Presbyterian Church, I had the privilege and honor to attend the Louisville, KY, Presbyterian Women's

Gathering. I was overwhelmed by the gathering women's love, compassion, and friendliness. I enjoyed the sessions and was glad to pick up material from the bookstore that I could use.

164_Photo: Bobbi Angie, Dressing Alike (2019)

My sister Bobbi and I were often headed in different directions, so being dressed alike among 1500 people surely helped us keep in touch."

Angie and I traveled from the airport to our hotel with two new acquaintances from San Jose, CA: Michael Walters and Joyce Summers, both Presbyterian women. We dined together and made plans for the following day, as the conference was scheduled to begin later in the week.

Tour of the historical houses

Wednesday was free, so we arrived in Louisville early to explore before the gathering. Our first activity was a tour of the historic houses. Our pre-tour manager, Michell, had arranged reservations with David Domine to guide us

through the numerous blocks of historical residences. The Victorian area's homes attracted wealthy individuals to Louisville, who then constructed the Victorian mansions we observed on our tour.

165_Photo: Victorian Mansion

We were particularly struck by St. James Court, where every house along the boulevard was a prestigious mansion.

This Court is still illuminated by gas lights, which were once lit nightly by a lamplighter. A carved old tree now stands as a tribute to this lamplighter. This reminded us of the song:

THE OLD LAMPLIGHTER
Here's a link to song sung by The Browns (https://tinyurl.com/yc24bvnb0)

A tree by one of the homes in another area is decorated with all types of items, denoting it as a place where spells occur. The legend states that City officials destroyed the tree for use in a May Day celebration. The witches curse the city for destroying their gathering place. Within a year, a tornado destroyed the City. It sent a magical tree in its place. The tree has burls, a twisted trunk, and craggy bark with dead branches and limbs overhead. This tree is better fitting for witches. The witches come back now in full force. Visitors from all over leave trinkets for good luck.

At this tree and one like it in the park, Angie and I sang Halloween songs:
"Halloween, Halloween, Oh what funny things are seen
witches on brooms with cats and bats
fly right after dark in their funny black hats
how queer are the noises on Halloween night
and then through the window, I see a strange light..
big scary eyes and a big red nose
i get close to mother and curl up my toes,
it's old jack-o-lantern; he peeks in the room
a worse looking spook than a witch on a broom.
halloween night is lots of fun
but sometimes i'm glad when it's over and done
it's good to have mother to kiss me goodnight

A three-mile walking tour in Louisville, led by the knowledgeable author David Domine, who has penned twelve books, including some on haunted history, offered an engaging hour and a half exploring the city's past through eerie tales of haunted houses and locations. Domine's recommendation led to a delightful lunch at a unique restaurant housed in a historic building, where each china plate boasted a distinct design and the service and food were exceptional.

Our visit to Louisville included a trip to the renowned Churchill Downs, which lived up to its reputation. I was particularly thrilled to find commemorative plaques for my favorite horses: Secretariat, Seattle Slew, and Mine That Bird. We enjoyed browsing the shops and tried on various hats.

Presbyterian Women's Gathering

The Gathering started on Thursday evening. Every day thereafter was filled with sessions and exhibits. Our Synod of San Francisco hosted us for a gathering to get to know each other better and let us know what will be in store this coming year.

We did get to use our room on the tenth floor of the Galt Hotel. The windows and balcony overlooked the Ohio River, and we could view all the bridges that crossed the river into Indiana. Touring boats docked on the river were old paddlewheel boats, and people could book dinner as they rode. Unfortunately, we had no time to take advantage of that entertainment.

Our friends could join us in our suite for breakfast each morning. Joyce informed us about a tour to Scotland in September 2018. The tour guide booking tours for 2019 informed us that there were still two places on the September 2018 tour, so Angie and I signed up.

Each morning, a bulletin gave a synopsis of the day before. This kept information before us and helped us store the multitude of experiences we had in our memories.

This Presbyterian Gathering helped me understand how the women of the church, through the organization of missions, have brought women into leading roles. Women's Church leadership is effective not only in their churches but also in communities, influencing societies all over the world.

REPORT OF THE PRESBYTERIAN GATHERING

Angie wrote a "trip report" for the trip and gave copies to all of our friends:

Angie: *"Angie Mitchell and Bobbi Batchelder just returned from the 2018 (August 2-5) 30th Presbyterian Women's Gathering in Louisville, Kentucky.*

Can you imagine being in a worship service with 1500 Women and a dozen or so men worshiping the Lord all day? The sessions ran from Thursday to

Sunday, with a half-day session on Thursday, all day on Friday and Saturday, and one-half-day on Sunday.

What a spiritual high! We sang, prayed, read scripture, and got to know our neighbors. We became acquainted with many Californians, Women from all over the US, and women from foreign countries. Some were interested in working for justice and peace, some in eradicating hunger, prejudice, gun violence, racism, and violence against women.

We chose from dozens of workshops, including Healing Trauma through Performance, Immigration, How to Get Unstuck, Poetry of Isaiah, Gratitude Can Lead to Compassion, How We Can Answer God's Justice for Children, and many others.

After praying and feeling God's urging, it was there that I chose to attend:

- *Let's be Bold Presbyterian Women Making a Difference.*
- *Lessons in Laughter, Flipping Tables, and Finding Sheep.*

From those one met, it was easy to get an overview of the workshops they attended. Thus, even if the same workshop was attended, it was interesting to see what resonated with other participants in the same session. Our workshop experience doubled as we sat and talked to others.

Our room was the best in the hotel, with a balcony and wrap-around windows overlooking the river. The food wasn't so good but adequate. We were not there for physical "goods" but for spiritual. So we didn't dwell on the food for our stomachs, just for the Spirit.

We hope and pray for women in every circumstance. We want to keep up with those we met in Africa, Korea, and the Philippines, and grow closer to those in our community.

We give God the Glory for our wonderful time from July 31-August 5, 2018, in Louisville, KY."

I added a few additional thoughts to Angie's trip report:

Bobbi: *"Angie mentioned something in her report that I want to expand on: 'Bobbi, my sister, and I were often headed in different directions, so being dressed alike among 1500 people surely helped us keep in touch."*

Indeed, we were having trouble meeting up after getting out of our different workshops. Once, when we caught up, Angie suggested we go into a store. She pointed out a dress she liked and noted one in my size. We bought one or two just alike and began to wear them when we knew we would be in different workshops. Even then, we had trouble finding each other as 1,500 women streamed from their different small group workshops.

To make it easy to get together, we would say, "Have you seen a woman dressed like I am?" The questioned woman would point to where she had seen the other one last. Workshops and exhibits were on different floors and parts of a long hall. It became easier not to say anything but just point with a questioning look, and women would point to where the one who looked like the other was.

We became wise enough to tell each other where to meet after a session. We were also smart enough to buy two sets of clothes. That way, instead of having just two sets, we could mix and match, making several outfits. I would stipulate what we would wear one day, and the next day, Angie would choose. That added so much to our experience.

Angie Joins Presbyterian Church

Returning from the Louisville Women's Conference, I asked, "Angie, do you think you could be a Presbyterian based on what you have experienced at the Presbyterian Gathering?" Her answer, "Yes," was followed by attending a Valley Elder's Meeting and giving this testimony:

Faith Story by Angie Mitchell:

"I was raised in a Baptist based home. I learned about God and was taught Bible lessons and worshiped in church every Sunday and Wednesday. I learned Bible verses from memory.

As I became older I married a man, who was not a person of faith. Yet I went to church and took my children with me. There they learned about God. However, my relationship with the Lord was not a personal one. I thought this would change but since my husband was in the service we moved around a lot making it hard to find help in growing my faith.

When my children accepted the Lord, I realized that my acceptance of Christ as my Savior many years ago was not enough. I needed to follow through as His disciple.

With the help of our pastor and a Bible Study Group which became my spiritual mentors I realized what Christ did for me personally. His dying on the cross meant He carried my sins with Him to the grave, He rose again without my sins thus giving me newness of life.

Through my baptism I symbolized what Christ did. He died, was buried, and rose again. I have the faith that through grace, I will live with Him forever.

I believe in one body in Christ, one God and the Holy Spirit. I believe in participating in the Lord's Supper, which to me is a reminder of what Christ did for me by shedding His blood cleansing me from my sins.

I am looking forward to being a member of Valley Presbyterian Church and taking an active part in it."

Upon her return, Angie and I decided to not repeat any of the things Angie had seen before when she helped me recover from my foot surgery, but to have new experiences::

- Seeing San Luis Obispo where two Batchelder kids and Harley Parson had attended school.
- Seeing all the California missions and taking away replicas
  - Creating a display map of all the missions,
  - Displaying replicas of each mission and its history.
- Traveling to Idaho to see
  - My son, Harley Parson,
  - The Idaho State Fair,
  - The sunset from the top of the mountain overlooking the area.
  - A total solar eclipse.
    - When the sun was hidden, the temperature dropped ten degrees. It was a once-in-a-lifetime experience.
    - Harley had chosen some games to play while we waited for the eclipse. He also brought all the items needed to cook our food and made everything comfortable while we waited for the great event. His hosting was very impressive.
- Attending two churches on Sunday:.
  - Menlo church met at 8:30 AM, and
  - Valley Presbyterian Church at 10:45 AM
- Getting involved in numerous church activities at Valley Presbyterian:
  - Angie: Teaching the Children and playing in the bell choir.
  - I became an usher.
  - Became members of a social group of women 50 and over.
  - Became acquainted with all the children at the church, from newborns through High School.
  - Tried to attend all the performances of the theater group connected to the church,
  - Became deacons,
  - Attended Valley Church's Women's Retreat in Santa Cruz and local places of interest
    - The Retreat Center was right on the ocean.
    - The first attendees got the best rooms overlooking the sea.
    - The Retreat was a spiritual renewal and physically restful.

- At Menlo Church:
  - We got to know the Harvey family.
    - One Sunday, we were standing around visiting after church when a photographer asked the six of us to stand apart. He then took our picture, which was blown up three feet by five feet and hung in the Church's front entrance, where it remained for 10 years. Recently, the picture was taken down and given to me. It is now hanging on the wall at my home. As was our custom, Angie and I were dressed alike.

166_Photo: At Menlo

  - Menlo Church began teaching the congregation about various spiritual subjects in small groups. One of these sessions focused on SPIRITUAL GIFTS. In 1 Corinthians 12:4-11, it states,
    - *"There are different kinds of spiritual gifts, but they are all from the same Spirit."*
    - *"There are different ways to serve, but we serve the same Lord."*
    - *"And there are different ways that God works in people, but it is the same God who works in all of us to do everything."*
    - *"Something from the Spirit can be seen in each person. The Spirit gives this to each one to help others."*
    - *"The Spirit gives one person the ability to speak with wisdom, and the same Spirit gives another person the ability to speak with knowledge."*

208

- *"The same Spirit gives faith to one person, and to another, he gives gifts of healing."*
- *"The Spirit gives one person the power to do miracles, to another the ability to prophesy, and to another the ability to discern what is from the Spirit and what is not."*
- *"The Spirit gives one person the ability to speak in different kinds of languages, and to another, the ability to interpret those languages".*
- *"One Spirit, the same Spirit, does all these things. The Spirit decides what to give each one."*

What Can I Give?

At the end of the teaching session, a Spiritual Gifts Assessment was conducted, and my most significant spiritual gift turned out to be "Giving." This sparked questions in my mind: What could I give? Who would be the recipient? How could I make the most meaningful impact through my giving?

Over time, it became clear that I could write notes and place them in a homemade paper box I had learned to make. I began handing these boxes to people, and soon the notes evolved into Bible verses. Each box contained a

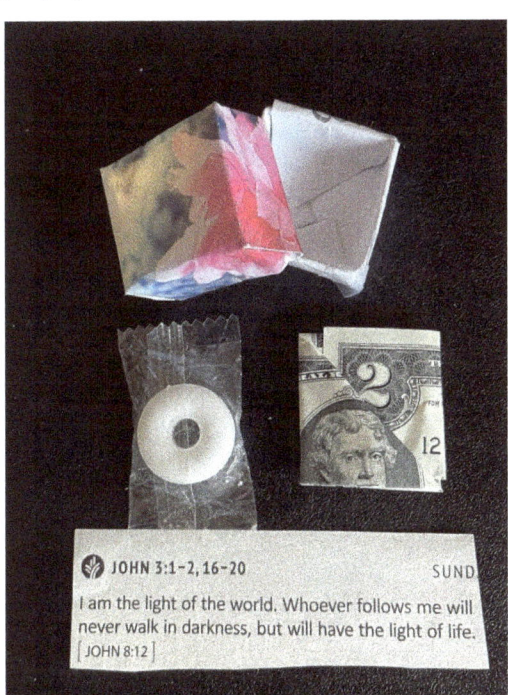

verse, a piece of candy, and often a $2 bill. I carried two or three in my purse and distributed them at church or when I encountered someone in a store.

167_Photo: My Gift Box
Eventually, I placed notes in boxes, gift sacks, or multicolored gift-wrapping paper and left them at each of the 60 doors in the condo complex where I lived. My sister Angie and I made about a hundred gifts each year, distributed at the Buckner Orphans Home Reunion. Church groups also received these gifts; the Parson

209

Batchelder Cropper family would get one at each holiday family dinner celebration.

It's hard to say when I started giving $2 bills in various ways, and I often wonder if I will ever stop. What keeps me giving is the joy I feel when I give. Since my time in the orphanage, I have wanted to share whatever I have with others. Honestly, I can affirm, "It is more blessed to give than to receive.

Becoming Special Friends with Patty and Jim Harvey

Patty and Jim Harvey became good friends with Angie and me. We were saddened when we learned that Patty had a severe form of cancer and became very sick.

168_Photo: Jim and Patty Harvey (2018)

When Patty Harvey became too ill to attend church, I would go during the week to help Patty. I would fix meals for the three of us and keep the bathrooms, kitchen, dining room, and porch clean. Patty had terminal cancer. With Jim's knowledge of how to treat her, Patty's life was extended. Jim and Patty's daughter came the last few days and took care of Patty until cancer took Patty's life. Patty was not afraid of death; she knew she would be with Jesus.

When Jim started returning to church after Patty died,, he and Angie became good friends. On Sunday morning, Jim would greet Angie by saying, "Good morning, Sunshine." In return, Angie would say, "Good morning, Moonbeam." After church, they would exchange information, laugh, and enjoy being together. Angie was popular with other people at Menlo. She was well-respected and sought after when exchanging information.

Daily Double

After our unforgettable trip to Louisville, the habit of dressing alike followed us home—and soon became a full-blown routine. Angie had lost

168_Photo: Matched Pairs

weight and needed a new wardrobe. My closet was already full, but that didn't stop her from encouraging me to buy something similar every time she picked out something new. Before long, my closet was overflowing—but I found myself only reaching for outfits that matched hers anyway.

We took turns planning our ensembles.Angie would choose what we wore one day, and I'd pick the next. Coordinating our clothes wasn't just a quirky habit; it became a delightful ritual, a way of saying, "We're in this together." Matching clothes, matching spirits.

When God Touched Me, My Cancer was Gone

Angie had been living with me for a while, helping me through what we both expected would be the final chapter of my life. I was supposed to get worse—but I didn't. Then one quiet day, I felt the unmistakable presence of God. It was as if His hand rested gently on me, and in that moment, I felt healed. I began praising Him with everything in me. It wasn't dramatic or loud—it was sacred. I didn't tell anyone right away. I needed to wait. I knew the truth would eventually come to light through a doctor's report.

When the day came, I went in for testing. The results came back—no sign of cancer. The doctor, still cautious, ordered more tests. But I told him what I knew in my soul: "I've been cured by the hand of God." He paused and said simply, "That happens."

From that day forward, something shifted in me. I wanted to live—truly live. I wanted to laugh more, travel more, and soak up every single day I had been given. I was so grateful to have Angie by my side, and I suddenly found myself dreaming again—dreaming of seeing the world. Life wasn't over. It had just begun again.

A Flourishing Faith Community

Angie and I became deeply involved in church life—both at Menlo Church and Portola Valley Presbyterian. At Menlo, I stepped into a leadership role with a group of women called "Presbyterian Women." What began as a small gathering quickly grew into a vibrant community of over 100 women. It brought

me so much joy to see the group flourish, united by faith, friendship, and a shared desire to serve.

169_Photo: Frank VanderZwan

Menlo was filled with gifted, charismatic leaders who inspired us to grow in our walk with Christ. One of the most memorable was Frank VanderZwan.

His sermons spoke directly to the heart, and his gift for connecting with people created a genuine sense of belonging. Angie and I always left feeling uplifted and spiritually renewed. We were deeply grateful to be part of such a vibrant and faithful church community.

Frank VanderZwan was the minister of the 8:30 a.m. service at Menlo Church. After each Sunday service, he led a Sunday School class in the Fellowship Hall that was so well-loved it filled the entire room. Once a month, he also hosted a Friday night dinner in the same hall, followed by a special program in the church auditorium. These evenings were rich with fellowship and spiritual growth. Frank introduced us to many remarkable people over the years, including Condoleezza Rice, former U.S. Secretary of State. Through his interviews, we learned about her upbringing, education, career in politics, love of music, and faith. It was inspiring to hear her personal journey and to witness how her belief in God shaped her life.

When Your Pastor Becomes Your Tour Guide

Quite suddenly, the much-beloved. Frank VanderZwan announced his retirement and moved to a small town in California's Central Valley, where he joined another church, but he didn't stop ministering. He began a new chapter—organizing and leading travel groups around the world. This new venture aligned perfectly with Angie's and my plans to see more of the world together. We eagerly joined Frank on three unforgettable tours—to Paris, Italy, and China. Traveling under his leadership deepened our appreciation for culture, history, and community.

Do You Want a Lick?

One afternoon, Angie and I drove to the Post Office at Woodside Plaza to mail some letters. Angie was still writing hers, so—worried I'd miss the 5 p.m. pickup—I left her in the car and hurried inside.

After mailing my letter, I stepped outside and hesitated—should I head back to the car or wait for Angie by the building? As I stood there, lost in thought, I noticed a man nearby, happily enjoying an ice cream cone.

Without warning, he turned to me and asked, "Do you want a lick?" Startled, I realized I was standing quite close to this stranger. I grinned and replied, "No, but I want to watch you eat it." He took a bite, and I added, "Oh, that looks so good." He paused, offering the cone again, teasingly. I shook my head. "I bet that tastes amazing." With a twinkle in his eye, he said, "Well, I'll just have to buy you one."

We made plans to meet the next day for ice cream. Just then, Angie came rushing into the post office to mail her letter, and while she was inside, the charming ice-cream stranger and I exchanged names and phone numbers.

And that's how I met Dennis Austin.

Scammed, Stood Up, and Saved

The next morning, shortly after breakfast, I received a disturbing phone call. A man claiming to be from the phone company told me I owed money on my account. I was confused—my phone bill was set to autopay, and I hadn't received any notices.

He said I needed to pay immediately using a gift card. "Go to the nearest store," he instructed, "buy a gift card for the amount due, and call me back with the number on the back. I'll wait."

In a rush, I drove to Rite Aid in Woodside Plaza—the same place Angie and I had been the day before. I picked up a gift card and headed to the cashier. He paused and asked, "Did someone ask you to buy this?" Cautiously, I replied, "Why do you ask?" He said, "This has been happening a lot lately—scammers pretending to be bill collectors."

I paid for the card but felt uneasy. I sat down on a bench outside the store, holding the card, replaying the conversation in my mind. Something wasn't right. Then it hit me—I was supposed to meet Dennis here... over an hour ago!

Frantically, I pulled out the slip of paper with his name and number and called him. "Were you at Rite Aid like we planned?" I asked. "Yes," he said. "I waited an hour. I thought I'd been stood up."

I quickly explained what had happened. Dennis didn't hesitate: "Don't call that number back. It's a scam. Go inside and see if they'll let you return the card."

I went back and found the same cashier. "We don't usually take gift cards back," he said, "but I'll make an exception." Relieved, I got my money refunded.

Just then, my phone rang again—it was Angie. "The phone company man just called," she said. "He wants the number on the back of the card—should I give it to him?" "No, Angie," I said. "It's a scam! Don't call him back."

And that, thankfully, was the end of that misadventure.

Is This a Date or a Disaster?

After I got my money back from the gift card fiasco, Dennis called and asked if I'd be open to giving dating a try. I asked point-blank, "Are you involved with anyone?" He said, "Well, I have a girlfriend, but I'm not married."

That wasn't the answer I'd hoped for—but still, I decided to see where things might go and agreed to have a date with him.

When Dennis picked me up in his convertible, he joked, "At least this time you won't have an excuse to stand me up!"

We went for ice cream at a shop on Santa Cruz Avenue in Menlo Park. It was nice enough that we made another date—and yes, it involved more ice cream. But something about it didn't sit right with me. He still had a "significant other," and I could feel that continuing down this path might lead to confusion or even heartache. I told him, "I'd like you to meet my sister Angie."

From then on, Angie and I began meeting Dennis for lunch at his home—with his girlfriend present. At one of those lunches, while seated at the table, Dennis started playing footsies with me under the table. I was caught off guard. Why was he making flirty gestures when someone else was right there? He hadn't shown that kind of attention when we were alone. The whole situation felt odd and uncomfortable.

Still, when Dennis invited us to lunch again—this time showing off the beautiful new gazebo he'd built with a full outdoor kitchen—I agreed. Other guests were coming, and Angie was with me, so I felt it was safe. What could possibly happen?

No More Travel, No More Angie, Just Me

COVID brought the world to a halt. Frank's international trips were canceled, and the joy of group travel disappeared overnight. Even church gatherings moved online, with Zoom replacing face-to-face fellowship. The vibrant community Angie and I had built now existed only through screens and phone calls.

I had already planned and paid for several trips for the two of us, but one by one, each was canceled. As the months dragged on, Angie began to speak of home—her real home in Texas. Though my family had become her family, and everyone she met in California adored her, something deeper was calling her back.

It was hard to accept. Angie wasn't just popular; she was magnetic. Wherever she went—grocery stores, Bible study, walks around the neighborhood—people didn't just like her; they loved her. She lit up rooms. Yet despite that, she longed for Texas. And so, with a heavy heart, I watched her go.

The laughter, companionship, and rhythm of shared life faded into quiet. I missed her terribly, but I knew she needed to be where her heart had led her. Suddenly, I was living alone again.

A Change at Residence #52

I wrote the note for those who became close friends with Angie and, hopefully, are still my friends without Angie.

"There has been a change in residence #52. My sister, Angie, has gone home to Texas.

Angie, a retired nurse, came to care for me when I was diagnosed with cancer in both lungs. Fast forward a year, and healing took place at God's discretion. Angie and I were busy traveling together. For four years, there were places to go. When COVID hit, we could not travel.

Even though Angie enjoyed widespread popularity, she decided to go home to Texas. She will reside in Amarillo, where two sons live with their families.

I am left with people saying, "How is Angie?" "Tell Angie I said I miss her." "When is Angie coming to visit?" It seems that every single day since Angie left, I have heard someone ask about her. Angie had nothing against the Enclave, any of my relatives living here or me, her sister, or even any of the neighbors. Everyone Angie met became a close friend.

What prompted Ange's leaving? She found that in California the taxes and insurance are just too high. She doesn't agree with California politics. She missed her family. She has three daughters, two in Texas, and two sons. Our brother is also there.

Angie's retired son-in-law from Arkansas decided to get the items we pulled together for her. She is renting a three-bedroom, two-bath home with a separate dining room. The house is on one floor and in a nice neighborhood with lots of yard space. She pays $1000 a month, with her son paying half. She works twice weekly as a receptionist in her son's business for pay.

As for me? I'm not going to leave California. I own a Condo here. My daughter is living in Woodside, another one is living in Redwood City and two great grandchildren are in the City. My son, from the Boise area has booked a flight to be with me for a week. Several of you count me as your friend. Therefore, I'm not moving.

I'm going to miss Angie, but I will be okay with: you, the duck family that has landed in the Enclave pool, Beth and her cat in #50, Barbara and her dog, Lucy in #47, and the two Mahjong players that play with me each week. "

"I kind of told my friends that you asked me to marry you."

Dennis called and invited Angie and me to lunch at his gazebo. I told him Angie had returned to Texas. Without missing a beat, he said, "Well then, why don't you come to lunch anyway?"

We set a time, and with great anticipation, I dressed nicely and arrived. I wasn't sure how this meeting would unfold. But our conversation was easy, warm, and filled with gentle laughter. He told me he was no longer seeing anyone—he'd broken up with his girlfriend—and wasn't interested in anyone else.

After lunch, we moved to the living room, where a fire was crackling. I noticed there was no coffee table between the sofa and the fireplace—only open space between us. I thought to myself, This man and I could make a good couple. I liked him. He seemed to like me. But I could tell he wasn't the marrying kind—he'd been single for 32 years. And I wasn't interested in being a "girlfriend." I wanted to be a bride.

We began dating, and one day I had to cancel a meeting with him because some of my relatives had come into town. I wondered if Dennis would take it personally—would this be the end of us? But he was understanding, even warm. That kindness told me all I needed to know: He's going to ask me to marry him.

The next day, when I met with my group of women, I said—somewhat boldly—"Dennis asked me to marry him!" The room erupted in congratulations and excitement. But when I met Dennis again, he hadn't proposed. Still, he gave every sign that he would. I decided to give him a little nudge: "I kind of told my friends yesterday that you asked me to marry you."

His eyes widened. "You didn't! Why would you say that? You don't even know me."

Embarrassed, I replied, "Well… I'll just tell them you didn't."

So back to the group I went, sheepishly: "He didn't ask me… but he will." And I added with a wink, "When he does, I'll make him come tell you himself!"

But time passed. I kept dropping hints. He kept saying, "You don't even know me."

Still, I didn't want to give up. When he invited me on a trip with him, I agreed. It was against my principles to live with someone before marriage, so I told my friends I was going away to think it over. I tried to keep it quiet that he was going too. I was walking a fine line—trying to respect my values, his perspective, and the curious eyes of my friends.

Dennis believed the only way to truly get to know each other was to live together, even for a short time. So we made arrangements to go away—to discover, decide, and perhaps…agree to get married.

Palm Desert Proposal

I had decided on La Costa in Carlsbad for our getaway, but I don't think Dennis was entirely on board. We spent our first night in a hotel in San Diego, and then settled into a two-week stay in Palm Desert. Each morning, I took group tennis lessons while Dennis played golf.

That first Sunday, we attended a Presbyterian church. After the service, the pianist, Daphne, approached us with a warm smile and said, "Come to our house for lunch." We accepted, not knowing this invitation would shape a core memory.

At Daphne and her husband Bill's beautiful home, dessert was served first, a tradition that immediately won me over. We gathered in a circle and each person shared who they were and why they were in Palm Desert. It turned out most were Canadians, and we were the only Americans at the table.

When it was our turn, Dennis and I shared our story—how we met and why we were away together. Someone asked, "So... how close are you two to making a decision?" I looked at Dennis, hoping for a revealing answer, but he skillfully changed the subject. Lunch followed—abundant and delicious—and then guests from the church arrived for an afternoon sing-along.

Daphne, who had played the piano in church that morning, now sat at her gleaming black grand piano and took requests from the group. Song after song filled the house with warmth and laughter. It was one of the most delightful Sunday afternoons I'd had in years.

170_Photo: Bill, Daphne Bobbi (2022)

The days passed quickly. Tennis in the morning, golf in the afternoon. I grew close to the tennis pro, a kind woman who later invited us to visit her home in Singapore—an invitation we haven't yet taken up, but still might.

Dennis and I were staying in a small apartment. We had quietly agreed that one day during this trip would be the day: Dennis would either ask me to marry him or explain why marriage wouldn't work.

That morning, I woke early, full of anticipation. "If you're going to ask me to marry you," I said, "please don't wait until after supper. Tell me before breakfast."

He smiled—and asked. "Will you marry me?" I didn't hesitate. "Yes!" I answered, my heart bursting.

171_Photo: Bobbi Dennis, Palm Desert (2022)

The rest of our time in Palm Desert truly felt like a honeymoon. We shared our joyful news with everyone we'd met—the warm-hearted Canadians, the welcoming church community, and the friendly folks at the tennis club. The celebration was heartfelt and sincere. Dennis and I strolled through shops hand-in-hand like teenagers, on a mission to find the perfect engagement ring.

At first, I had my heart set on a classic single diamond. We browsed the upscale jewelry stores, but nothing felt quite right. Then Dennis gently guided me toward Macy's. "You already have a single diamond," he said. "Let's find

something a little different—something that's ours."

And we did. The moment we saw it, we both exclaimed, "This is it!"

172_Photo: The Ring (2022)

The Presbyterian Church community in Palm Desert was the first to see my ring and hear our engagement story. Among our new friends were Daphne and Bill—Canadians who, like us, seemed to be falling in love all over again. Despite being the only Americans in the group, Dennis and I were instantly welcomed as if we'd always belonged.

Why would we be the only couple, not from Canada, who became solid friends with all members of this group? "God certainly works in mysterious ways His wonders to perform."

In God's Hands: A Courtside Miracle

After returning to our homes in the Bay Area, Dennis and I began planning our wedding. He was back at his place, and I was in my condo. His soon-to-be daughter-in-law, Loryn, kindly offered to be our wedding planner. We set the date: July 9, 2022, at Valley Presbyterian Church.

In the meantime, the Alpine Hills Tennis Club announced a pickleball tournament. Dennis and I signed up and arrived early to warm up. He was playing far better than I was, so when the teams were assigned, I suggested he join the intermediate players while I stayed with the beginners.

The courts were divided into two sections: beginners on one side, intermediates on the other. Sixteen players filled four courts. Among the onlookers was Rita Williams, a retired KTVU-TV reporter.

Warm-ups had barely begun when commotion broke out on the intermediate side. Rita came rushing over to me. Without explanation, she took my arm and began steering me toward the other court. As we approached, she gently placed her hand over my eyes. When she removed it, I saw Dennis lying on the ground.

He had collapsed mid-play. His opponent, Dr. Tina Molumphy, a medical doctor, rushed to his side. She immediately laid him flat, assessed him, and began CPR. She called out for Karen Giordano, a cardiac nurse on the next court. Together, they worked as a team, issuing calm but urgent instructions: "Get the AED!" "Call 911!" "Clear the court!"

173_Photo: Dr. Tina L. Molumphy MD
They worked on Dennis for over 20 minutes. Rita let go of my arm. I stood still as the others were cleared from the courts.

The tennis pro retrieved the Automated External Defibrillator (AED) from the clubhouse.

174_Photo: Automated External Defibrillator

Dennis's body jolted with each shock from the defibrillator.

I kept whispering to myself, He's in God's hands now.

Eventually, I was asked to step aside. As I rejoined the others watching from a distance, I tried to lighten the heaviness by saying, "He was losing!" The group chuckled gently. I added more soberly, "But truly—he's in God's hands." Another player walked over and said, "I can tell you're a Christian. May I pray?" And right there, in the middle of it all, he offered a beautiful prayer that comforted everyone.

When I was called back to the court, Dennis was breathing—oxygen mask in place. The paramedics arrived and worked carefully to stabilize him. Chuck Woo, the Swimming Director, arranged for me to ride with Dennis in the ambulance. As we headed to Stanford Hospital, I sat in front while the medics in the back tried to keep Dennis conscious.

"Dennis, it's Bobbi. Open your eyes. Talk to me. Dennis—say something," I called out, but he didn't respond.

We reached Stanford in under 15 minutes. In the emergency room, doctors confirmed that Dennis had suffered a sudden cardiac arrest—a far more dangerous event than a heart attack. The odds of surviving such an incident outside of a hospital are less than 5%. Even in a hospital, survival rates hover around 40%. The ER doctor said that if not for the immediate CPR, the cardiac nurse, and the defibrillator, Dennis wouldn't be alive. His ribs were broken, but CPR had done its job.

She explained the surgical plan: a triple bypass and valve replacement. Dennis, remarkably coherent, gave his consent.

Almost Mrs. Austin: A Wedding Postponed, A Faith Renewed

Dennis's two sons, Adrian and Derek, and I were allowed in Dennis's room, but only two at a time. Dennis seemed awake and coherent. While Dennis' boys were visiting, I met with my daughter, Joni, and her husband, David. They had brought my car to the hospital.

175_Photo: Bobbi: Stanford Hospital (2022)
I visited Dennis often while waiting for his operation on Monday, June 20, 2022. Adrian was also usually present. He seemed to be handling all the business related to Dennis' affairs. I was most interested in Dennis' comfort and kept him current on our relationship and the upcoming marriage planned for July 9, 2022.

It was Saturday, and Dennis knew he would be operated on in two days. On one of my visits to his room, Dennis awoke and said, " Let's get married before the operation." I was so happy. This meant I would be Mrs. Austin the next day, Sunday. I asked the nurse if it would be possible to hold a wedding in the hospital. She, in turn, asked the Head Nurse on the floor. It was "okay, " so we started planning. The nurses working with Dennis were excited.

Joni ensured our minister, Jenny Warner at Valley, was available at 3 p.m. Joni would be the Bridesmaid, and Adrian would be the Best Man. The nurses reminded us we could not have real flowers, so one nurse made the boutonnière and the bride's bouquet with " look-alike real flowers" (see picture above).

Everything was set for Sunday at 3 p.m. The minister would finish the Sunday morning service and make it to the hospital before 3 p.m.

On Sunday morning, I did not go to church; instead, I went to see Dennis at the hospital. What a surprise to hear him say, "I don't want to get married in the hospital today." In our discussion, Dennis noted that getting married before the operation is a lack of faith. He was hopeful that, with God's will, he would survive the operation. He did not want a hospital marriage. He wanted a proper wedding and marry in the Church with our friends.

That made sense, even if it meant undoing what we had just done. I agreed with Dennis' decision and accepted the fact that I would not be married on July 9th, 2022; Dennis would still be recovering from his operation. So a new date would have to be set. I could wait until he had completely recovered, but I was eager to be Dennis' wife.

Still Sharp, Still Standing—Dennis After the Storm

The operation went well. Dennis stayed in the hospital for a few days. He was sent home with a schedule for a nurse to be with him during the day. Dennis' two sons, Derek and Adrian, could be with him at night if he needed one of them. I wouldn't live with Dennis until we were married.

Despite having recently undergone a cardiac arrest and triple bypass surgery, Dennis' Palo Alto Medical Foundation (PAMF) cardiologist was unaware of his condition a month later. She suggested a different medication plan than the one the Stanford Hospital doctors used. Navigating conflicting medical advice, Dennis researched online, applied common sense, and aligned with the shared recommendations of both medical institutions. Ultimately, he took charge of his recovery, showcasing that his intellect remained sharp.

Dennis Meets with a Life-saving Doctor and Nurse

Six months after Dennis' cardiac arrest, we had a heartfelt reunion with the

two women who had saved his life: Karen Giordano, a cardiac nurse, and Dr. Tina Molumphy, a medical doctor.

176_Photo: LR Bobbi, Karen Giordano, Dennis, Dr. Tina Molumphy

During their conversation, Dr. Molumphy shared just how extraordinary Dennis's recovery was. She explained that his heart had stopped for over 20 minutes—a scenario in which most people either do not survive or suffer severe cognitive impairment. And yet, here Dennis was: fully coherent, deeply grateful, and very much alive. He thanked both women with heartfelt words, acknowledging their swift action, exceptional skill, and unwavering dedication as the reasons he was still here.

Dennis Back to Health

It didn't take long for Dennis to return to many of the activities he had enjoyed before his cardiac arrest. With determination and renewed energy, he resumed building and fixing things around his property. One of his first tasks was climbing a ladder to finish the second gazebo—the very project he'd left incomplete on the day of his collapse during pickleball.

Soon after, he tore up the den floor and oversaw a team of workers as they laid down beautiful new hardwood—managing the entire renovation without ever having to move out of his house.

Then came my birthday, August 24th.

Dennis surprised me with a gift I never expected: a 1935 Steinway Model S baby grand piano.

177_Photo: Bobbi Playing Her "New" Piano

I was speechless. The sheer thoughtfulness of the gift left me stunned. It was something I had never dared to dream of owning—but deep in my heart, it was something I had always desired. And somehow, without me ever saying a word, Dennis knew.

What a marvelous man I was about to marry.

Must-Dos Before the I-Dos

Thanks to the unique skills and assistance of Loryn, Dennis's future daughter-in-law, we could do all of the many things that had to be done before our wedding. For example:

- Valley Pres Church, the Church we chose for our wedding, had restrictions on allowing couples to hold weddings during COVID-19.
  - Initially, they insisted that guests agree to wear masks, but they finally decided to make that "optional."
  - We had to sign up for a date.
  - We had to hire our musicians. The church musician told me she didn't play at weddings, but since we were such good friends, she would be pleased to perform at our wedding.
  - We had to have had so many sessions of church-approved counseling with a recommendation from the counselor for the marriage before it could take place.
  - We had to get a pastor to do our wedding. Jenny Warner, who on the day of our wedding, was in transit rom a trip out of town. Fearful she would not return in time to perform the wedding, Bobbi asked Frank Vanderzwann to perform our wedding. He agreed enthusiastically.
  - We had to meet with the church's senior pastor and get her blessing, even though she wasn't going to "do" the wedding.

- ○ We had to get approval from the church to have Frank Vanderzwan do our wedding.
- There was so much to accomplish.

From Guest to Hostess

Dennis was pleased to have the engagement party at his home's poolside. The catered party was open to those in the wedding party and the people who came from a long distance to the wedding. Family and Friends had a good time "table hopping" to get to know everyone. The weather was excellent, and the ambiance was perfect.

The first time I came to Dennis's house with Angie was so Dennis could show his construction work and entertain his friends. Now, I would entertain Dennis and my family and friends there. What a special gift God was giving me! It was almost more than I could fathom. My joy and gratitude were "over the top."

<u>She'll Never Make It (But She Did)</u>

Dennis's soon-to-be daughter-in-law ensured everything was done for my September 10, 2022, wedding day. Angie drove me to Valley Church, where we

took our dresses. We didn't want Dennis to see me, so we ensured he wasn't visible as we went to the Bride's room. Joni helped me dress, do my hair, and do my makeup.

178_Photo: Joni, Bobbi

It seemed the photographer was shooting me every second. Of course, she was there to take informal pictures of my every move.

Angie and Joni went to stand in position for their "cue" to enter the auditorium. I was not to be seen, so I hid away. After everyone had entered, I stood next to the flower girl.

180_Photo: Bobbi Flower Girl

How precious this flower girl looked. I had known her since her birth, and having her be a part of this wedding was a joy.

On cue, the flower girl entered the auditorium and dropped the flowers on the carpet, but then, inexplicably, she would pick them up again. She didn't want to give the flower petals away. When she finished with the petals, it was my turn.

I walked into the auditorium and was amazed at how full the pews were. I started walking down the aisle, thinking, "Yes, that family, "as I pointed my finger at them, was invited, and they came. Wow! "

181_Photo: Bobbi, Stopping to Greet Guests

On the other side of the aisle were others who were invited and came. I was overwhelmed by the number of my personal friends in the pews. I waved to each of them, pausing to thank them for coming.

Seeing that I was taking an inordinate amount of time coming up the aisle, Frank Vanderzwann said to Dennis, "Go get her, or she'll never make it." Dennis left the altar to "get me."

I was surprised to have Dennis take my arm and be so serious. I hadn't greeted all who were present, so as he walked me to the altar, I kept pointing and greeting people.

As I approached the podium, I saw my close family sitting on my left and Dennis' family sitting on my right. I was so happy that I verbally said," I'm so glad you came." With that, I had finished acknowledging each side of the pews. I was ready to be serious. I took Dennis' arm, and we joined Frank at the front of the Church.

The proceedings were short. Barbara Grant played the harp as everyone came in. Then she sang while Anton Nel, from the Menlo Church, played the piano.

When Frank pronounced us man and wife and introduced us to the congregation as Mr and Mrs. Dennis Austin, we started down the aisle, and Anton played a rousing tune. Midway to the door, Dennis turned me and gave me another kiss.

182_Photo: Bobbi, Dennis

It was a grand celebration. I was indeed Mrs. Bobbi Austin. I praised God.

Toasts, Tears, and $2 Bills

There was a limit to the number of people who could attend the wedding at the Church (250), and even fewer were allowed at the Town Center for the reception. How could we eliminate people from the reception if we had them attend the ceremony? There was no way to do it.

We turned the problem over to Dennis's son Adrian's fiancée, Loryn, to solve, and somehow, she solved it.

Almost everyone had drinks and appetizers outside when we arrived at the reception. They came in and were all seated when we walked into the room. The food was served, and the speeches began.

What Dennis' sons had to say was very impressive. Their words touched Dennis.

Adrian's Wedding Speech

"I want to start with a story because the internet said it was the right way to do for these speeches.

For those that don't know, my Dad is a pretty adventurous guy. From multi-day Winter backpacking, to unguided white-water rafting (with no training), he has done a lot! I encourage you to ask him about it, because it is certain to be a good story.

But this story is set in Syracuse NY, where my dad grew up. Every summer and winter, my dad would take my brother, Derek, and I to see our grandparents on their 7-acre farm in Syracuse. And in between all the yard work, and plowing snow, and other no-so fun things that kids are asked to do at a farm, my dad took us on adventures too.

One summer my dad packed Derek and I into the car and headed out on a road trip. The road trip brought us to a hilly part of the state, and as we were driving, we saw a group of people. These people were clad in head-to-toe protective leather, like you would see on a motorcycle racer.

So, my dad, being the person that will talk to just about anyone, slowed the car and yelled out the window, "Hey! What are you all doing?" "We're doing Road Luge!" For those of you that aren't aware... Road Luge is just like Ice Luge, like you would see in the Winter Olympics. But instead of a sled, they use a long flat skateboard. And instead of slippery ice, they use cement like this hill.

So my dad then says, "Cool! Can my son do it?" To which the guys says:, "Sure! I think I have a kid's suit in my car." At this point I'm terrified. I'm not sure about anyone else in the room, But my road luge experience is pretty limited. "Dad, I'm not doing that!" "Come on! It'll be fun. And look, there's hay bales on the side of the road." "...No! Not going to happen."

And so I didn't do it. I regret not doing it! Just think of how much better this wedding story would have been if I did do it. It was something that seemed wild at the time and I was scared, but my dad had an eye for things that are bold but ultimately great.

What's the point of that story?

My dad is someone who does not live with regrets. When he knows something is important, special, meaningful, he doesn't wait around. He takes the moment head on, and doesn't let it slip.

While I am still acquiring more stories with Bobbi, I can share one about when we got to meeting her family. One of our first times meeting Bobbi's family was at a dinner she hosted at my Dad's house in Woodside. After the usual getting to know each other and food, Bobbi came out with a stack of fresh $2 bills and said "OK now it's time for games." The game was liars' poker, using the serial numbers.

Everyone got their bills, But! They turned out. Since they had never been circulated, they were all in sequential order. Which if you know the rules of Liars' Poker, doesn't allow for much mystery. That put an end to that game quickly. But not to worry, Bobbi had more games than that to play.

Because that's what I'm learning about who Bobbi is; she's someone who brings people together. And just from the number of people here today, we can see how good at that she Is. And the more I learn about Bobbi, the more I realize what a special match her and my dad are.

My dad is never one to let something special pass him by, And Bobbi with her uncanny knack for bringing together soon-to-be friends. It is really something extraordinary.

So, in closing, I want to leave you with a simple toast:

"Life is better when you are living to the fullest. So follow in the steps of the two people that we are celebrating today, and strive to make every day something special."

Cheers to Dennis and Bobbi.

What a nice speech. I felt "warm and fuzzy feelings for Adrian.

I think Derek's speech was lost. Derek gave such glowing accolades that I'm sure it would be worth having a copy.

Joni and Angie spoke. My heart was overflowing with love and tenderness for these two women. I surely hope we are able to find their speeches..

When we cut the cake, we fed each other and served dessert. Loryn orchestrated the cake cutting and the music so Anton, our piano player, could eat.

The Best Wedding Ever (According to Everyone)

Anton played the piano again, and we had a sing-along. Dennis and I went to each table, handed out two-dollar bills as favors, and thanked people for coming. The guest commented, "Best wedding I've ever been to." "This wedding was so much fun." "You put on an unusually entertaining wedding."

When we started to leave, the guest made two lines, and Dennis and I moved between the lines, saying, "Thank you and goodbye."

Our "getaway" car was decorated with "Just Married."

Dinner, Dresses, and Deep Gratitude

Where Dennis chose for our honeymoon was a complete surprise. I think I barely let him finish parking before blurting out, "This is the place!" We had arrived at the Frisco Hotel in San Francisco. The room was beautiful, the service impeccable. Every time we left the room, someone would come in and freshen it up—like magic.

Because I wasn't sure what clothes to pack for a honeymoon, we made a quick dash back home to pick up a few things. I hadn't lived at Dennis's house before the wedding, but just before the ceremony, he had thoughtfully moved all my clothes into his beautifully expanded closet. Everything was perfectly in place, waiting for me.

The hotel's restaurant was so lovely, we didn't even want to leave the premises. But we did have one special outing in mind.

We were beyond grateful for everything our amazing wedding planner, Loryn, had done to make our big day unforgettable. We wanted to thank her in a meaningful way. So Dennis and I decided to treat Loryn and Adrian to a truly special dinner in San Francisco. It also happened to be convenient—they lived nearby.

The dinner with Loryn and Adrian was wonderful—excellent food, good wine, great company. As a final touch, Dennis and I gave them a heartfelt thank-you card… and a generous check. Loryn hadn't expected anything, certainly not a gift of that size. But we were so grateful. It felt good to give, especially after receiving so much.

A New Home, A New Husband, A World to See

Dennis and I were ready to settle down at 130 Kenmore Way, Woodside, CA 94062, two miles from where I had lived since 1979.

Photo: 130 Kenmore Way, Woodside, California (2015)

I lived at 50 Horgan Avenue, Unit #52, in Redwood City for 36 of the 43 years I was married to Bill. It became my anchor through life's many seasons—four years with Angie, and three years on my own after Bill passed. When Dennis and I married, I chose not to sell the condo. Instead, I rented it out. The real estate agent found a wonderful tenant—a single professional lawyer with good taste. It felt like the perfect match.

Dennis's home in Woodside, at 130 Kenmore Way, seemed to satisfy everything I had hoped for. At least, that's what I thought at first.

I quickly bonded with Raphael, the gardener. Though his English was limited, we found ways to understand each other. Dennis gave weekly instructions, and Raphael kept the gardens looking lovely. But then came the news—Raphael was returning to Mexico to visit his parents and would be gone for three months. We waited. And waited. Sadly, he never returned. The replacement didn't work out.

After trying several others, Dennis finally found Eulogio—a gem! Not only a skilled gardener, but also a capable handyman and trusted friend. Problem solved.

As for inside the house, we've had no trouble. Our weekly house cleaners, Ana Maria Mendoza and Magdalena Mendoza, are top-notch. Everything runs smoothly.

That year, 2022, brought another major milestone—one unlike any of the 60 or so Buckner Reunions I had previously attended. This time, I wanted to introduce Dennis to my Buckner friends and to my extended family in Texas and Arkansas. Fortunately, Dennis's family lived nearby, and he agreed to join me.

So in September 2022, Dennis and I—now officially Mr. and Mrs. Austin—headed to Texas for the Buckner Alumni gathering. We stayed with

Dennis's brother David and his wife, Gaye, in Wylie, and also visited Sue and Terrell Landry, as well as Hank and Pam Hood in Plano.

Pam, the daughter of my cousin Barbara Parson Ridley, has always been part of my reunion visits—even before her daughter Jordan was born. This time, Jordan joined us for dinner and a movie. It brought back memories of when we'd seen a film together featuring my grandson, Adam Cropper (Joni and David's son). Adam has been in several movies—never as the star, but often in meaningful roles. My favorite was the one where he played young JFK's best friend. He was also in a movie with Meryl Streep.

While I visited with Sue, Dennis played golf with my brother Bill Richardson and Terrell. It was a meaningful introduction—my new husband spending time with my brother in the Texas sun.

We made a pact to travel regularly and visit places neither of us had seen, "while we're still healthy." That became our motto. Even as we stayed committed to both our families' traditions, we carved out time for adventures together. In fact, during our first two years of marriage, we averaged one trip per month.

Some of those trips were simply to help Dennis meet my far-flung family. But they all became part of the rich fabric of our new life together.

Travel and special events

The following lists some of the places we've been from September 2022 to July 3, 2024:

Buckner Reunion (Sept and early Oct 2022)

- Dennis and I visited Buckner Reunion, Landry's, and the Hoods.
- We stayed with Dennis' relatives in Wylie, TX-"Yes, the place of the murder in LOVE AND DEATH." My Grandson, Adam Cropper, played the lawyer.

Adrian's wedding (Oct 2022)

- We attended Dennis' son (Adrian) and Loryn's marriage in Bodega Bay, a 3-day celebration. Loryn was our wedding coordinator and did an outstanding job.

183_Photo: Austin Family

LR: David (Dennis' brother), Gaye (David's wife), Dennis, Bobbi Adrian (Dennis' son), Loryn (Adrian's wife), Derek (Dennis' son), Mallory (Derek's wife), Mark (David's son)

Palm Desert (Mar 2023)

We celebrated the birthday of our good friend Daphne.

Dennis's First Grandson (Apr 2023)

Dennis's first grandchild, Atticus, son of Derek and Mallory Richards Austin, was born.

184_Photo: Bobbi Atticus (2023)

SpaceX, Boca Chica, Texas (May 2023)
The Day We Were Nearly Deported from Texas

During our visit to my relatives in Texas, they kindly offered to take us on a sightseeing trip to Boca Chica to see the SpaceX facilities. The scale of it all was breathtaking—massive structures, and towering rockets.

185_Photo: Dennis Bobbi at SpaceX (2023)

We drove all around the complex, marveling at everything we could see. At one point, we found ourselves at a special access area where a rocket was being assembled. Dennis, always the curious adventurer, hopped out of the car and walked right into the assembly building, snapping photos of everything that caught his eye.

Security personnel arrived quickly and, without much conversation, called the local police. The officers arrived, took Dennis's phone, and deleted the photos. Apparently, we had wandered into a restricted area—something we hadn't fully realized.

Dennis, unfazed, pointed to the lone "Restricted Area" sign and made the case that its location was highly ambiguous. After inspecting the sign's placement, the police agreed—it was technically unclear. In the end, they let us go with a warning. But not before one officer leaned in, gave Dennis a pointed look, and said sternly:

"Leave Texas—and don't come back." We couldn't tell if he was joking.

Don't Sell Past the Sale

As we were getting ready to leave—relieved we hadn't been arrested—my "niece" began pleading our case to the police officer, insisting we hadn't done anything wrong and had no idea we'd entered a restricted area. She launched into a passionate defense just as the officer, who had been ready to let us go, began to bristle. Realizing things might take a turn, we gently asked her to shush, offered a final, sincere apology, and eased away as calmly and quickly as possible. Dennis turned to me and said, "Don't sell past the sale."—when the police have decided to let you go, stop talking and drive away.

Brownsville, Texas (May 2023):

We visited some of Bobbi's first husband Glenn Parson's relatives: Laurie, Scott, Paula, and Chris. Laurie is Glenn's sister's daughter. Her husband is Scott

Bernard.. Paula is Glenn's brother's wife. Chris is Paula's son.

186_Photo: Laurie, Scott, Bobbi, Paula, Chris (2023)
Runge, Texas

We visited Bobbi's first husband Glenn Parson's relatives; Bronwyn and Elgan (Buddy) Ridley. Elgan (Buddy) Ridley is Glenn's sister's son, and Bronwyn is his wife. They live on a cattle ranch that has some active natural gas wells on it.

187_ Photo: Bobbi, Bronwyn, Buddy

Iceland (June 2023)

We took our first trip out of the US as a married couple. We spent 10 days

touring the Icelandic coast and were amazed at the number of waterfalls.

189_Photo: Bobbi Iceland (2023)

Iceland is known as the Land of Fire and Ice and is famous for its Waterfalls, Volcanoes, and Glaciers.

Home concert (July 8, 2023)

We had a concert at our house featuring Anton Nell (Piano), Barbary Grant (rythm, vocals), and Jeff Buenz (guitar). Approximately 40 people attended.

190_Home   Concert (July 2023)

Bobbi's 90th Birthday Party (Aug 24, 2023)

I celebrated my 90th birthday with a BIG BASH at the Alpine Hills Tennis Club, beautifully planned by Dennis's stepdaughter, Loryn, and my daughter, Joni.

191_Photo: Bobbi's 90th (2023)

It was an extraordinary event filled with joy and surprises. A magician amazed the crowd with an act featuring a floating table. My grandson, Adam Cropper, delighted everyone with his piano playing and singing. We were also treated to performances by vocalist Barbara Grant and pianist Anton Nel. The decorations were exquisite—every detail thoughtfully arranged. It was truly a birthday celebration to remember.

Carmel-by-the-Sea (September 2023)

We rented a place in Carmel-by-the-Sea to get some "family time" with Dennis' two sons, their wives, and his new grandson, Atticus. The boys played golf while the girls went shopping.

192_Photo: Mallory,
Atticus, Derek

193_Photo: Dennis Bobbi

194_Photo: Adrian Loryn

Italy, Slovenia, and Croatia (Oct 2023)

Thinking I had been disappointed for not having traveled with Frank Vanderzwan and never having been on a Cooking Tour, Dennis suggested we sign up for a culinary tour of Tuscany, but then go on our own around the Adriatic sea through Trieste, Slovenia, and Croatia. I agreed.

Before joining the group in Tuscany, Dennis and I flew to Rome and spent time at QC Termeroma, a luxurious spa near the airport—an unusual and memorable place unlike any we'd visited before. The property featured a variety of water experiences, with pools of warm, hot, and cold water cascading over the body in different ways—whether clothed or unclothed.

One of the most unexpected events was the pre-dinner cocktail gathering, where street clothes weren't allowed. Instead, guests were required to wear bathing suits and bathrobes. It made for a lighthearted and relaxed atmosphere, and the food was hearty enough to serve as our evening meal.

The spa even offered waterbeds for post-soak lounging. We enjoyed it so much that we returned again after our trip to Croatia. It became a special, restorative bookend to our Italian adventure.

After QC Termeroma Spa, we stayed at the Terme di Saturnia Spa in northern Italy, which featured a huge warm water mineral-rich pool, and a restaurant where everyone wore white bathrobes.

195_Photo: Terme di Saturnia, Italy (2023)

237

After joining the tour group in Tuscany, Italy and enjoying his Culinary Tour of Tuscany, which featured winery tasting, cooking lessons, and trips to Siena and

196_Photo: Frank and Tuscany tour group

Florence, we drove on our own through northern Italy and around the Adriatic Sea through Trieste, Slovenia, and Croatia.

197_Photo: Bobbi: Croatia (2023)

198_Photo: Bobbi in Siena

199_Photo: Bobbi Cinque Village, Italy

Texas and Arkansas (Oct, 2023)

We traveled to Eureka Springs, Arkansas, and took the "Holy Land Tour."

We visited Cheryl and Frank Dunlop, my sister's daughter and son-in-law, and Angie Mitchell. Dennis and Frank built things, so they had a lot in common.

Cheryl and I teamed up to provide for Angie's life when she needed total care, but this was not acceptable to her. As her person, Angie has provided for her own "present and later life, " just as I have.

We visited relatives (Curt and Bren) in Rockwall, Texas, and Dennis played golf with them in Lewisville, Texas.

Curt showed us his toys: a Big Mobile home, a "cigarette style" racing boat, and two Corvettes (one for him and one for his wife)

200_Photo: Curt Raney (2023)

Home Concert (11- 12-2023)

We had a home concert featuring Anton Nel on the piano, Jessica Morgan on vocals, and Benjamin Chen on the violin. About 42 people attended.

201_Photo: Concert Program

December 17, 2023- Christmas sing-along
Our annual Christmas sing-along home concert featured Anton Nel, Benjamin Chen, and Barbary Grant.

PROGRAM NOTES

Since the mid 2000's Anton (piano), Jessica (soprano) and Benjamin (violin) have been a part of the Traditional Services at Menlo Church. Through the years all three of them have been actively involved in the music industries in South Africa, Texas and California.

This is a unique opportunity to hear them share a pat of their musical journey. They will cover repertoire from movie and Broadway themes, spirituals, and love and war songs from yesteryear.

Anton Nel

Jessica Morgan

Benjamin Chen

My Grandkids, their Significant Others, and My GreatGrandKids

Adam Cropper and his wife, Chelsea

Adam is my daughter Joni and her husband David's son.

Brian Cropper, his wife Rachel Heredia, and their son, Beck. Brian is my daughter Joni and her husband David's son.

←

Russell, Celiste, Evan, and their daughters Everly, and Theodora,. Evan is my daughter Corinne and her husband Dave's son.

→

Haley Cropper and her fiancé Luis

Haley is my daughter Joni and her husband David's daughter.

My Step Grand kids and Others

 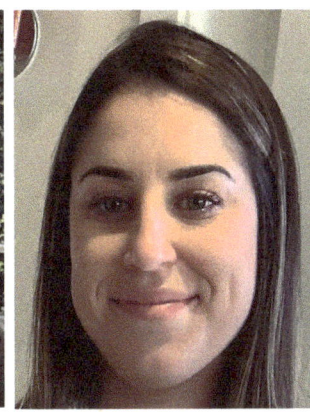

Eric Garcia and his fiancée Sabrina

Eric is my stepdaughter Mary Ruth's son.

Tracy Cropper

Tracy is my daughter Joni's husband David's Stepsister

Faith
Faith is Tracy's daughter

Ixtapa, Mexico (December, 2023)

I had traveled many times with Frank Vanderzwan's group, most recently to Italy, and I thought we would probably join them on their next trip, a boat trip on the canals in the Netherlands. But we had both been to the Netherlands.

Dennis surprised me by booking a five-star hotel in Ixtapa, Mexico. I don't think I have ever taken a trip so luxurious and relaxing. We were waited on like a special envoy, without the responsibilities.

202_Photo: Bobbi Ixtapa, Mexico

Tahoe (February, 2024)

We wanted to go skiing and hang out with Dennis' sons and their wives.

202_Photo: Bobbi in Tahoe

When we found out the sons couldn't come, we invited every couple we knew. Many agreed to go but backed out at the last minute. However, Dennis' friend, Michael, and his son said they would come for a day and a night.

203_Photo: Michael, Bobbi, Dennis, Son

A piano was in the house, and Michael's son played it every moment he wasn't eating, skiing, or sleeping. The place was beautiful. Our mistake was booking it during the week when everyone had to work. When our only visitors left, we again felt like we were having an extended Honeymoon.

Home Concert (March, 2024)

Our Spring home concert featured Sandra Shen, a 'world-class' piano player.

204_Photo: Sandra Shen (2024)

Palm Desert (March, 2024)

We hung out with our good Canadian friends, celebrated Daphne's birthday, and Dennis played golf while I worked on this book some of the time.

We also visited Anza Borrego, which has sculptures in the desert.

205_Photo: Dennis, Bobbi, Anza Borrego (2024)

Egypt (April, 2024)

Instead of joining Frank VanderZwan's group tour to the Netherlands, Dennis and I decided to travel to Egypt—a place neither of us had been before. Wanting a more personal and flexible experience, we chose to hire a private guide rather than join a large group.

Our guide was everything we hoped for—knowledgeable, fluent in both Egyptian Arabic and English, and deeply familiar with the region's history and culture. One of the best parts of having a private guide was skipping long lines. We were often ushered straight through gates and crowds to the sites our guide wanted to highlight, receiving insightful commentary in a friendly, conversational tone.

Our tour of Egypt was extensive, and we stayed in some truly exceptional accommodations.

The contrast between modern and ancient life was astonishing. In the city, the tourist areas were sleek and contemporary—but out in the countryside, it felt like we had stepped back into biblical times. Camels, donkeys pulling carts, and old cars all shared the same dusty roads.

206_Photo: Bobbi and Sphinx, Egypt (2024)

And then there was the traffic: chaotic, wild, and somehow functional. Few traffic rules were followed—except for one: the vehicles on a given side of the road were usually headed in the same direction. Cross-traffic seemed to follow no rules at all, yet somehow, collisions were rare.

207_ Photo: Bobbi on the Nile River, Egypt (2024)

We loved the experience—except for one upsetting moment. During a camel-cart ride, we were disturbed by the driver's repeated whipping of the animal. That part left a sour note in an otherwise unforgettable journey.

Stayed Home! (May 2024)

Dennis worked on a small gazebo, had the strawberry patch demolished, and rebuilt the area. Derek and Mallory bought a new house. We started babysitting at the new place rather than bringing Atticus to our house. All three

of us enjoy the park close by. We put Atticus in a stroller and walked to and from the home.

On one trip, Dennis picked up a chair and a stool from the sidewalk. Thinking they were leather, he took them, but they were plastic and soon began to disintegrate. We were disappointed!

208_Photo: Atticus (Dennis' grandson) Bobbi (2024)

Home Concert (June, 2024)

Our fifth concert was held on June 2 at our home. Three singers and Anton performed, with Tiffany's husband pantomiming, 'The man watching the girl from Ipanema.' These concerts have been successful; between 35 and 40 people enjoy each. One of the girls who cleans our house, Magelina, has been serving the catered food and cleaning up afterward, making the evening much more enjoyable for Dennis and me.

Dennis's second grandchild (June 2024)

209_Photo: Bobbi Viola (2024)

Dennis's First Granddaughter, Viola MaraBeth, daughter of Derek and Mallory Richards Austin, was born.

Pollock Pines (June, 2024)

I rented an Airbnb in Pollock Pines, California, to work on this book uninterrupted. Dennis ensured everything went smoothly while I wrote the story of my life.

210_Photo: Bobbi Writing (2024)

I wrote using my computer's text editor app, and Dennis converted my writing into Google Docs.

Conclusion

I have often told my story in parts, using it in devotionals, conversations, and lectures. I have now told it from beginning to end as clearly as I recall. Since my aunts and uncles, grandparents, most of my older cousins, Daddy, and two older siblings are dead, there is only one person besides myself who would have known the early part of my story. That person is my brother, Billy Dean Richardson (b.1931), who is 2 years older than I (b.1933). I've checked my story with him. Nothing in his recollection conflicts with what is written here from his point of view.

Telling this story has been a soul-wrenching experience that has brought me to my knees, face to the ground, and heart beating fast. Sadness and gladness combined bring this story to its final resting place.

With Dennis Austin, a new life story begins. It may never be written, but believe me, it will be the most uplifting, exciting, spiritually lived life any two people in my time of life could have. We are a paradox, and a pair-of-docs :-).

Permissions Acknowledgment

Every effort has been made to obtain proper permissions for the use of copyrighted materials appearing in this book. All photographs, articles, and quoted materials are used with the express consent of the original copyright holders or are believed to be in the public domain.

Special thanks to the individuals, families, and institutions who graciously granted permission to share images, letters, and stories from their collections. Your contributions help preserve and illuminate this personal and historical narrative.

If any material has been included inadvertently without proper attribution or permission, please accept our sincere apologies and contact the author or publisher so that the oversight may be corrected in future editions.

Photo Credits

The author gratefully acknowledges the individuals, families, and organizations who generously granted permission to include personal photographs and archival materials in this book. Each image enriches the story of Me, Bobbi Nell and brings greater depth, context, and humanity to the journey told within these pages.

Special thanks to the Buckner Home Alumni Association for granting permission to include photographs numbered 39 and 46, which were originally published in *The Orphan Chronicles* (2000), compiled and edited by Jerre Graves Simmons.

Deep gratitude is also extended to Buckner International (www.buckner.org) for permission to use photographs numbered 17, 19–37, and 40. These images were drawn from *Home Sweet Home: A Pictorial Memory of Buckner Baptist Children's Home Buildings* and from photographs generously provided directly to the author.

Finally special thanks to the Fairfield Recorder Newspaper for permission to print the front page of the Fairfield Recorder Newspaper March 30, 1939 edition in photo # 10.

Following this introduction is a listing of the some of the personal photographs used in the book along with the individual who granted permission for their inclusion. To each of you: thank you for your trust, your generosity, and your contribution to preserving this legacy.

If any photographs have been included inadvertently without proper credit, please accept our sincere apologies. We welcome your communication so the oversight may be corrected in future editions.

Contributors	Photo #s	Contributors	Photo #s
Adam Cropper	117, 145, 146, 148	Frank VanderZwan	169, 196
Adrian Austin	194	Gaye Austin	183
Andy Wiessner	126	Haley Cropper	118, 145
Angie Mitchell	7, 11, 13, 45, 119	Harley Parson	100, 101, 113, 130
Anton Nel	190, 201	Helene Parson	140
Athena	180	Ira Lee Henslee	53, 80
Atticus Austin	184, 208	Jeff Buenz	190
Beck Heredia	201d	Jessica Morgan	201
Benjamin Chen	201	Jim Harvey	168a
Bill deHaas	170	Joni Cropper	103, 105, 142–144
Billy Richardson	6, 12, 62	Jordan Hood	116
Bronwyn	187	Karen Giordano	176
Chelsea Cropper	201c	Laurie Ridley	185
Chris Batchelder	120, 122, 170	Loryn Ferrari	183, 194
Daphne deHaas	170	Luis	201f
Dave Pleger	115, 131, 133, 135	Mallory Austin	192
David Austin	183	Mary Ruth Batchelder	112, 121, 127, 129
David Cropper	117, 146	Michael Schneider	203
Dennis Austin	171, 182, 186, 193	Paula Parson	185
Derek Austin	183, 192	Rachel Heredia	201d
Dr. Tina Molumphy	173	Rosaline Fisher	153
Erasmo Garcia	129	Sandra Shen	204
Eric Garcia	125, 157	Scott Bernard	185
Evan Pleger	134	Tracy Cropper	201i
Faith Cropper	201j	Viola Austin	209